AF248751

The Book of Dolores

The Book of Dolores

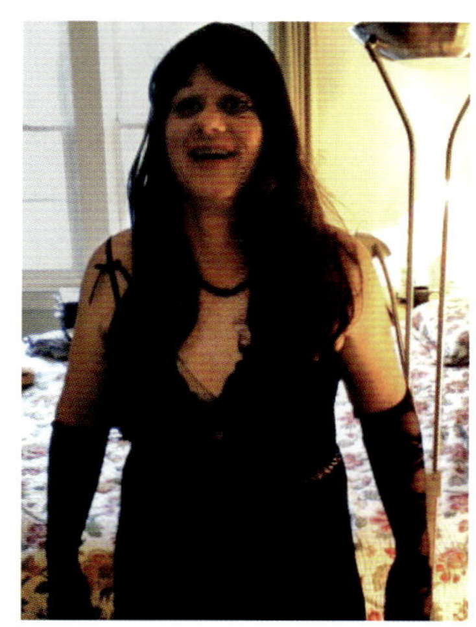

by William T. Vollmann

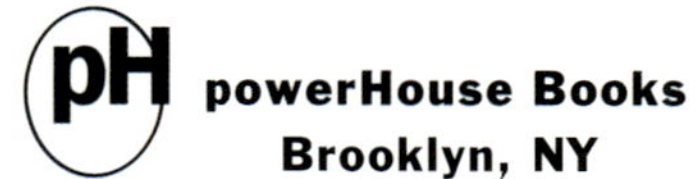

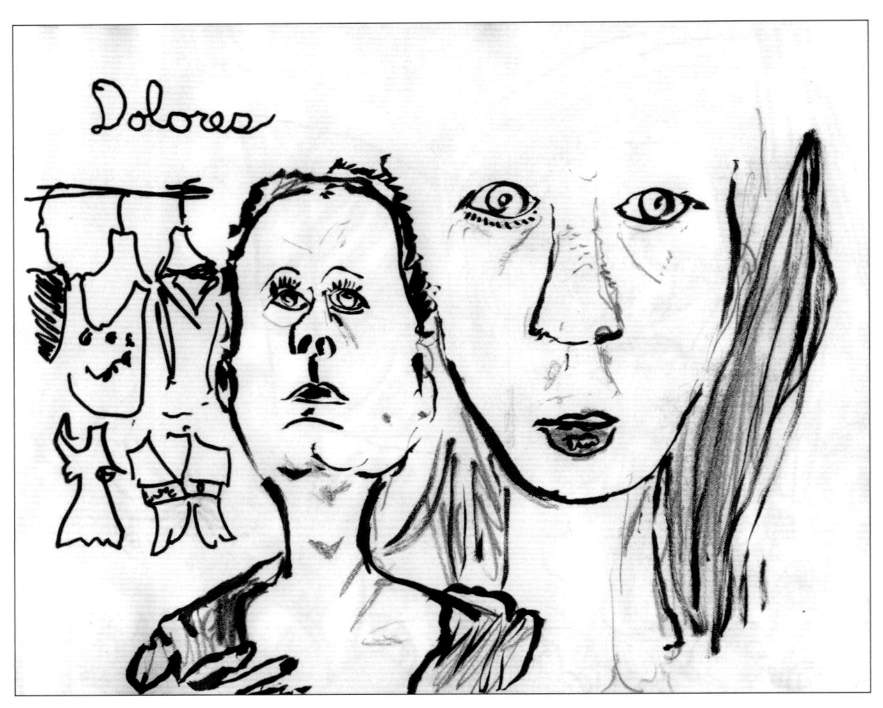
Dolores

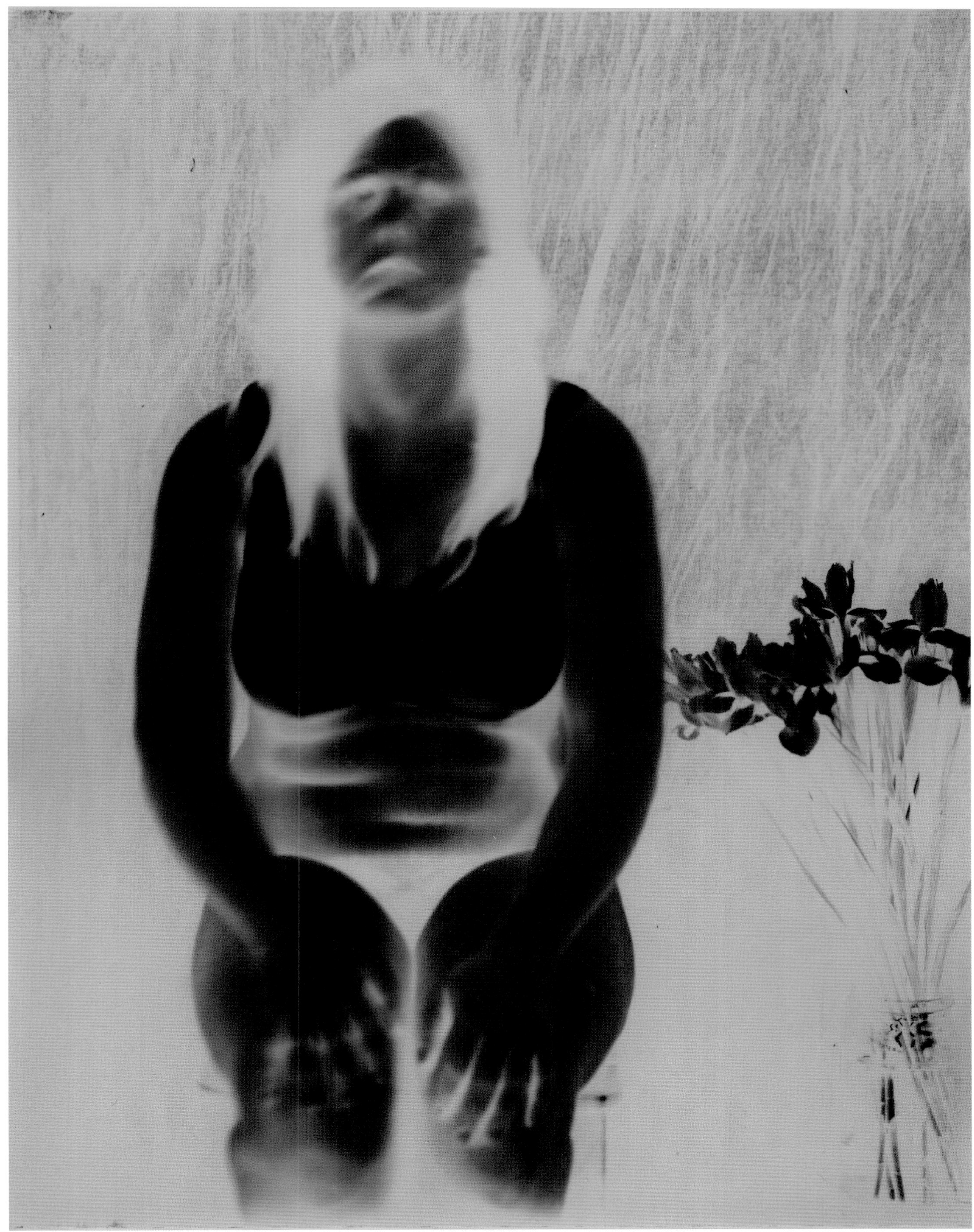

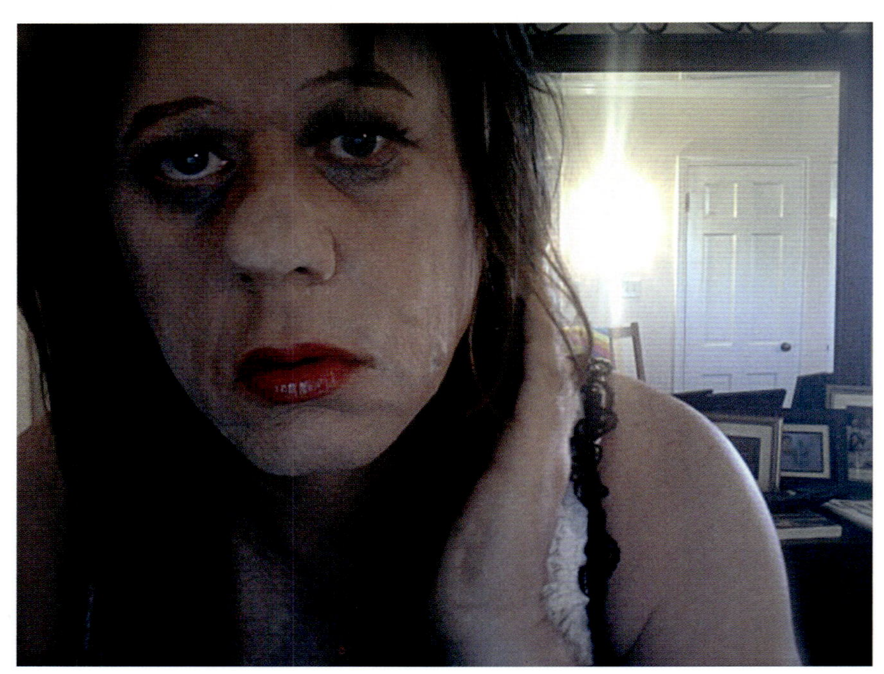

This book is dedicated to the gum bichromate printer Stephen Livick, whom I have never met but whose genius, known to me only through reproductions in books, has inspired my years of effort in the darkroom. I never achieved his mastery but I did learn to please myself.

1 CONSTRUCTIONS

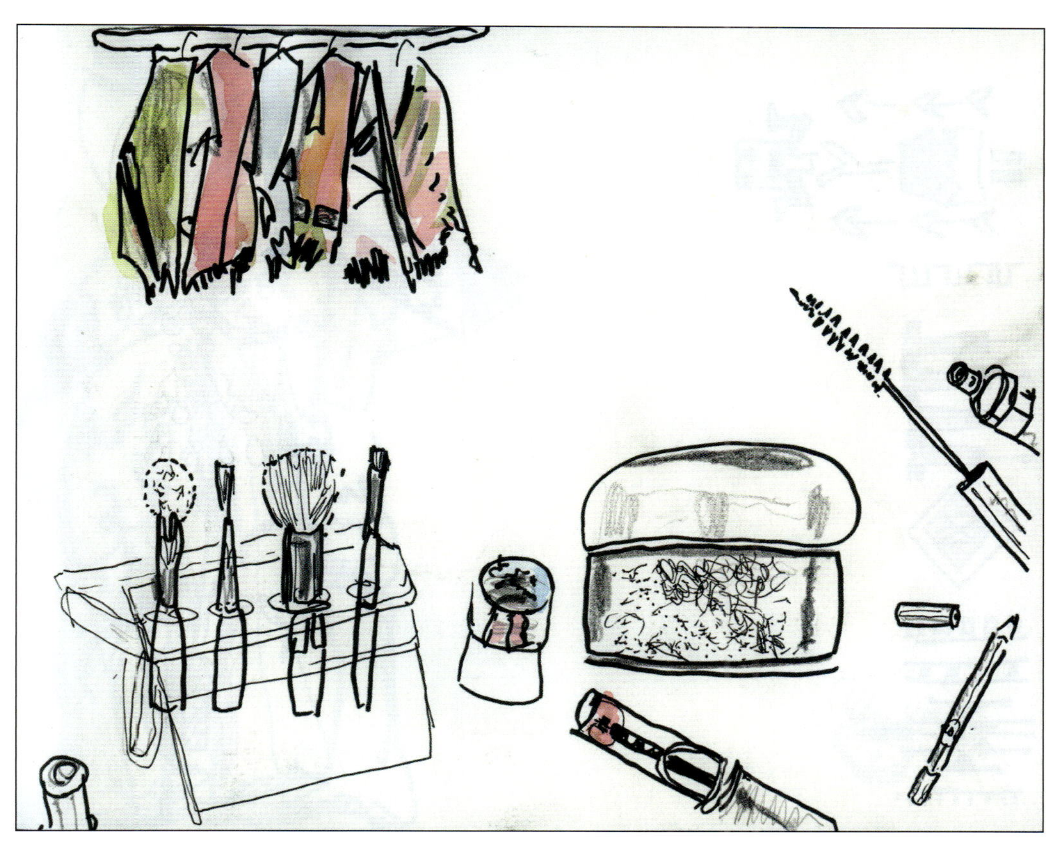

1.1: Denial, and Other Cosmetics

The young woman whom you see on the facing page, somewhat veiled by the flash of her 35 millimeter Contax camera, is feeling quite excited, curious and happy with herself, like a teenaged girl who has locked herself inside the bathroom in order to covertly and inexpertly, hence all the more earnestly apply her elder sister's makeup. The photograph was made in a tiny second-storey studio, less clandestine than merely discreet, where certain men in Tokyo make appointments to be professionally made up as women.*

This woman's name is Dolores, and she imagines that she has never looked so good — which is to say, so much herself. And this rather murky print (on account of its murkiness) does her hopes justice. Not only are her foundation and concealer fresh, but the collusion of flash and ambient dimness suppresses the ageing midtones of her skin. She exists only in episodes, and even her youth arrived rather late in life.

Beaumont Newhall once wrote: "The fundamental belief in the authenticity of photographs explains why photography of people no longer living and of vanished architecture are so melancholy. Neither words nor the most detailed painting can evoke a moment of vanished time as powerfully and as completely as a good photograph."** Let us forgive the man his overstatement; he loves what he knows. And because I likewise love photographs, and other images, I have made this book. How "authentic" is the photograph now exposed before you? The person it depicts was certainly present on that rainy day in that little room, not so many years ago. Since then I have lost one of Dolores's best earrings, and the new black dress of which she felt so proud has worn out, and my hands are more wrinkled. Meanwhile Dolores has made herself real to me even as I wonder when she will disassemble herself for the last time.

Among my photographic teachers I count Ansel Adams, whose books I read and reread. Quite often his final print appeals to me less than one of the trial versions reproduced beside it, just as I sometimes prefer a study to a finished oil painting. It used

---

* For a more complete account of this establishment, see my book *Kissing the Mask* (New York: Ecco, 2010).
** Beaumont Newhall, *The History of Photography*, 5th ed., 6th pr., rev. (New York: The Museum of Modern Art, New York, distrib. Bullfinch Press / Little, Brown & Co, 1997; orig. ed. 1982), p. 94.

to unnerve me that people disagree as to the best form of a picture (or of almost anything). Now it makes me feel free. The main thing is to know what one likes. Next in importance (although it may come earlier) is learning what one can do. More inspiring than his coolly brilliant prints is Adams's insistence on previsualizing the image and its tonal scale before snapping the shutter. To the extent that I sought to obey his advice, my large format work benefited, and even my 35 millimeter negatives improved once I comprehended what a light meter can and cannot see. I have published another book of pictures, called *Imperial*, which shows, I hope, that I tried to think through my compositions and exposures. Adams might not have been impressed by the choices I made. Many an inferior worker is too easily pleased, and I frequently did please myself. I remember opening my tripod one hot day in a grapefruit orchard on the shores of the Salton Sea. Pale moons of fruit shone against the dark leaves. Thanks to previsualization, I knew that I wanted a green filter, and I chose to increase my exposure by two and a half stops. I felt excited when I opened the shutter, elated when I saw the developed negative, and calmly joyous when I produced my first platinum print from it. Whether or not it was the best grapefruit picture ever made, it was certainly my best, and I take pride in it. When I see it now, I remember that May morning, and the woman who was with me, and I reexperience them together. Perhaps a locket of her hair would serve me as well; as for the grapefruit picture, people sometimes tell me they like it, but of course for better and worse it is a different picture to them because there is no woman in it. Andrew Wyeth's occasional practice of portraying someone in, say, his meat cellar and then painting him out, leaving only the depicted setting to represent him, proves how effectively context can haunt a picture; and if the joke were on us, and Wyeth had never actually concealed a person beneath the final layers of paint, would it matter?

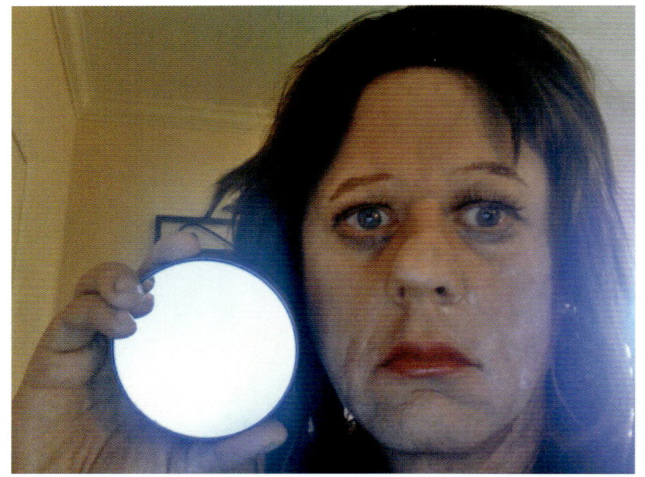

With landscapes, I took my time. But when I photographed people for *Imperial*, I plucked their vanishing moments more straightforwardly after Newhall's sense. Most of them I would never get to know; thus their portraits became all that you and I could have of them. I think that when they were posing for me in their asparagus fields and in the doorways of their sun-dazzled dusty streets, they sensed this. What they gave me cost them little to give because, like the sun, they kept giving it simply by existing. This left me no less covetous. The longer I live, and the more *past* their portraits become, the more I will cherish them.

My previsualizations on those occasions were simple: Stop down the lens for maximum depth of field, set the shutter speed as high as feasible (generally around an eighth of a second), and refrain from stage directions, since I remember how a photographer once posed *me* against the churchwall of his choice, in his leather jacket; I never liked that picture.

Dolores was, at first, just such a stranger as these others. And I could not previsualize her even as superficially as I had them, because I could not *see* her except in a mirror, and she mostly refused to let me wear my glasses. Well, her moments were certainly vanishing ones, all right.

To be sure, the portraits in this book are by their nature posed. (Sometimes I posed her and sometimes she posed herself.) They are also discoveries. What I discovered I frequently wished were different. Well, didn't that make it all the more authentic?

When I look at the woman on page 13, I remember how thrilled with herself she was, in that ignorant, innocently narcissistic way of hers, and I feel tenderly toward her and her enthusiasms, as I would toward the self-exaltations of any small child. When it comes to myself, I rarely hold such tolerance. I live in an ageing, expendable male body. My intellect, such as it is, I consider to be one of my tools, not something I deserve credit for, or even something that is more a part of me than, say, the Contax camera riding at my belt. My body and mind deserve my care and, perhaps, my gratitude. But they exist to be used until they break, not to be cherished.

I do not exactly cherish Dolores, who is, after all, an aspect of myself. (When I looked closely at myself, I began to see what I was made of. I was more like me and less like Dolores than I had imagined, or perhaps it was the other way around.) Anyhow, I would help her if I could.

In the same spirit in which Nixon once assured the nation that "I am not a crook," I advise all my readers that I am not a narcissist. Why this work, then?

Transgendered people sometimes make extreme commitments to selves which could never exist but for effort, pain, anguish, humiliation and isolation. Dolores is no such individual, for I have never believed myself to be a female born into the wrong body. I am a heterosexual male with a hypertrophy of the empathetic organs. Not only am I physically and emotionally attracted to women, I also wonder what being a woman would be like.

Recently I wrote a novel in which I imagined myself as a transgender woman.[*] The more some acquaintances saw and heard of what I will call my research, the more

---

* When I first began the research for that book, I did not understand the difference between cross-dressers and transgender people. In brief, the latter often tend to have believed since childhood that they were born into a body of the wrong gender. Their resulting misery, or gender dysphoria, impels them into painful, expensive surgery in hopes of rendering who they are consistent with what they have. Cross-dressers, on the other hand, may or may not become transgendered. Frequently they enjoy the use of the genitalia they were born with, and step in and out of their acquired gender as easily as they do their lingerie.

degraded they considered me. This encouraged me to embellish what they called my degradation. So in the book I became a physically unattractive Mexican street prostitute. How could anyone believe that women, Mexicans, prostitutes, street people are by nature inferior? But multitudes do — among them, sad to say, members of those very categories; not to mention the rich and selfish, who have no justification not to know better, and the circumstantially ignorant, whom I excuse. In fine, I found that because there were some who looked down on me, I grew ashamed. When I put on my dress and prosthetic breasts, it felt frightening to go out into the night. This was, as a good friend would say, information. Precisely which other information I sought by becoming Dolores is not entirely transparent to me, but I might have learned it, or other things, in the course of this experiment. For a summation, I refer interested parties to the novel, which is called *How You Are*.

To repeat, what I felt while wearing feminine clothes, wigs and other things differs from how I looked, both "objectively," to a camera, and, let's also say "objectively," to myself, with a watercolor brush in my hand and my spectacles off. The camera saw Dolores in one way. I saw her in another. Previsualization became a joke.

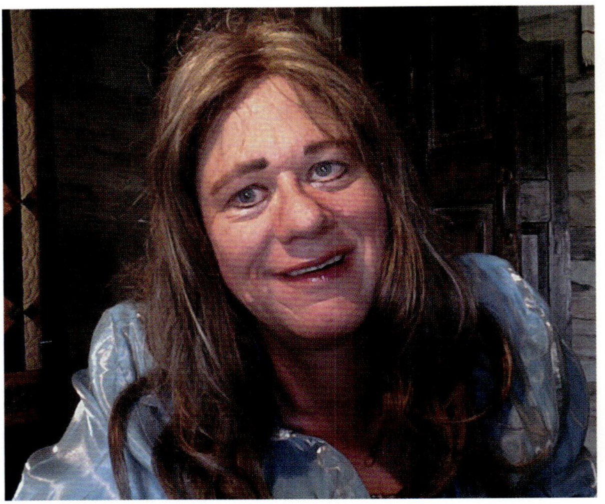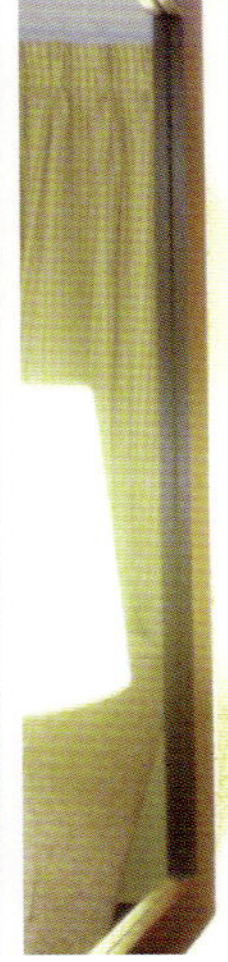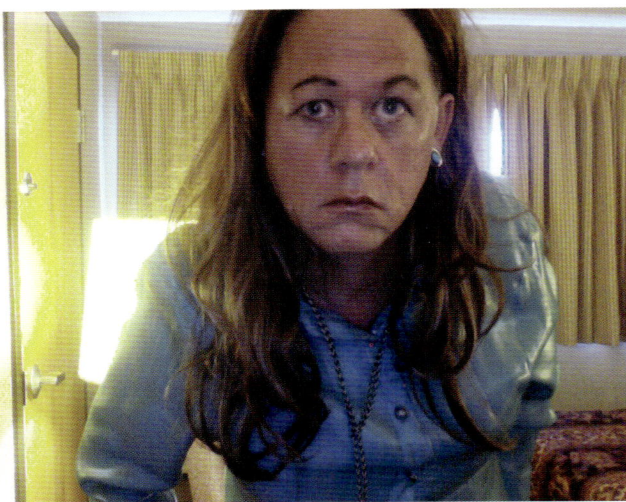

This vain, young, inexperienced woman thought that she looked better than she did. Who was I to tell her otherwise? I would not say that my watercolors flattered her, exactly, but many of her pores and wrinkles became invisible to this well-meaningly nearsighted old watercolorist, who might perhaps have believed in what the women's magazines sometimes spell "glamour."

In the 1980s my friend Ken Miller used to photograph prostitutes with his big camera while I made watercolor portraits of them. Ken once said: "Man, I envy you, because you can just make your background the blank white of the paper. Me, no matter how shallow I set my f/stop, there's still going to be some texture or off-white from the wall." Ken's photographs were cruelly beautiful, every stretch mark and abscess in place. As for me, I was benefitted not only by my paper's blankness but also by my poor vision. As I said, many of the fine wrinkles around a sad old street-whore's eyes I could not see. And I did not mind missing them. One of the greatest compliments I received in my distinguished career of harlot-painter was when a hotel girl whom I had paid to pose offered me the ten dollars back if she could keep her likeness. When I declined, she snatched it and ran laughing down the hall, with her money tucked safely in her underpants! As an old commercial photographer used to tell his clients, "Ma'am, when you look good, I look good." I guess she looked good then.

So when it came time to make portraits of that sad old lady named Dolores, I recollected my talent for not seeing wrinkles. By then Dolores had had many humiliating experiences of taking off her glasses, primping and posing for the camera, exposing herself to truth's light, and then, her glasses back on, inspecting the portrait, only to discover that she did not look as pretty as she had felt. If only the camera had envisioned her as she did! When I put on a dress and wig, sat down before a mirror, with a pad or notebook in my lap, a palette on the table and a brush in my hand, I could see only what Dolores could. After a few such sessions, I began to know my face a little, for the first time in my life. I noticed, for instance, that at the outer edge of each eye, a crease curved downward. I learned the shape of my mouth, which was neither thin nor full; the line between my lips consisted of two diagonal segments and three curves. I had no eyebrows (the result of an accident at the North Magnetic Pole). I became conversant with my ovoid head. Of course I could rub concealer over my eye-grooves, enlarge my lips with red gloss, draw on the eyebrows of my fancy, and give the sides of my face any shape I liked, thanks to wig-hair. But the eye-grooves and mouth, at least, I generally left alone. I wished Dolores to be recognizably me as well as herself. And so I drew my eyes with their downcurving side-creases, and I sketched the lips that I have. By then it scarcely mattered whether I wore a wig or any makeup, unless I chose to do so in order to regale myself with that "feminine feeling" so delicious to cross-dressers. Did I want to be a longhaired blonde like my youngest sister, or a greyhaired butch lesbian? I could paint those details in.

Ken was quite right; my paper gave me help. Even more helpful were my dreams, suppositions and imaginations.

One afternoon in Oaxaca, I was sketching an old clay figurine in the anthropology museum. The thing gaped its thick-lipped, beautiful mouth and widened its eyes. It wore a thick headdress and massive ring-earrings. I had wished to render it more carefully and completely, but the establishment was closing. Returning into the sunlight a little sorrowfully, I kept thinking about that lovely female image and longing to see it again. Suddenly I wondered how Dolores would appear if she attempted to impersonate it. Opening the sketchbook to the quick drawing which I had just completed, I sat before the mirror and began to model. The clay lady had opened her mouth. My lips did not go in quite the same way, but I drew them the way they did go, plumping them out, however. Next I drew my nose, and my eyes with their downcurving creases, accompanied by their undershadows. I invented a collar from which a grinning, gaping pendant hung by a chain studded with Dolores's earrings. And when I stopped to study the effect, I felt that "Dolores the idol" was me, but also someone alien. I experienced a sense of freedom, pleasure and power.

At this time I had not worked out how my novel would end. The picture-play with that indigenous figurine convinced me that Dolores would somehow come into her own in Mexico. I accordingly awarded her the capacity to speak perfect Spanish and a half-reliable supply of hormones and methamphetamines, upon which everything took a suitably extreme direction.

No, as much as she might have hoped I would, I never flattered her. And yet in these drawings and writings I did get to be what I pretended. Hence the drawings and woodcuts are in my opinion fair representations, which is to say self-portraits by a nearsighted person.

So I played and played with poor Dolores, who had little to say about any of it — not that she objected, either. It is possible (although I cannot say for sure) that at times she liked to get a trifle high and kinky; unlike me, she could be an exhibitionist.

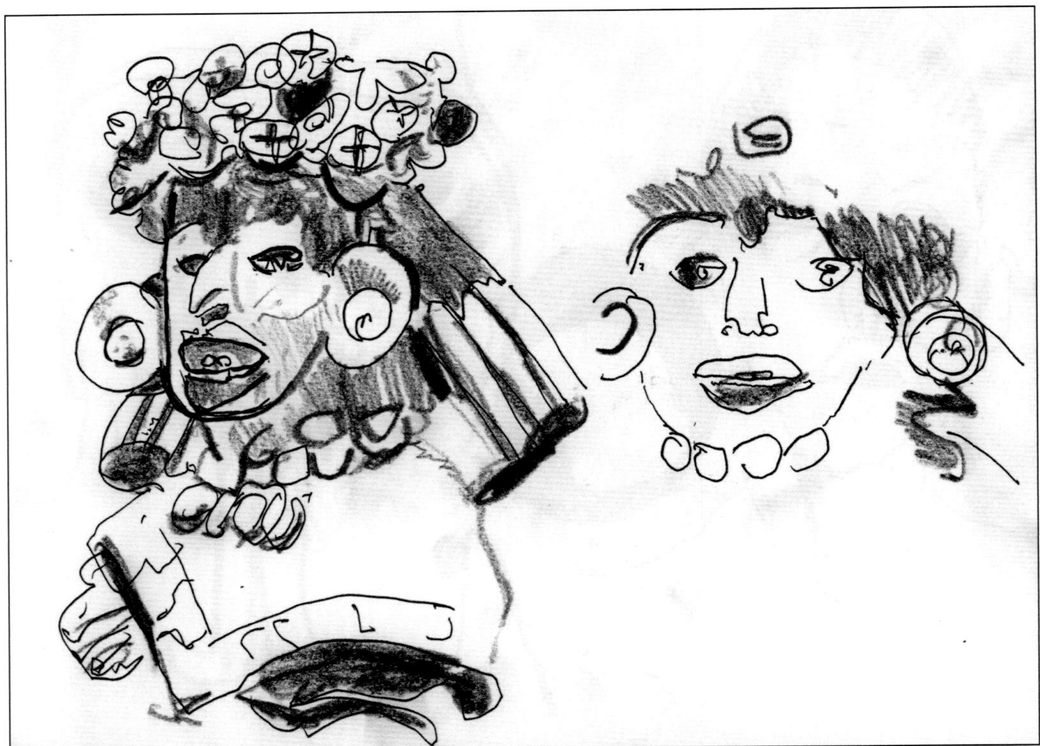

Statuette, and Dolores imitating it

At those times I wondered whether she knew her own interest. If the word got out, what kind of person might she be taken for? All the same, I clicked the shutter.

Just what a photographer owes his subject is an eternally unresolved question. I suppose that what Michael Walzer remarked on the subject of just and unjust wars pertains here: "Whatever the rules may be is less to the point than the fact that there are rules." In any event, throughout my career I have sought to show respect and gratitude for the people who pose for me, asking and thanking, paying those who need it, and refraining from making nonconsensual images except under very particular circumstances such as the following: a person is dead, unconscious, or otherwise a victim, and the picture is about his situation; a person is part of life in a public place, etcetera. For me such photographs are exceptions. Mostly, I ask. I would rather fail to get a good photo than fail to be a good neighbor to others.

In commencing this project, of course, I looked forward to exploiting myself with ruthless abandon, without regard for courtesy, dignity and all the rest of it. Since Dolores belonged entirely to me — was in fact my construct, who came and went only at my will — how could she stop me from posing her as I chose?

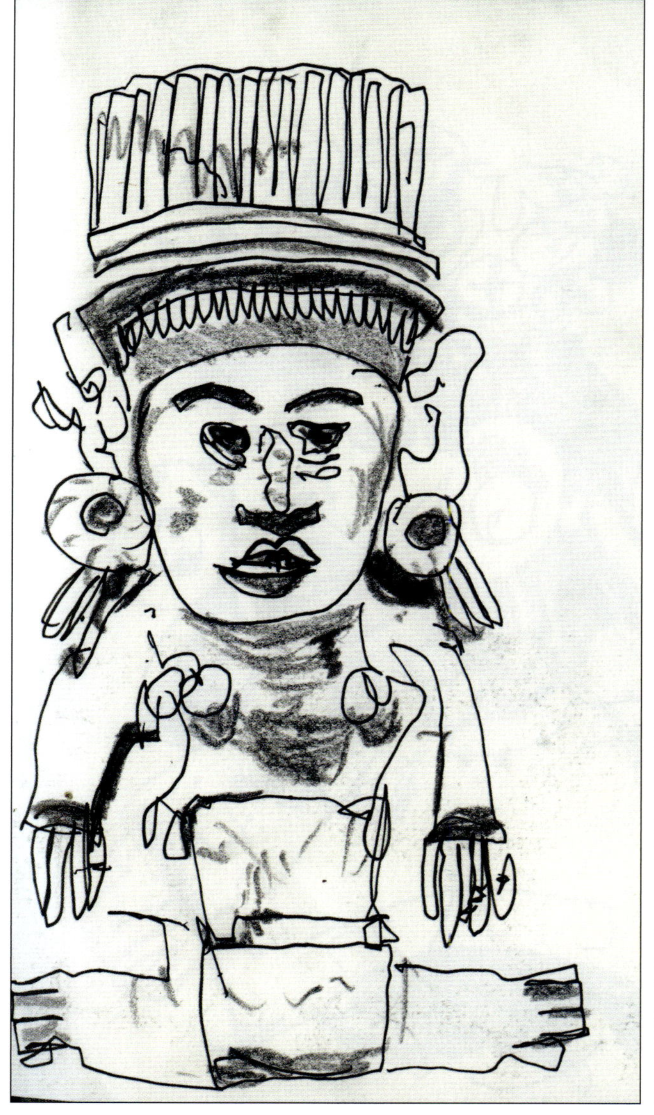

Indigenous idol

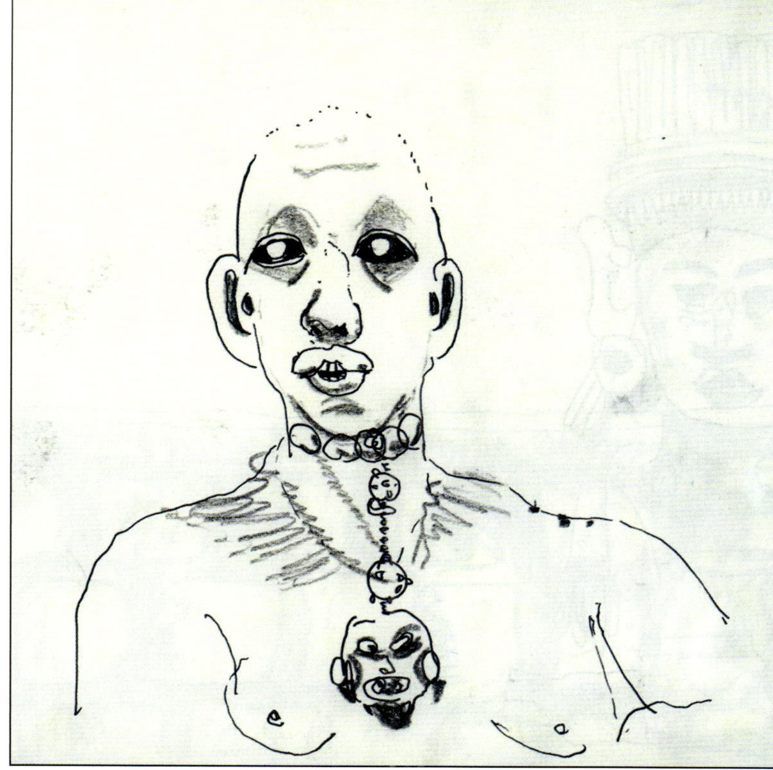

Dolores as idol

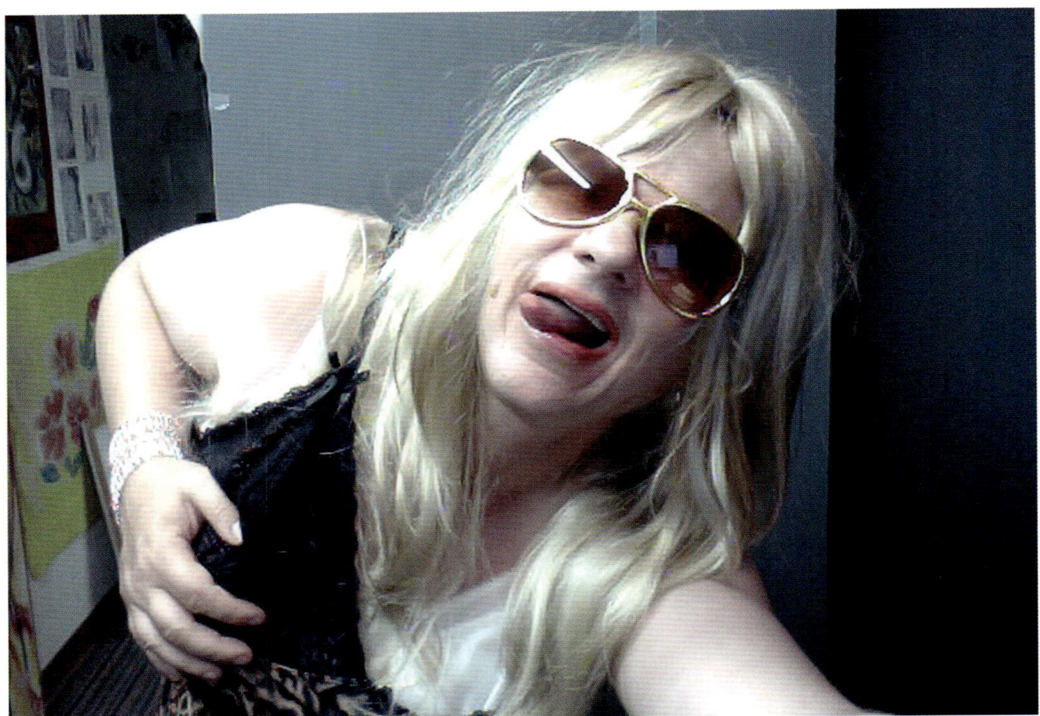

Party girl

All the same, in certain respects she turned out to be a difficult model. Like me, she could be stubborn and unrealistic. As I keep remarking, she expected to look beautiful, posed with what she fondly supposed to be a come-hither look (derived, I suspect, from half-remembered glances at fashion magazines and pornographic pictures), and offered my camera what was in fact the vacuous simper of a wall-eyed, jowly man of late middle age. When I put my spectacles back on and saw these pictures for the first time, I felt embarrassed on her behalf. Poor Dolores! But, after all, I owned her, so if she appeared ridiculous, grotesque or pathetic, there was nothing she could do about it, and it certainly didn't affect me.

(My friend Jeff, who develops my film, laughed at the pictures and said: "You know, Bill, you really are awfully ugly." He and I both eventually got used to it.)

I would have liked to photograph her nude, out of curiosity or empathy. Unfortunately, Dolores nude would have been nobody other than myself. — Or am I mistaken? Precisely because she is blinder to her faults (or merely because she is newer), she appears more at ease with herself than I. Although people do sometimes inform me that the pictures of her tend to look "sad," and in my condescension I think of her as such, she may well be more gleeful than I, or at least freer. Had I asked her to pose without clothes, I am sure that she would have done it. (Perhaps I did ask; maybe the pictures didn't come out.)

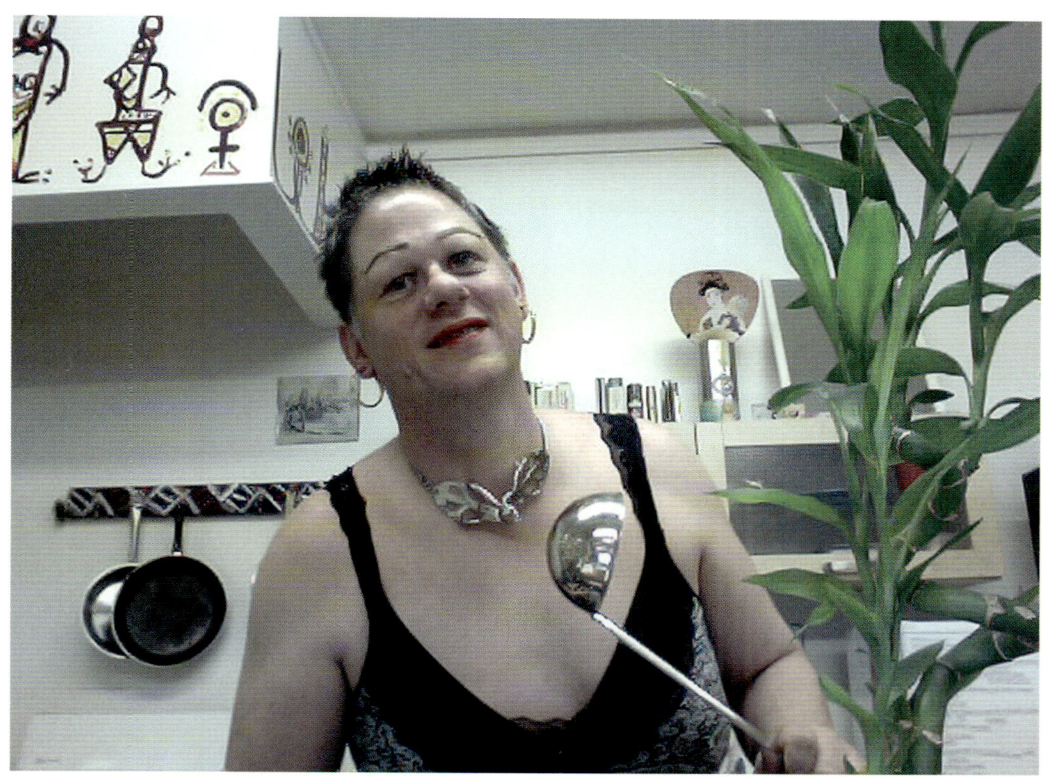

Housewife

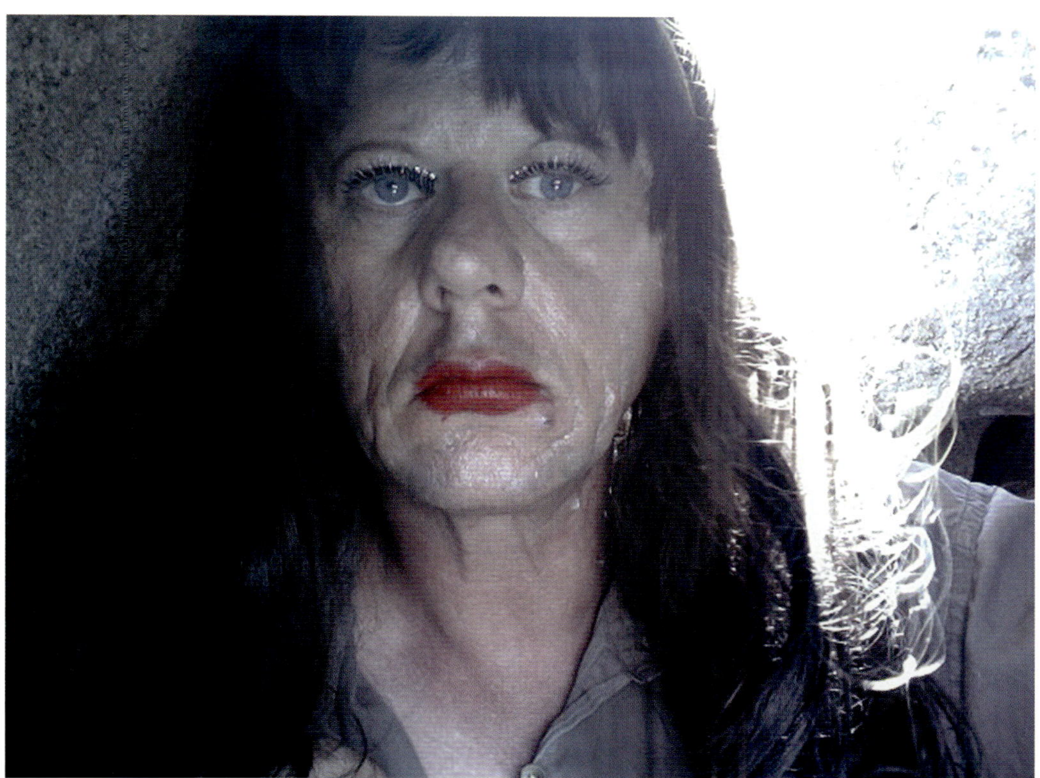

Geologist

I compassionate Dolores in her pathetic vanity, her peculiar determination to be what she is not (for she is not anything). With the publication of this book she will doubtless receive her just deserts: laughter, pity and contempt.* Foreseeing that, I find myself almost touched by the long defunct moment when she still supposed she was pretty. Thanks to her, I have begun to learn how much it might be possible to become happier or sadder by means of a definition.

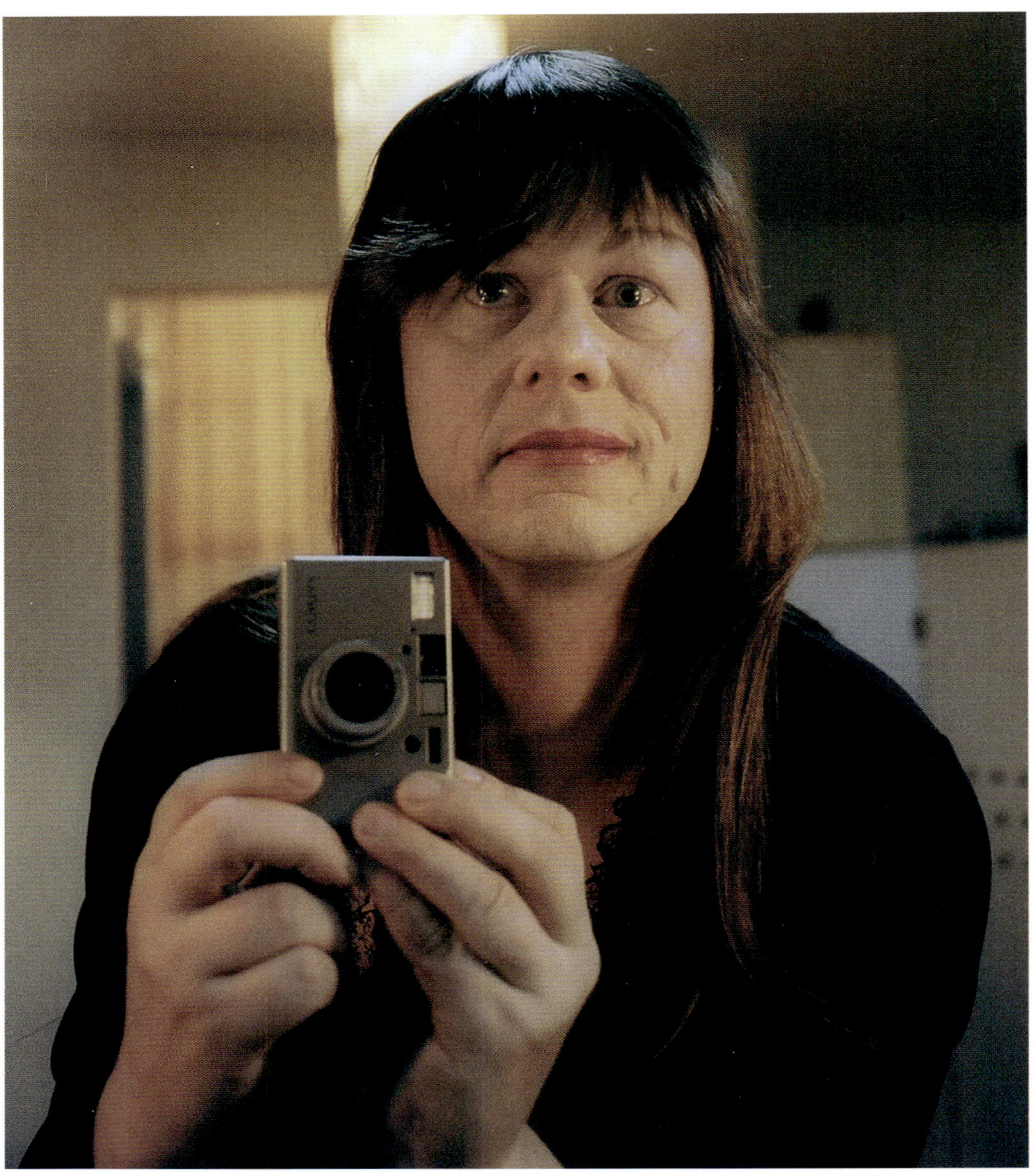

* Among her less expected humiliations were the cattily invasive comments she received from certain women. If she presumed to return the favor, in however mild a form, her tormentors took offense. (As for certain men, they threw rocks.) By and large, it was the women who were kindest to her, at least to her face. When they complimented her outfit, or, better yet, her makeup, Dolores glowed. Among this experiment's many rewards was rediscovering the tactful generosity of others.

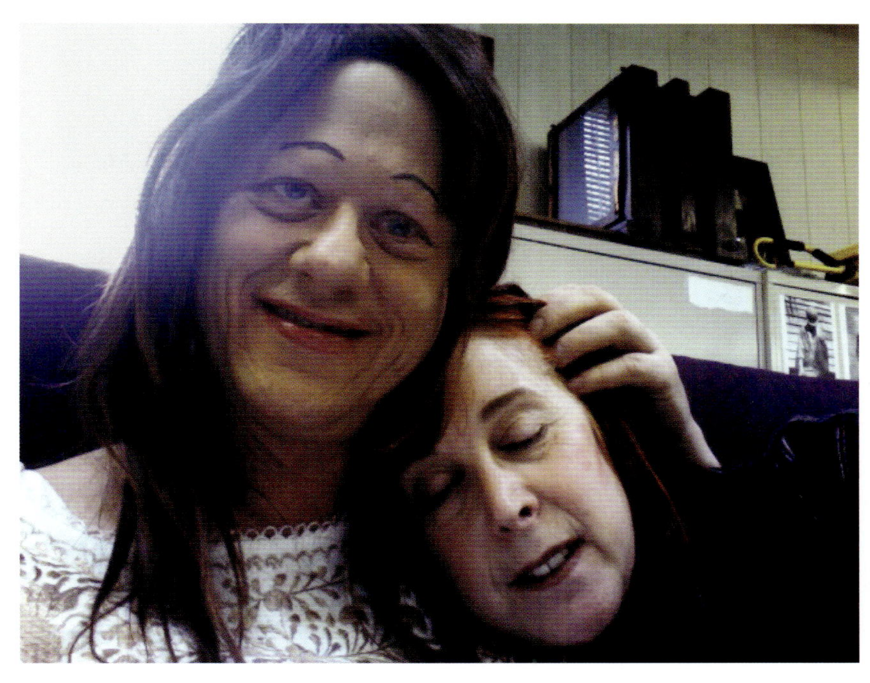

dolores and her friends

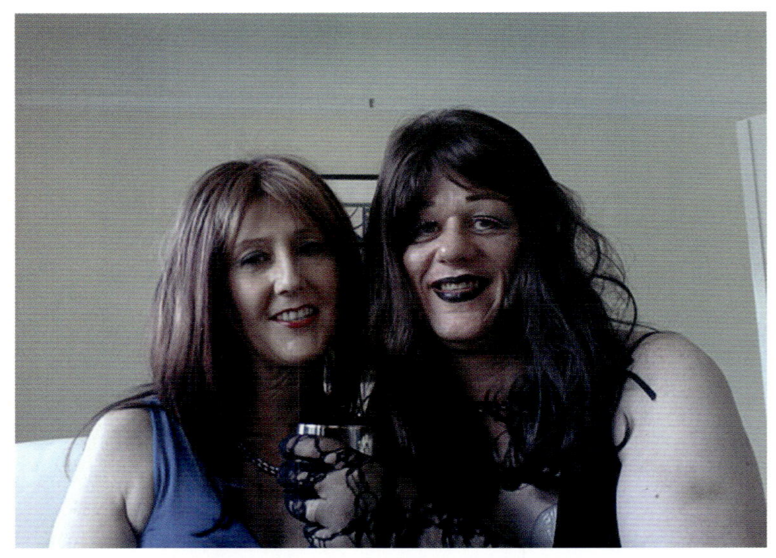

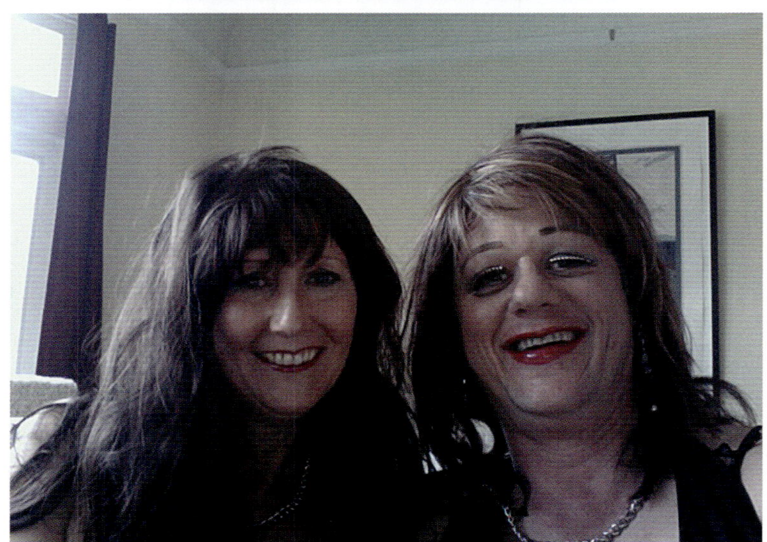

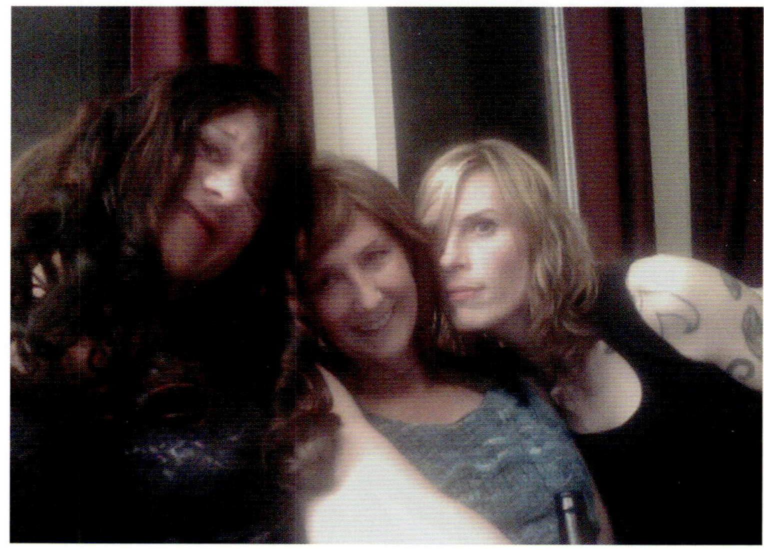

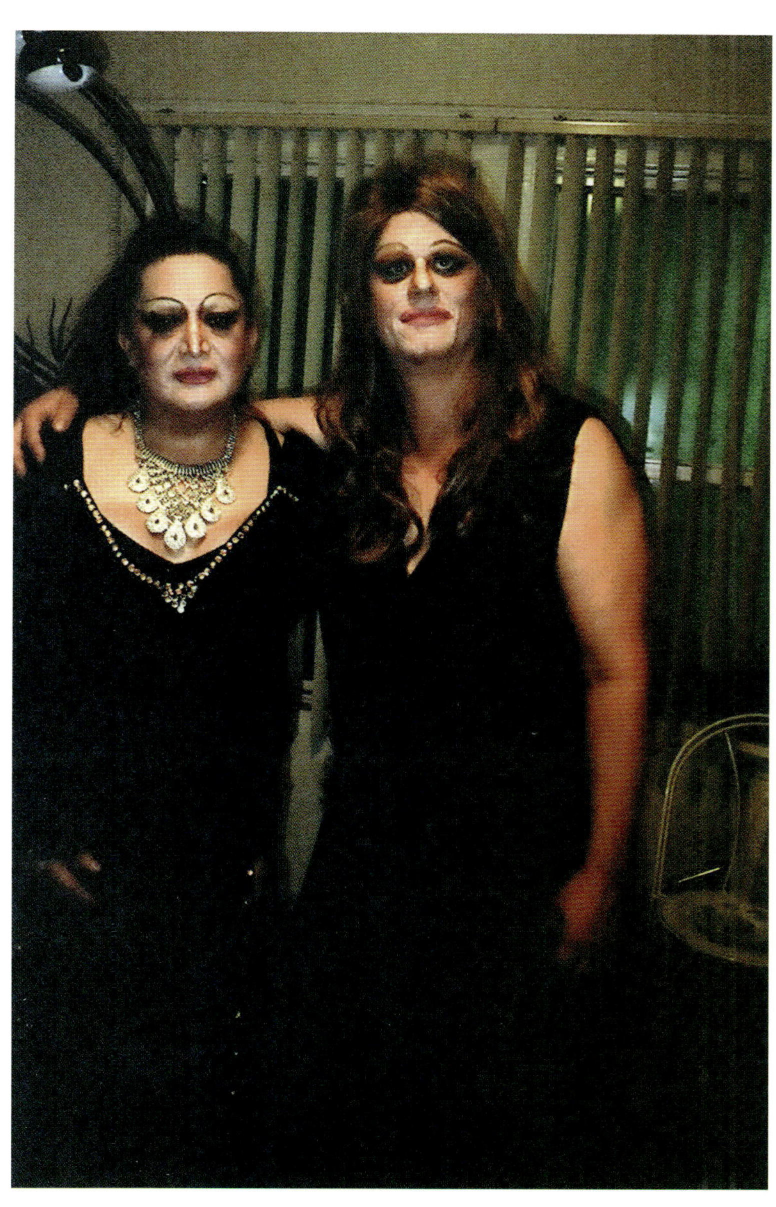

1.2: Practicing and Recording, *or*, Confessions of a Lady's Tailor

"We don garment after garment, as if we grew like exogamous plants from addition from without."* Thoreau, perhaps, did not have cross-dressers in mind when he wrote that fetching sentence. Nor would he have approved of them, I fear, but to quote him again: "I do not mean to prescribe rules to strong and valiant natures, who will mind their own affairs whether in heaven or hell."** However well or poorly I might have minded my own affairs, I certainly kept myself busy, sometimes by inventing little tricks: For instance, since Dolores could not seem to learn how to hook her brassiere from the back as most women do, I used to hook it on in front for her, after which she swung it around. Although half the human race (I forget which half) were of Dolores's kind, the procedures and props to which she aspired were poorly understood by me, no doubt because whenever I had previously kept company with a woman who happened to be undressing, her lingerie was no more to me than the bread in a sandwich, and I 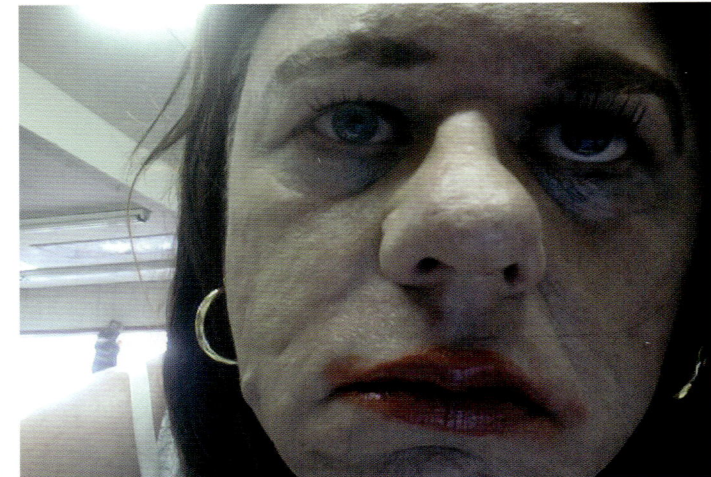 have never been one for starch; as for the reverse operation, at that point I tended to be more sorry to see her body vanish than interested in how she covered it. But in Dolores's case, what was she but the things she put on?

In short, a good portion of my effort went into learning how to become Dolores, becomingly (at least by her standards). The rest consisted in photographing her without getting in her way. Hence in this section you will first find some snapshots under the rubric of "Becoming Dolores," and a few others to show some of my recording processes, whose final results appear in the second part of this book. Here they are:

On occasion I have made paper negatives of myself with an 11 x 14" film camera,

---

* Henry D. Thoreau, *The Illustrated Walden, with Photographs from the Gleason Collection*, ed. J. Lyndon Shanley (Princeton: Princeton University Press, 1973; orig. ms. finished [8th version] 1854), p. 24.
** Ibid., p. 16.

but the lens is very slow; my shortest exposures (outdoors, in bright sunlight) are 4 minutes. I more frequently used one of my three 8 x 10"s. The Kodak 2D field camera proved itself to be the most practical of these, although I have permitted the slightly grander-looking Wisner to parade itself in the chapter on paper negatives.

Often I merely point a 35 millimeter camera at my face.

Most frequently, however, I have managed with a rather poor quality laptop camera (JPEG, 80-odd kilobytes). The picture below depicts this simple procedure, as caught for your edification in the bathroom mirror. Dolores had just been made up by a transgender prostitute named Melissa in a hotel in Mexico City.[*]

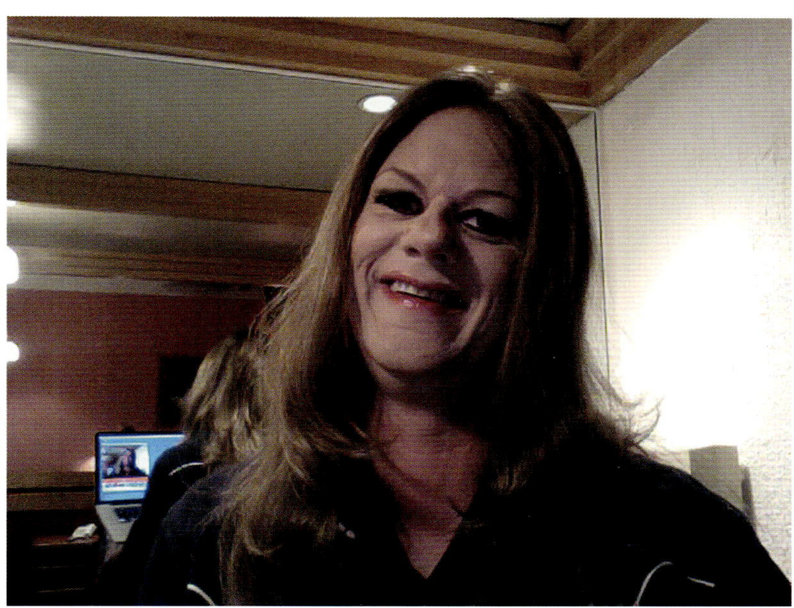

The peculiar photographic device I had chosen constrained her poses extremely. Unless some reliable surface happened to be available at the appropriate height and distance, she had to hold the laptop out at arm's length, gripping it in her right hand while her left forefinger or middle finger held down the shift key in order to suppress the primitive flash, which tended to bleach images beyond redemption. This pose could be (especially when, for instance, standing on a chair with heavy breast forms, a tight slip, pinchy earrings and a noose around one's neck) tiring and distracting, as one can tell from her frequent expression of stoicism, strain or even bewilderment. And, of course, this circumstance ruled out most full length portraits.

So there was Dolores, trying to be a sport, grimly gazing at me with her arms outstretched, sweating in her makeup, which she never learned to apply excellently with-

---

* See "Melissa's work" on its two versions on pp. 81 and 175

out help (mascara troubled her especially, because when I was three I underwent an operation on my left eye which infected me with a revulsion against bringing anything too close to it).

I have picked out a few snapshots to illustrate this all too characteristic quality of my female gaze. (Most of the laptop portraits in this book partake of it to some extent.) On another spread are some complementary male self-portraits. Since I rarely hoped to "pass" as a woman, Dolores's forays into public spaces were brief and uneasy. But "in drab," as some T-girls call their state of maleface, she attracted no remark. On those occasions she could pose more or less as she pleased in the light. That is why the male portraits are in that respect more varied.

* * * * *

It might be argued that whatever Dolores is she reveals most essentially partway through her transformations. She begins to represent what she wants to be, but has not gotten there yet, so that through all her mediocrity and awkwardness her hope glimmers. Confronted with the photograph of her with the asymmetric eyelashes, smeared lipstick and pores bursting through the face powder, one has to wonder if she understands how poor a job she did. Since this particular making-up occurred early in her life, my guess is that she did not. What will these heavy blue eyes express once they see the truth? I have documented this situation in the section "In Between."

Of course the construction of femininity must address secondary sexual character-istics, whether or not it chooses to represent them. While not every inch of Dolores is necessarily everyone's business, I am willing for the sake of sincerity to show you certain incarnations of her breasts, in a final eponymous section. — Hormones, falsies or trick photography? — Only Dolores knows for sure.

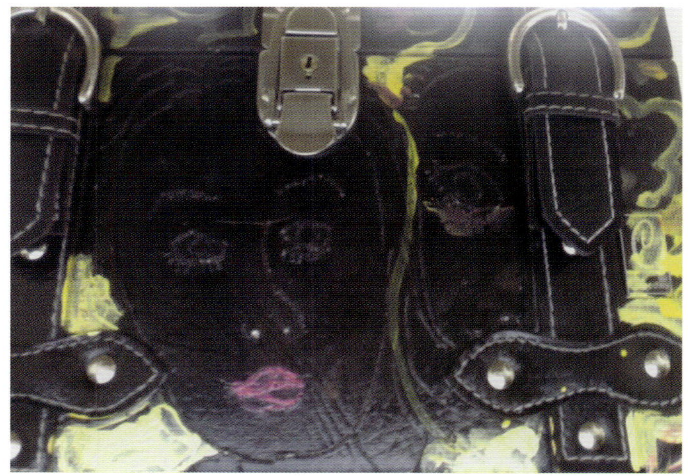

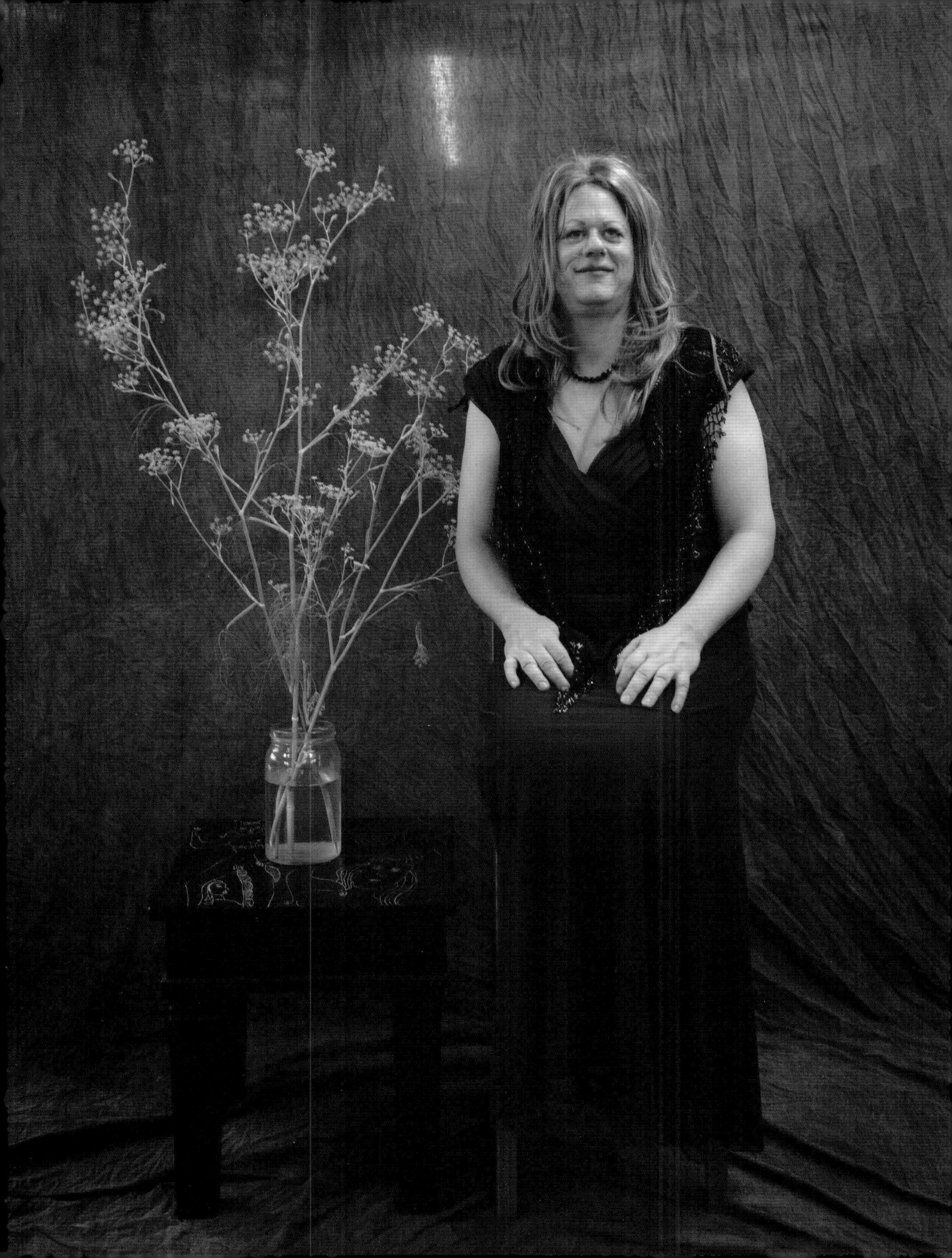

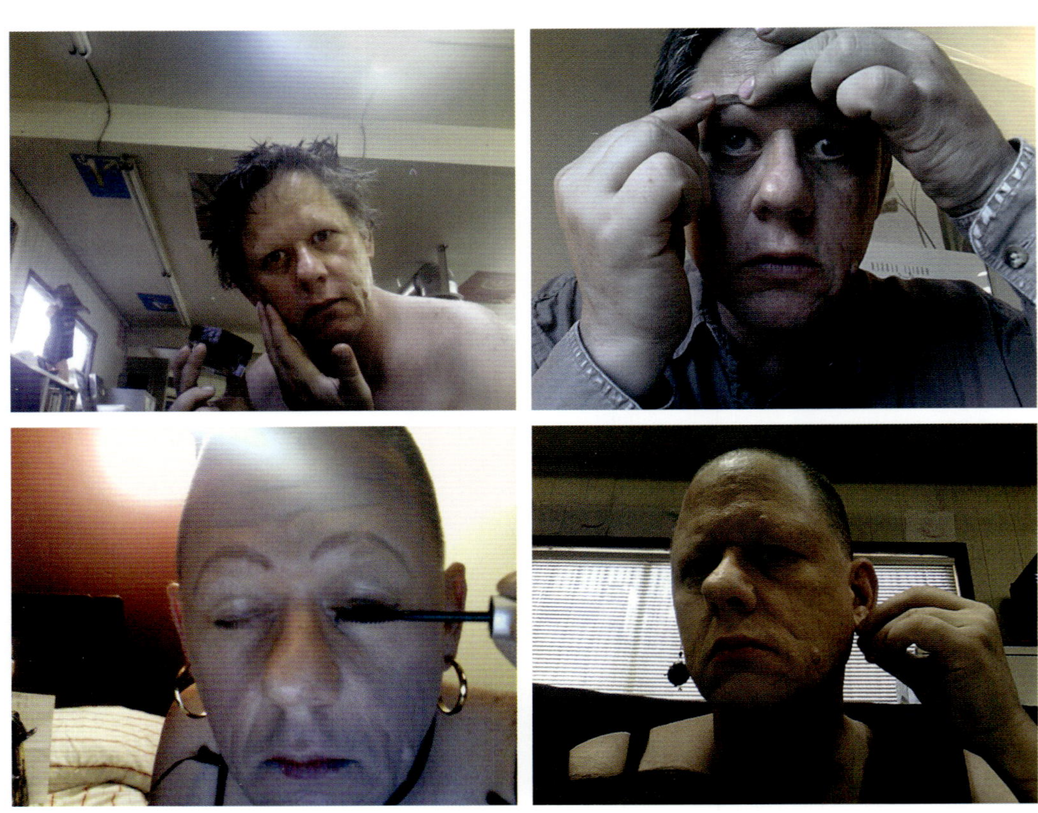

becoming dolores

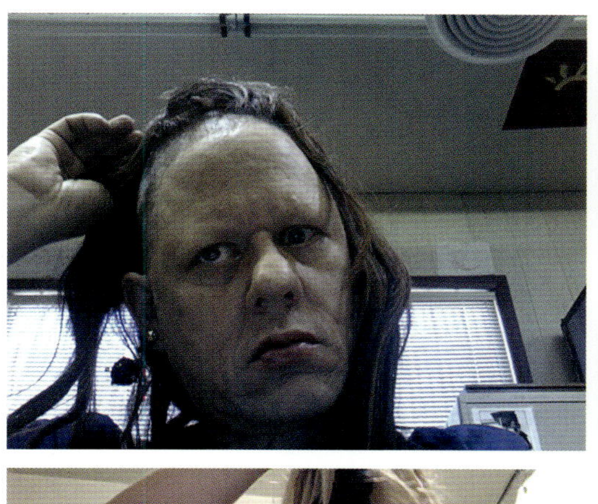
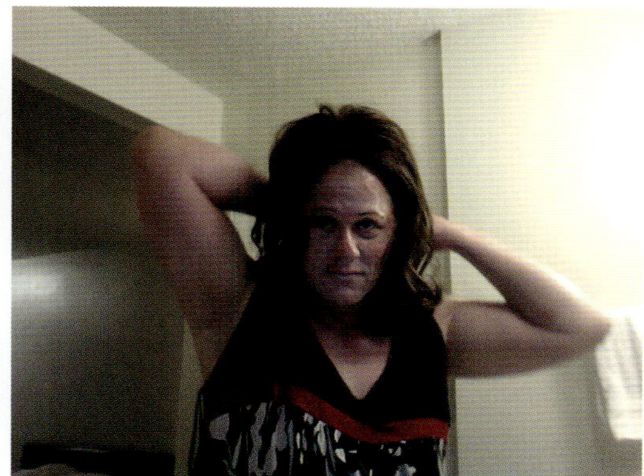
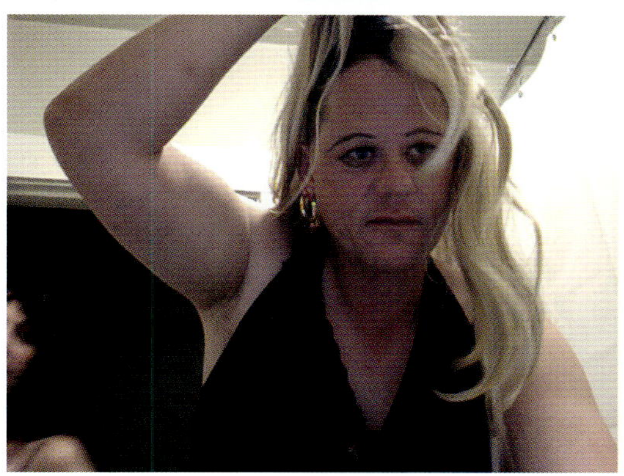
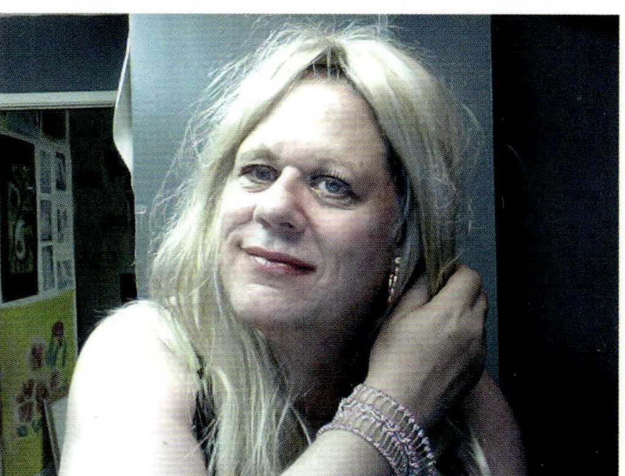

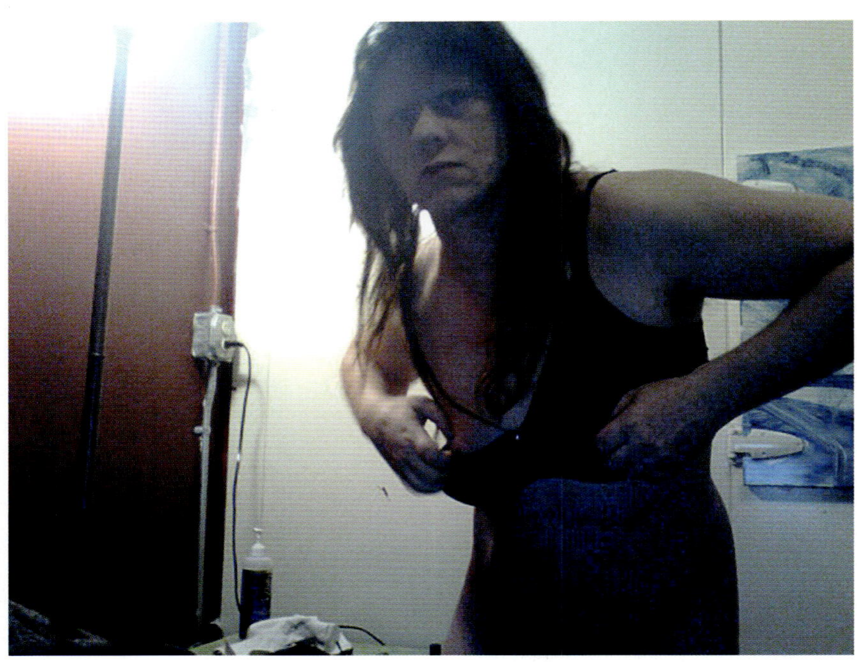

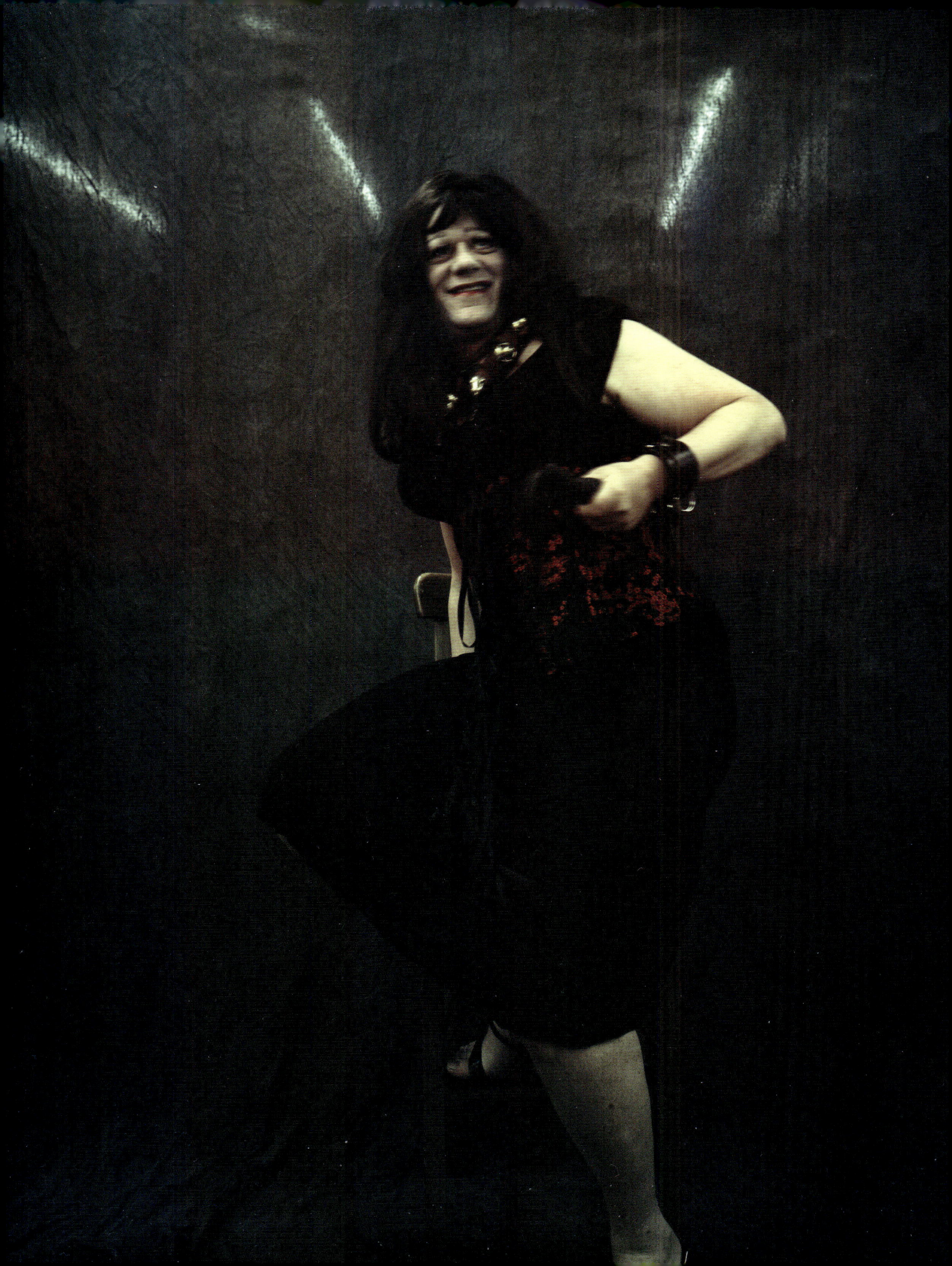

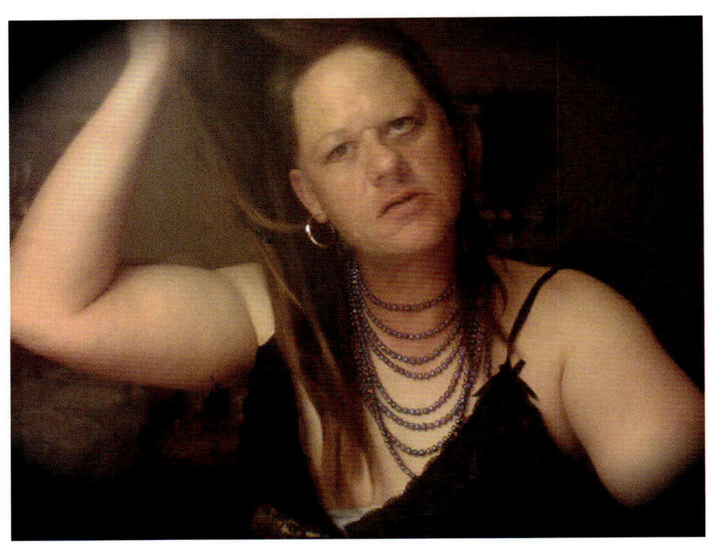

in between

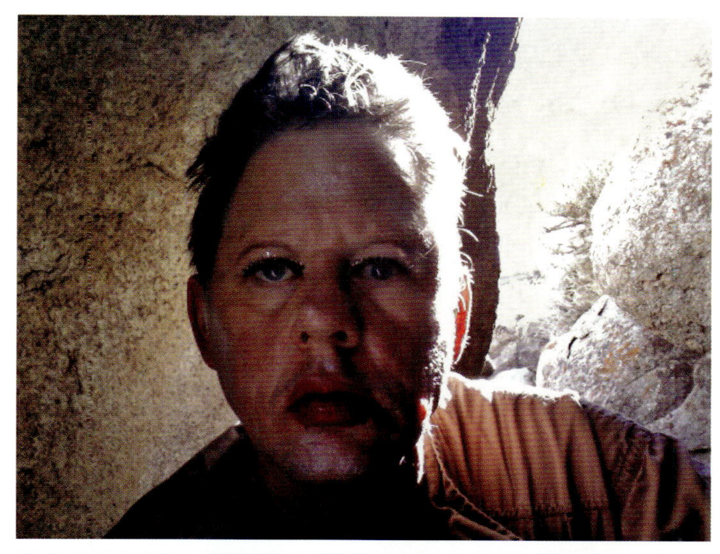

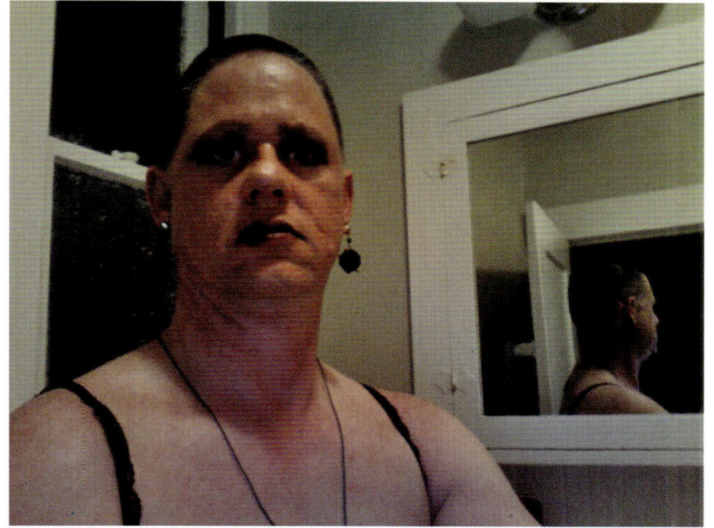

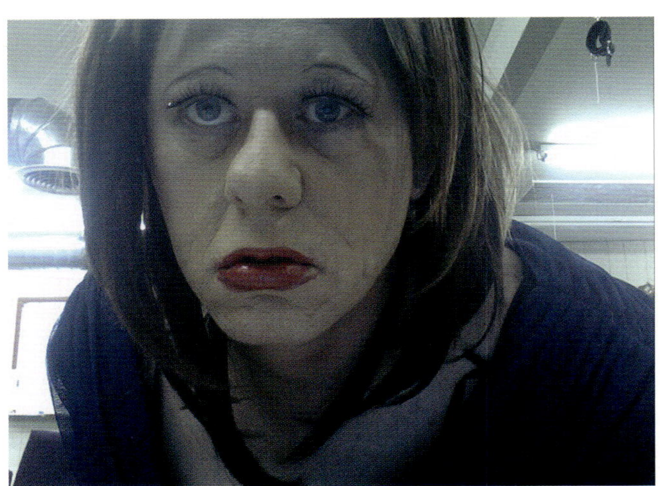

first female gazes

And as long as he sat on the bed, stroking Dolores's hair, feeling the articulated swings of her Christmas-ornamental earrings . . . he felt that he was she, and so happy in her existence; but should he gaze at himself in the bathroom mirror he would see Dolores's sad, sad eyes looking out at him from a bespectacled man's wide and stubbled face.

from *How You Are*

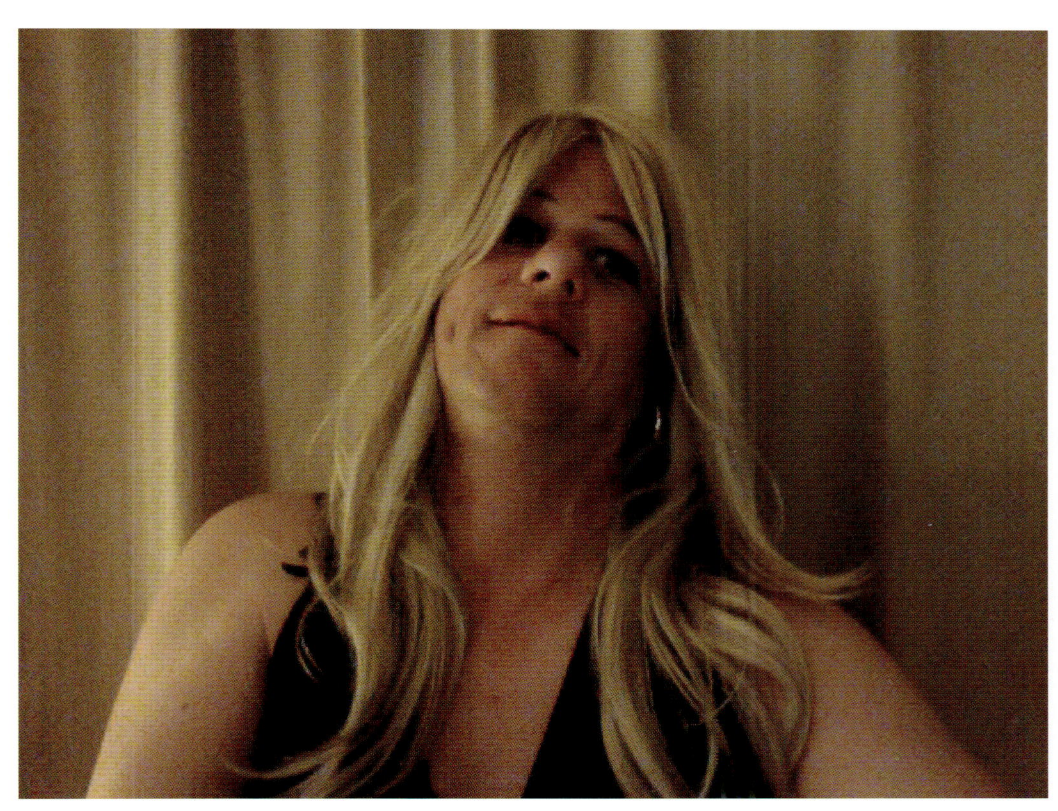

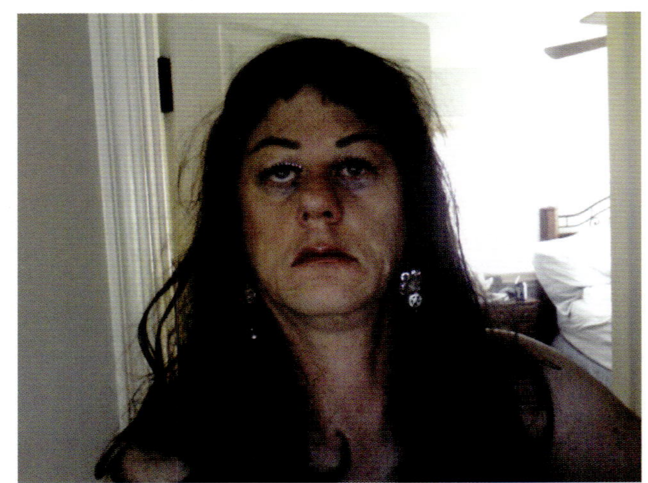

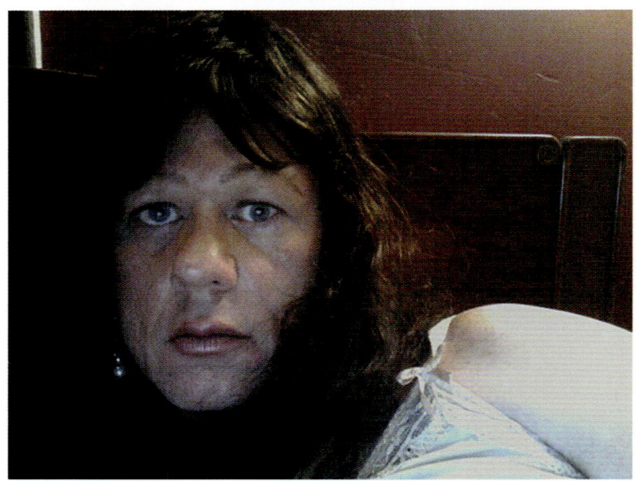

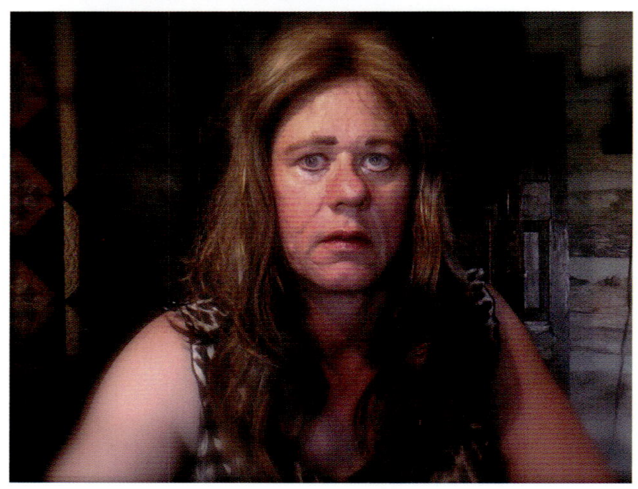

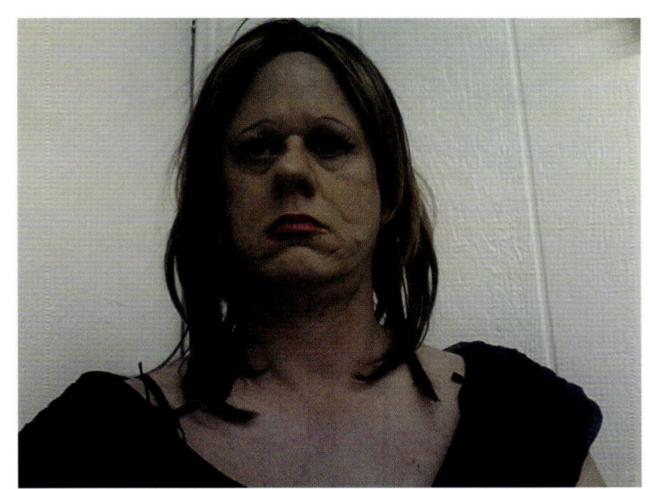

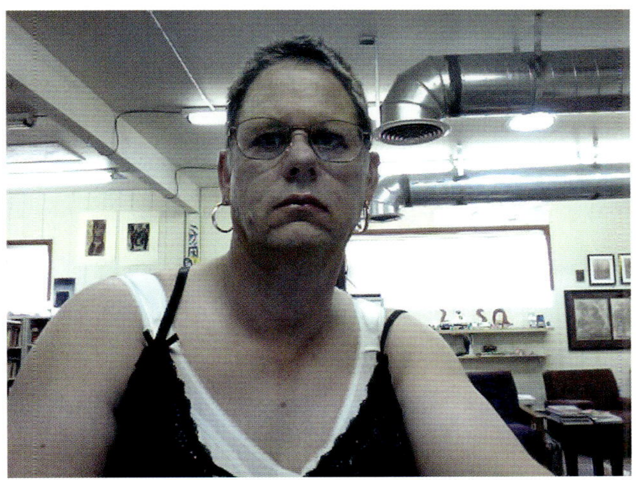

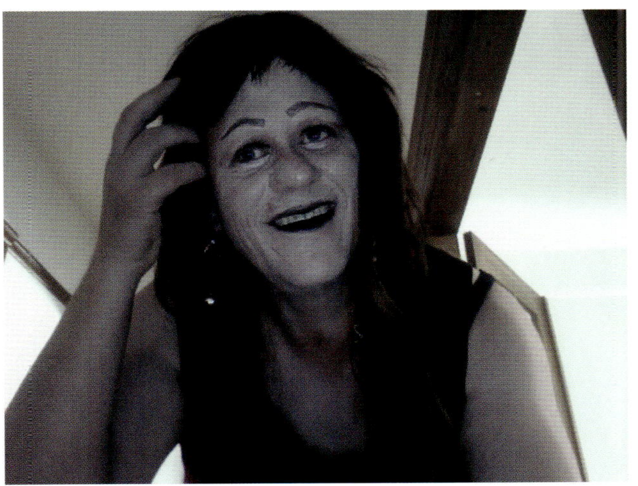

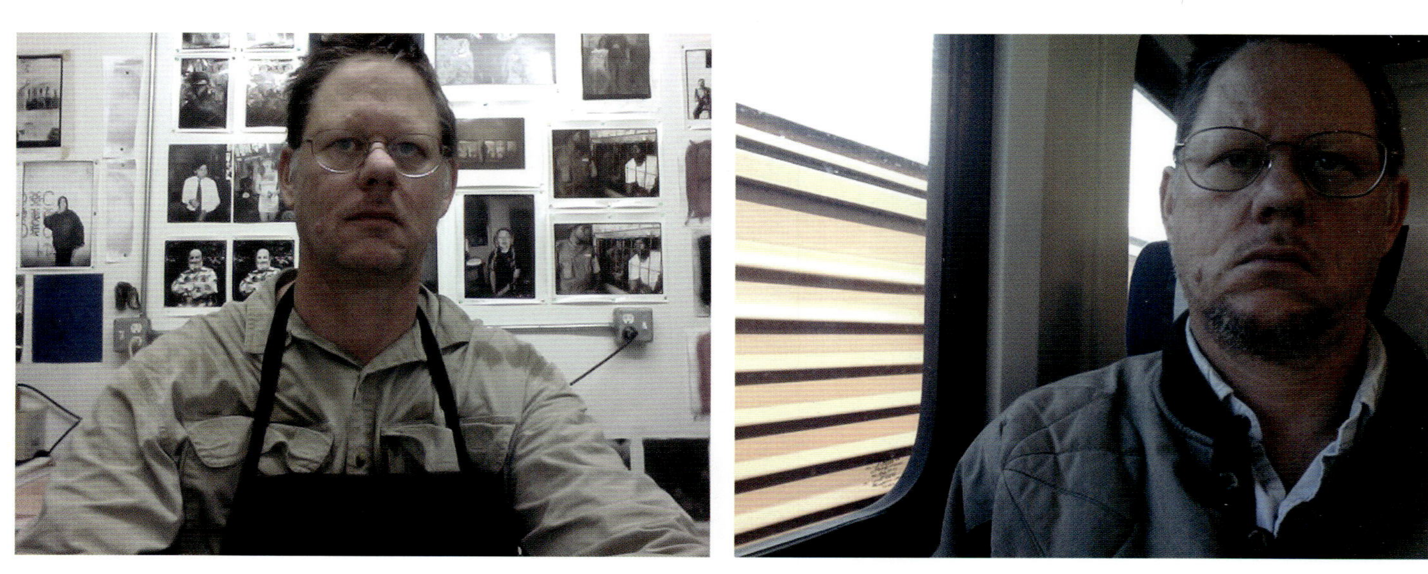

male gazes

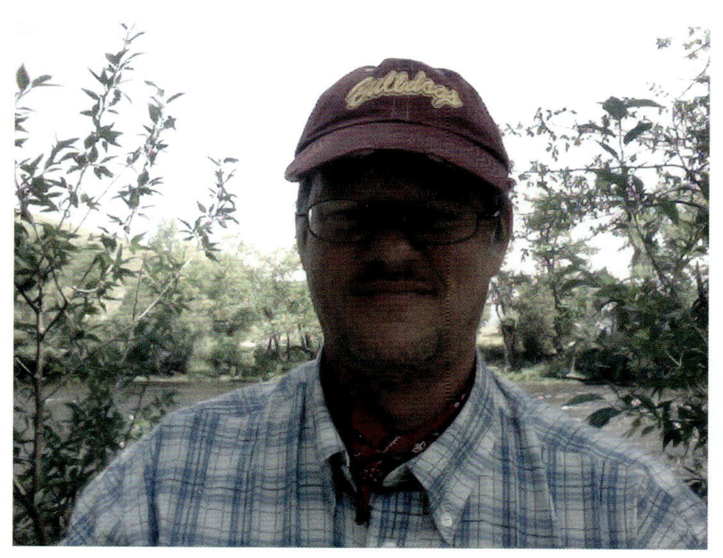 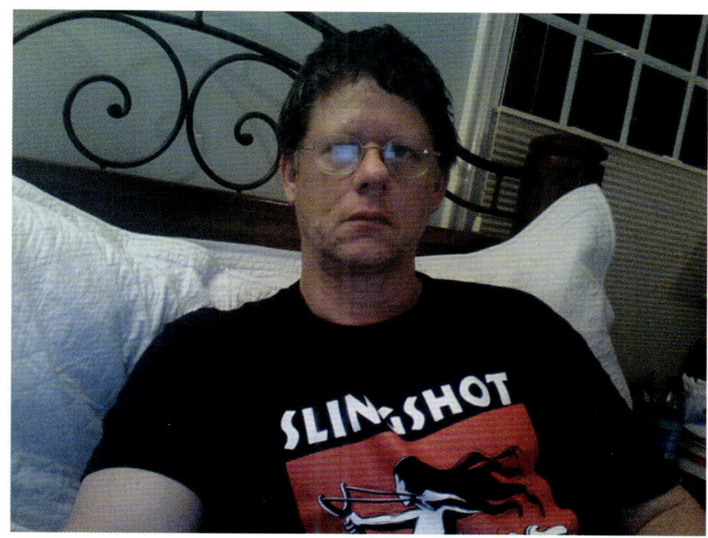

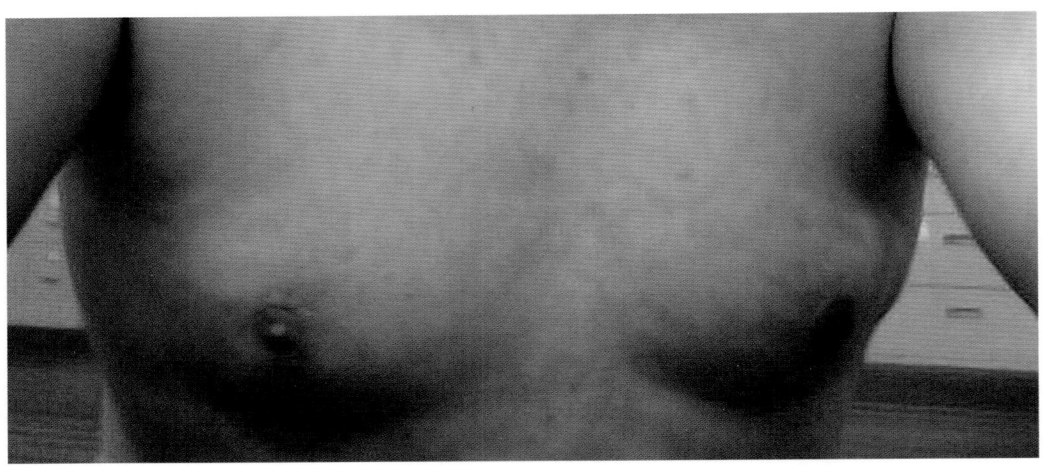

breasts

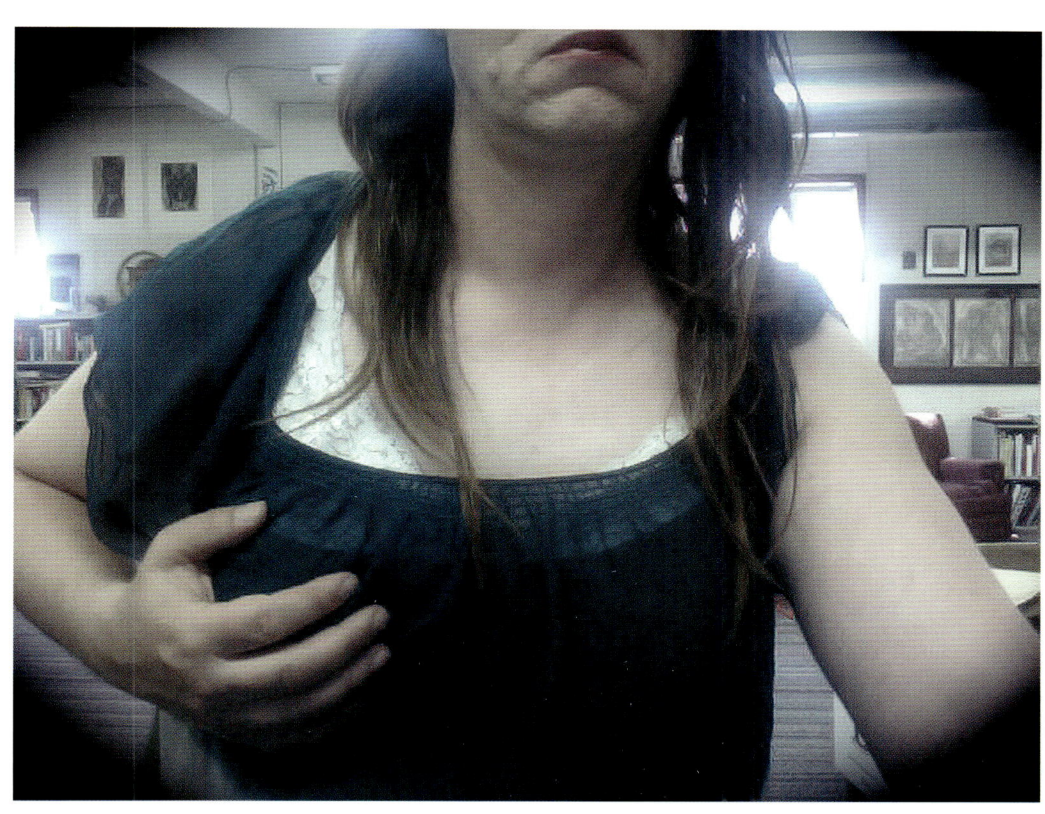

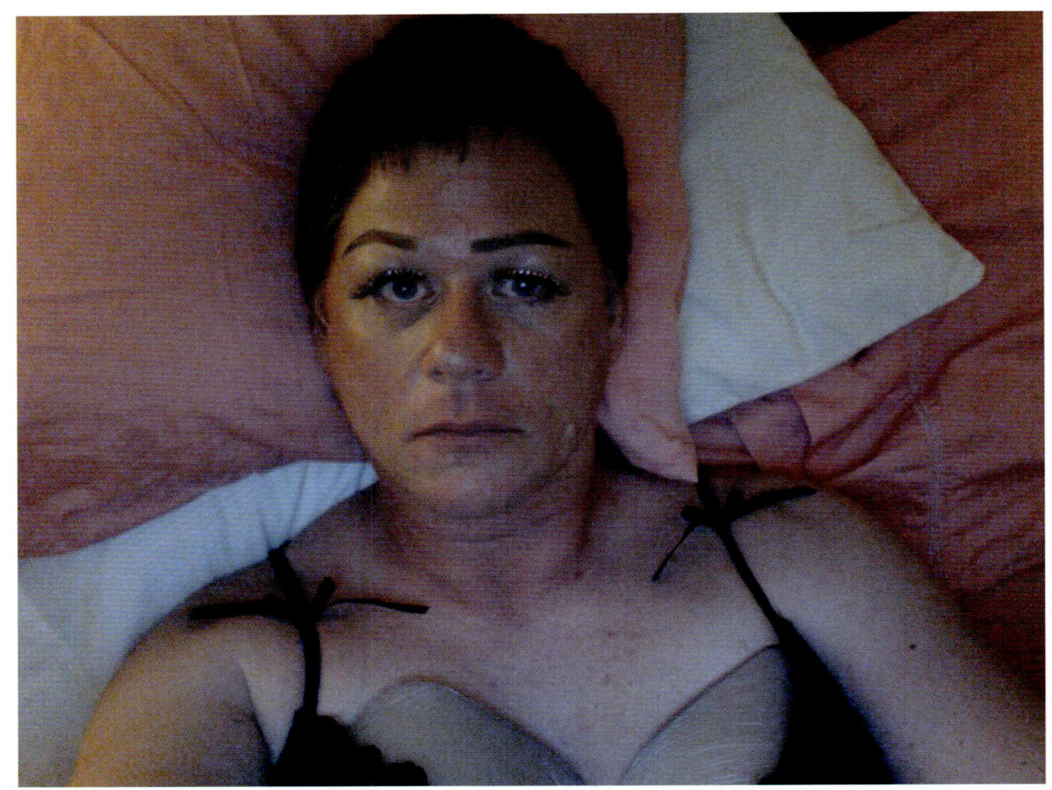

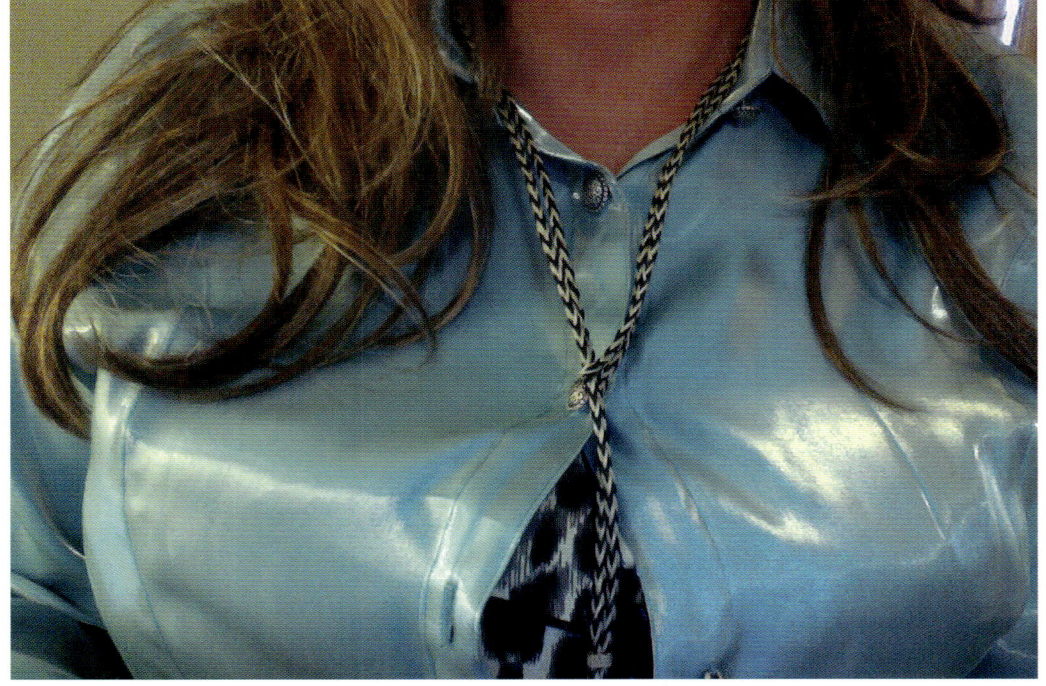

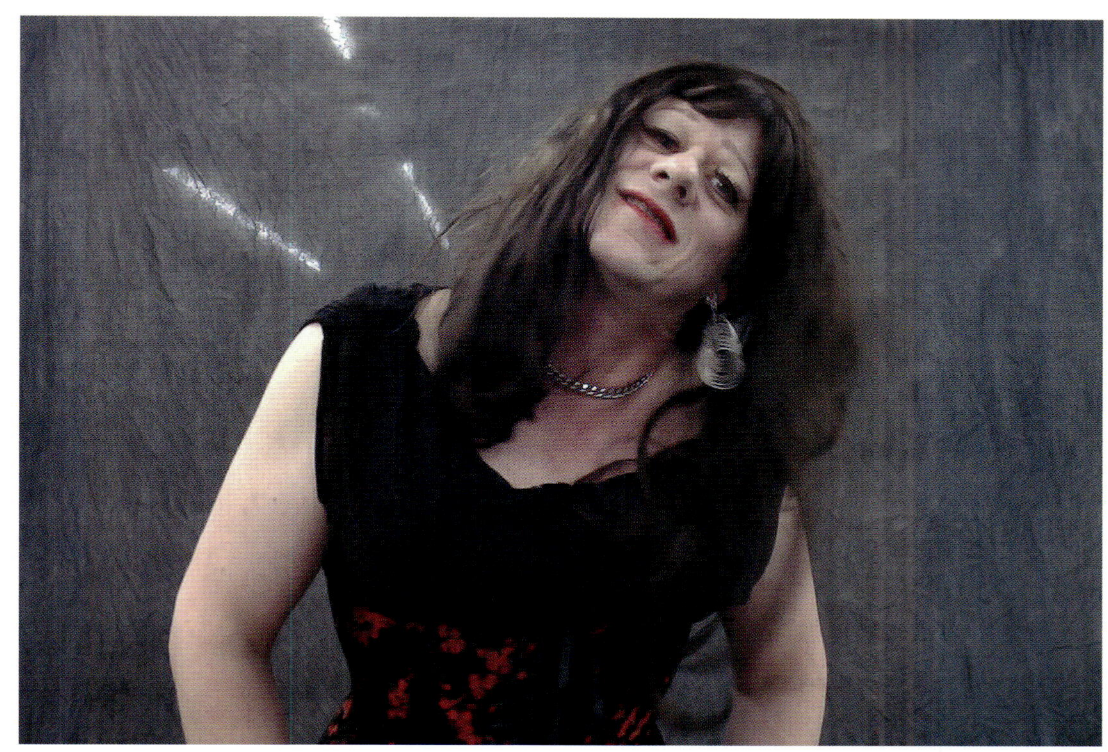

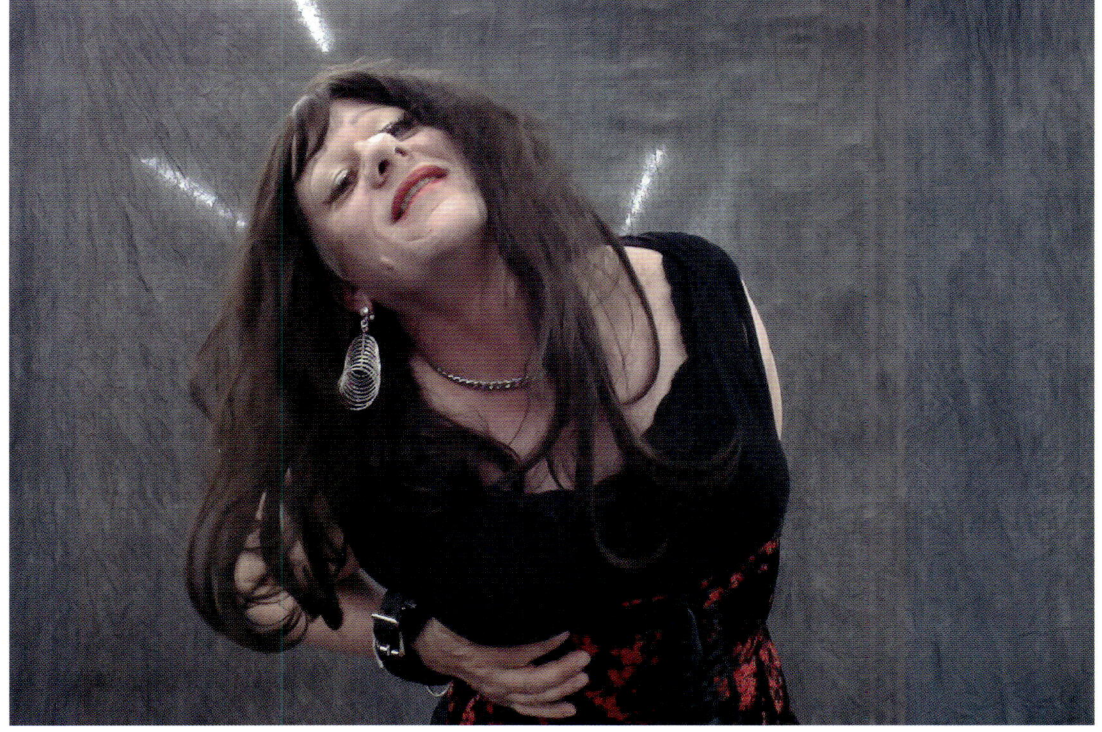

1.3: How You Are

Herbert Marcuse, 1955: "The individual comes to the traumatic realization that full and painless gratification of his needs is impossible. And after this experience of disappointment . . . the reality principle supersedes the pleasure principle."* Complete submission to the reality principle would simplify our lives, which might grow accordingly sad, but only to third parties who still keep faith with the pleasure principle. When I was writing a book about poverty I visited Yemen, among other places, and one of the people I met was an old beggar-lady named Annah, who was sitting on the street in Al-araf, Lahij governorate. She informed me that her children were "far away" and "always needed money."

"Where do you sleep?" I asked her.

"Outside."

"Why did Allah allow some people to be poor?"

"Allah chose. For me it's no problem. And I am happy."

"If you became rich what would you do?"

"Allah knows! I don't know."

"How old are you?"

"Allah knows."

"What do you think about politics?"

"Allah knows."**

In contrast to her I remember the leader of an Afghan insurgent band whom I interviewed during the Russian occupation.

"What weapons do you most need?"

"Anti-aircraft guns. And if we get anti-air missiles, you will see what a lesson

---

* *Eros and Civilization: A Philosophical Inquiry into Freud*, with a new preface by the author (New York: Vintage Books [Random House], 1961 repr. of 1955 ed.), p. 13.
** *Poor People* (New York: Harper Collins [Ecco], 2007), p. 30.

we can give the Soviet invaders!"

"How bad is the food situation in your part of Afghanistan?"

"Very bad."

"What will you do if you cannot get what you need?"

"Why, perhaps we will kill ourselves, but we will certainly never surrender."*

His magnificent answer proves that the reality principle defines itself only negatively,

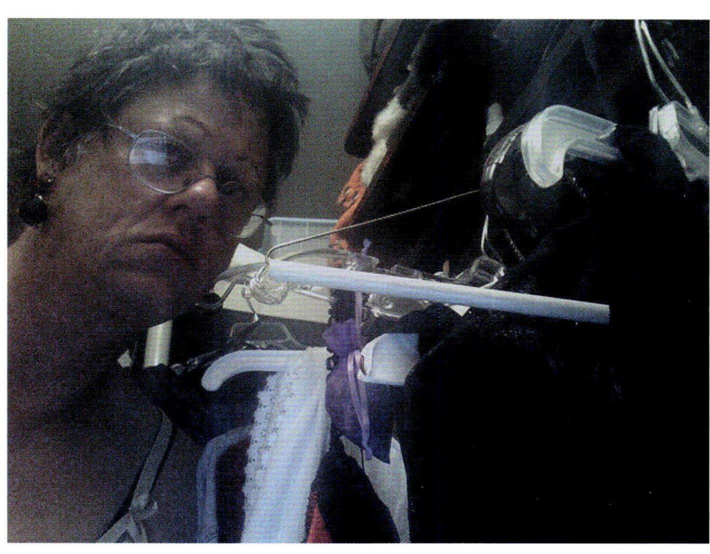

for we can never know how immutable reality is until we contest it. The Afghans did not surrender, and in the end they beat the Russians as they will beat the Americans, who of course are contesting that manifestation of the reality principle and will deny it to the end.

Defiance is the continuum between submission and triumph. We might say that defiance is more noble to the extent that its object is more impossible, for the defiance by the strong of the weak must always be ignoble, whereas he who stands up to authority is, if nothing else, brave. I have always liked Gandhi's admonition to treat the powerless with respect and the powerful with familiarity.**

The dichotomy between the pleasure principle and the reality principle underlies the normal losses, lacks and disappointments in any life. As a reader, writer, lover, artist and citizen who interests himself in character on and off the printed page, I study what literary critics name ambiguity, Marxists call dialectic, Orwell pinpointed as doublethink, and Bildungsromans present as growth, maturation and decline. One of the points where all these entities overlap is defiance.

Of course reality versus pleasure is far from the only conflict in life. People often get

---

*   Quoted in my *Afghanistan Picture Show, or, How I Saved the World* (New York: Farrar, Straus and Giroux, 1992), p. 238.

**   When I said these words to a Norwegian audience in 2011, a few months after a certain mass murderer took action there, I added: "Perhaps this is where Anders Breivik went wrong. However much one might pityingly disagree with his fear of Islam and multiculturalism, his point of view, like any and all opinions, deserves a hearing. Indeed, the more hateful the point of view, the more crucial it is to understand it, for the sake of self-defense. Being a foreigner, I cannot presume to tell you very much about Norway, much less about Mr. Breivik. However, we all know that beneficial or not, change cannot be dissociated from loss, nor can it be escaped — two more corollaries of the reality principle. Hence his rage against change in Norway could not have been utterly causeless. But in his defiance of power, he forgot who was actually powerless when he murdered children."

crushed to pieces between the grindstones of conflicting realities, as did the Poles during the Nazi-Soviet pact. And one can certainly be torn between two pleasures, tragically or not. Moreover, the specific qualities of both reality and pleasure alter as we live, so that whatever submission, victory or defiance we enact must itself change.

As I think about the life I have lived so far, it strikes me that the reality principle, which well-meaning people would have us believe is "just a part of life," is actually an extrusion of death. The nature of all life is self-assertion and aggrandizement. My daughter's pet lizard will theoretically grow as large as his cage, they tell me. Traditional American economists wish for steady growth forever. And I myself desire what I desire, in as considerable a quantity as I can get. If I could, I would restore my dead father to life and I would protect my child from ever dying. In these examples the pleasure principle seems no more or less than life-assertion. As such, it is not good or bad in itself; neither is death. My task as a literary writer is to describe the interplay of life and death as beautifully and accurately as I can. I may, if I wish, defy the entire meaningless process, as did Ivan in that famous passage of *The Brothers Karamazov* when he cried out against the suffering of innocents:

> When the mother embraces the fiend who threw her child to the dogs, and all three cry aloud with tears, 'Thou art just, O Lord!', then, of course, the crown of knowledge will be reached and all will be made clear. But what pulls me up is that I can't accept that harmony . . . I don't want harmony. From love for humanity I don't want it. I would rather be left with the unavenged suffering . . . And so I hasten to give back my entrance ticket . . . It's not God that I don't accept, Alyosha, only I must respectfully return him the ticket.[*]

To me this defiance is as admirable as the Afghan Mujahideen commander's, since it is warmhearted. I myself only rarely adopt Ivan's position, because if God ever gave me an entrance ticket, I must have mislaid it. My despair about the general category of unmerited suffering has become resignation. I see no justice in the natural order, and so I seek to present the struggle, if that is what it is, between life and death, as equivalent to the dancing of a flower in the wind. When a child is murdered, whether or not the murderer is tried and judged, nothing will bring about the harmony in which Ivan would still craves to believe. If it comforts us to explain the matter coldly, we can say that when the child died, the pleasure principle was superseded by the reality principle. Lead won out over flesh. And we can accept this, defy it, or defy the murderer and his ideology, but in any event we cannot prevent some other child from getting murdered tomorrow. To know this and to go on living, what is that but adherence to the pleasure principle? With our mouths we agree that death possesses ultimate power over all life, but our hearts have been fashioned to forget or defy this

---

[*]   Fyodor Dostoyevsky, *The Brothers Karamazov*, trans. Constance Garnett (New York: Modern Library, n.d.; orig. Russian pub. 1879-80), pp. 253-54.

fact. I myself feel called upon to remember it but not to insist on it. In other words, my personal bent is to submit to the reality principle but in my own way, standing up to bullying when I can and forgiving myself when I cannot. As I get older, I may be growing a little braver, perhaps because I need less or have less to lose. Once upon a time the reality principle cowed me more.

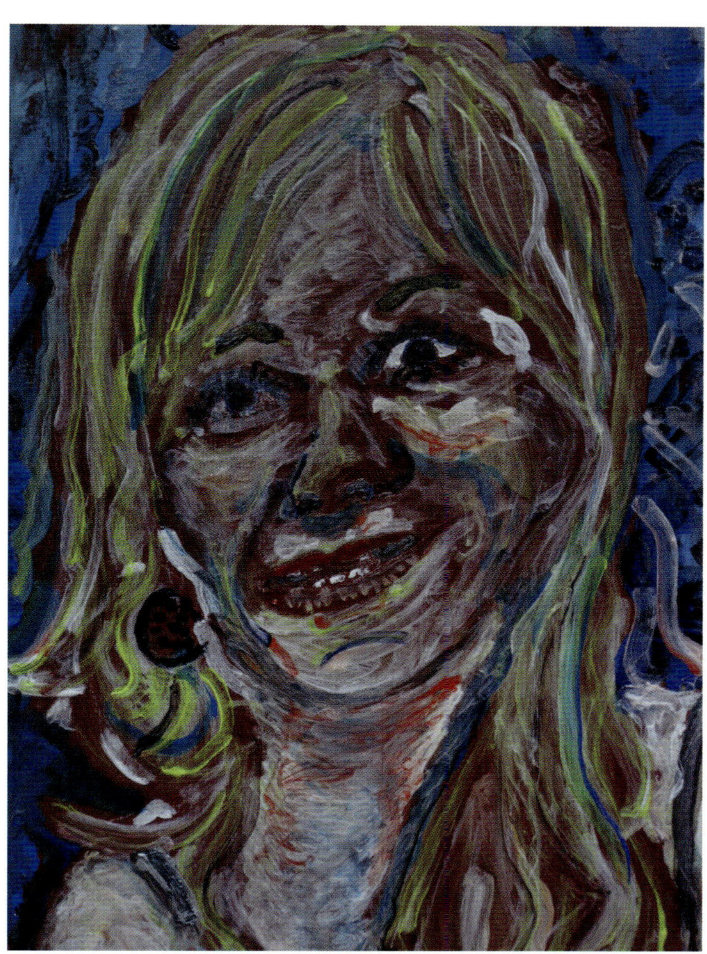

My early childhood was nearly friendless, which goes far to explain why Dolores mostly prefers to lurk indoors. I used to wonder how to enter the crowd — an impossibility, for my taint was incurable: I can see only out of one eye at a time, and so I could never catch a ball. In the place and time where I was raised, that failure was not only contemptible but nearly unforgivable. At school I was always last to be chosen for any sports team, and whichever one had to take me booed. Worse yet, I loved to read and could spell, which rendered me worse than defective: I was a subversive, a pervert. Among American children, an inclination toward the life of the mind is perceived as a blasphemy against the worship of the average. It is defiance, and therefore must be struck down. Year after year I was humiliated and physically attacked. Had it been within my power to catch a ball and hate books, I would have done so, for wouldn't most children sell their souls to be loved? But I could not. Although my nature was an insult to theirs, I never felt defiant, for my circumstances asserted that there was some wrongness about me. All I could do was exist, and seek to hide who I was. I had already reached adolescence before I realized that my nature could scarcely be changed; hence I might as well accept myself. At once I felt relief. I could not be like others. Very well; I need not try. Strange to say, I then began to be liked, and since then I have been blessed with as many loyal, loving friends as I could wish. As for Dolores, she has kindly well-wishers, but she still hopes to be what she is not.

No one is utterly free from vanity or anxiety, but in my own various projects I resist defining myself on the basis of others' judgments. While I like very much to please others, I decline to depend on their pleasures. A vitriolic review of my latest book might cause me five minutes of embarrassment; a friendly one might buck me up for an instant; either way, it goes in the scrap paper box; my books remain as good or bad as they were before. Call this defiance if you will. I call it acceptance. As for Dolores, the blandly damaging remarks of women or the menacing obscenities of men cause her misery, and the poor thing is happy whenever someone compliments her hair. Thus I live out my childhood. Fortunately, Dolores does not exist; I can lock her in the closet whenever I wish; I'm the man around here.

When it comes to affairs of the heart, I have not always been able to achieve so convenient a distance. Most of us experience disappointment in love, and in my case there were several relationships whose ending I experienced as a sort of death. I often found it easier never to see the woman again than to interact with her in the shallowness of some semi-intimate friendship. This is defiance of a sort. I honored the pleasure principle by remembering the woman as she was in my heart, preserving her. Really it was cowardice or immaturity. Had I managed to accept that the reality principle killed this particular attachment, then I might have been able to continue benefiting from other aspects of the woman — her intellect, her friendship — and to show her kindness. But I could not.

Near the end of my forties I began to discover that my winning ways, such as they were, had become less effective with the opposite sex. Once I might have been a prospective bed partner. Now I was a nice old uncle. It began to seem that my mirror was defective, because this plump, greying fellow with the double chin could scarcely be me. So I defied my mirror. Strange to say, that made no difference; and when I went out in public I began to experience the phenomenon so often mentioned by ageing women: invisibility. We have all met angry, bitter old women-hating men who cannot make sense of the fact that there is no one to blame for their own diminished attractiveness. I did not care to become one of them. Since, as I said, I do like to please people, being a nice old uncle was not so bad; it certainly ranks above being a silly old cross-dresser. Moreover, as a novelist in search of new material I find it convenient to be invisible. So I accepted the reality principle in this instance, thank goodness, not least because my female friends who got facelifts informed me that even those procedures couldn't save them.

At around the same time I began have more difficulty in making friends when I went overseas. Realization of the cause saddened me: I was an American, and America was not what it used to be. Dolores spends too much time mugging in the mirror to concern herself with politics; as for me, here was how I saw it: The rich democracy to which so many of the people in poor countries and war zones longed to emigrate had always been a nest of chauvinistic ignoramuses, but now our minders prosecuted unjust wars, legalized torture and impoverished themselves for the convenience of the rich. Shortly before he died, my father told me: "I used to be proud to be an American. Now I'm ashamed." Shame is hardly my own feeling, since I have not given up on my country. Within my heart lurks the baffled love of an idealist. Therefore, in this instance I find myself defying the reality principle in small ways, speaking out here and

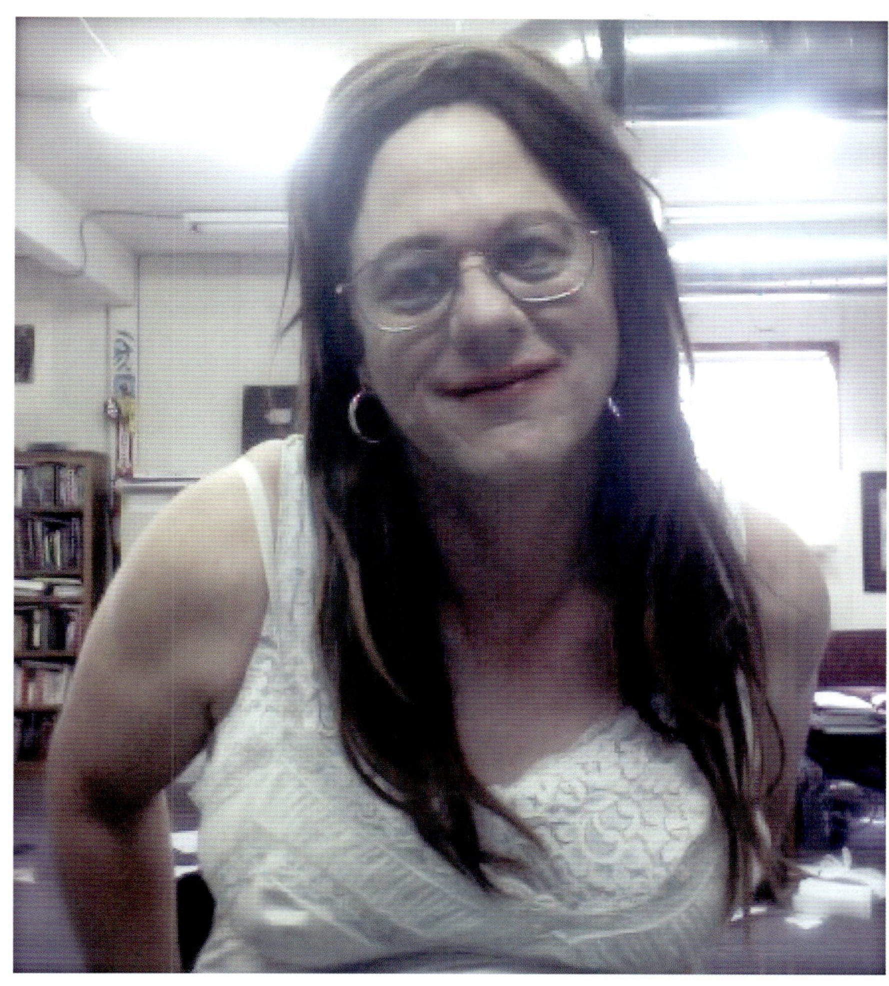

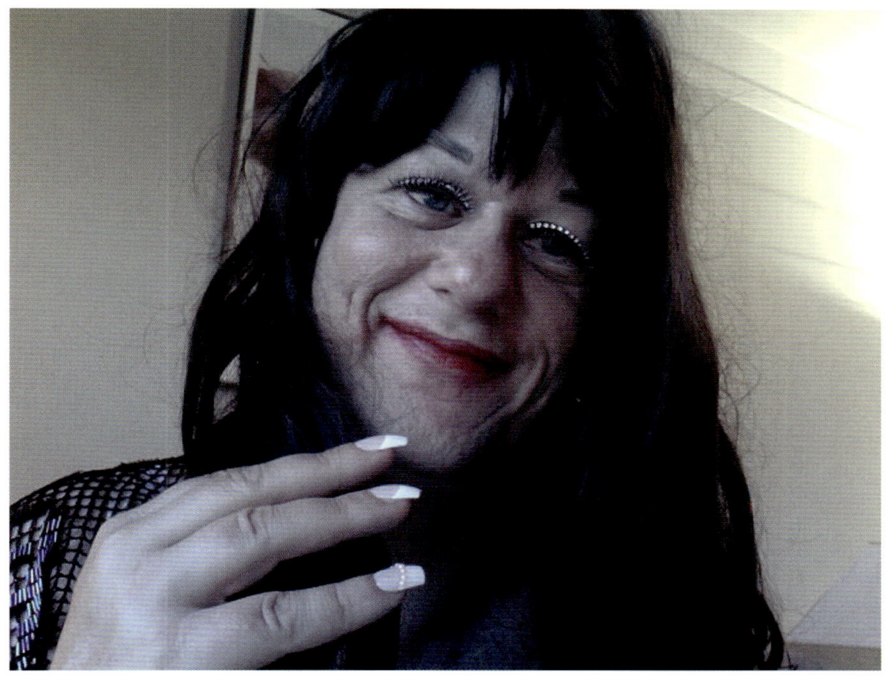

there against the crimes of my government. That this is futile I know full well. The only result I might conceivably accomplish is to invite a raid on my studio or a microscopic tax audit.* But this knowledge is one more chilly shadow of the reality principle, which I prefer to resist unless it gets too inconvenient. I am a man who likes to be left alone. The pleasure principle calls upon me to do what I consider righteous, but the reality principle frequently dissuades me.

So that is who I am. In my imagination, of course, I am any number of other people.

Defiance might justly be called a sort of fantasy, because until the defier has prevailed (if he ever does), the reality principle's insistence that he cannot prevail appears true. Copernicus and Galileo were egomaniacal heretics, lying criminals in thrall to the pleasure principle, until reason and observation finally proved otherwise. Life is itself a fantasy, which defies death but inevitably loses. Because I am myself a fantasist, in my capacity both as a fiction writer and as an empath, someone who considers it the duty of a world citizen to step into the other person's shoes, I discreetly defy preordained places and identities. Earlier on in this book
I mentioned my novel *How You Are*, in which I tried to
imagine myself, or a character based in part upon myself, as a woman. My reasons for undertaking this project
were various (and not identical with my motives for cross-
dressing). I told you that marginalized people have always
haunted me, and in my country the transgendered may
suffer discrimination and worse. Secondly, I had recently
completed a book about feminine beauty, especially as
expressed by geishas and Noh actors in Japan. Since my
subjects were professional performers of womanhood,
I couldn't help but wonder to what extent femininity is
itself a performance. Hence, having in previous novels
imagined the personas of a seventeenth-century Huron
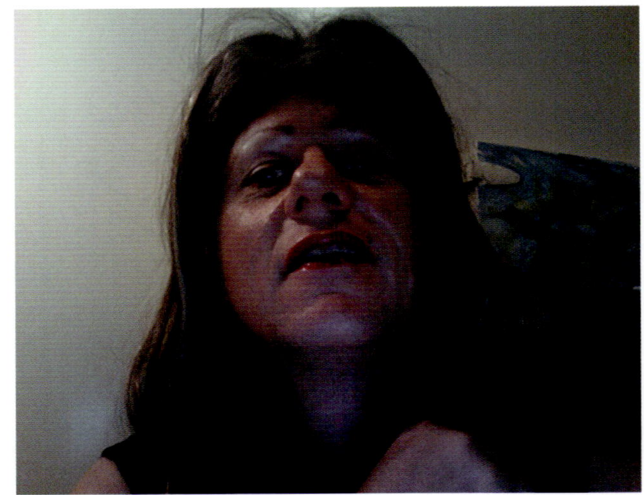
Indian, a twentieth-century Russian composer, a tenth-century Norse outlaw, etcetera, I thought to embody some of my new conclusions and meditations about gender in the form of a woman whose circumstances require her to define herself in relation to maleness. Being a man, and therefore by the reality principle unable for all eternity to know what it is like to be a woman, or even to know how different the experiences of men and women may actually be, I chose to obey the pleasure principle instead, and perform femininity for myself.

In my novel, the protagonist becomes a woman in a far more extreme way than I ever did. Beginning as a cross-dresser in order to gratify first his mistress and then himself,

---

*   Since writing this I have read my (redacted) FBI file. My case might be a trifle worse than I imagined.

he discovers that his personality is splitting. I decided to bless or afflict him with auto-gynephilia: attraction to himself in the image of a woman. Reader, if this runs contrary to any of your own principles, congratulations; you have the Buddha on your side:

> A bodhisattva-mahasattva should not preach the Law to women . . . if he enters the homes of others, he does not converse with any girl, virgin, widow, and so on; nor again does he become on friendly terms with any hermaphrodite . . . *

At any rate, an autogynephiliac defies the reality principle with a vengeance. Not only must he imagine himself in a body of another sex, but he must also double himself in order for the two bodies to embrace and experience one another. *How You Are* thus becomes a somewhat metaphysical tale.

Having finished both *How You Are* and this book of photographs, I owe it to the subject (and perhaps to you) to compare the "real" Dolores whose portraits you see to the heroine of *How You Are*, who happened to be called Dolores.

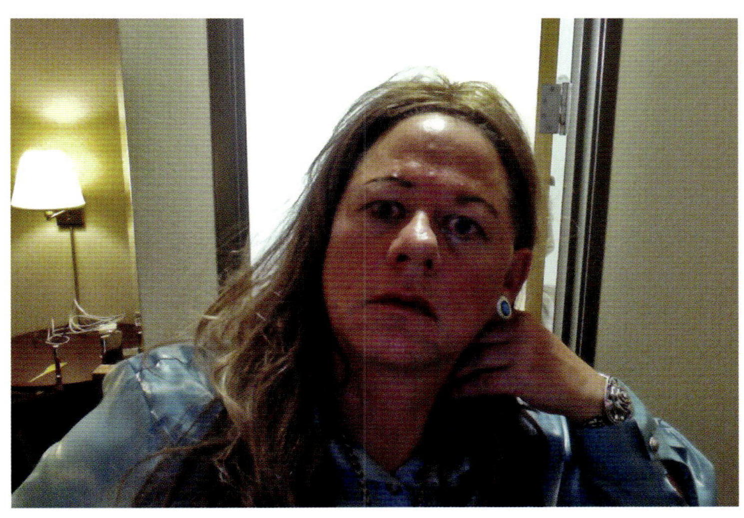

The great expressionist artist Käthe Kollwitz came to use herself as a model. For better or worse, I have done the same. The Dolores of *How You Are* lives a life more sad and lonely than mine. But the other Dolores (I was going to say "my" Dolores, but both are me) simply found it interesting to pose as her for the camera.

The photographs in this chapter both illustrated and engendered (you know what I mean) passages of *How You Are*. Sometimes a spontaneous experiment — particularly when it failed — gave rise, when I put my glasses back on and saw the result, to an idea. The black lipstick and calliope sequences are examples. And occasionally I would ask myself: "How would the Dolores of *How You Are* appear, or what would she do, if this or that happened?" (Hence the birthing cave sequence, abbreviated below.) Although I cannot answer all such question, I can at least guess her whereabouts: That girl spends much of her life in hotel rooms.

---

*   *The Threefold Lotus Sutra: Innumerable Meanings, The Lotus Flower of the Wonderful Law*, and *Meditation on the Bodhisattva Universal Virtue*, trans. Butto Kato et al (Tokyo: Kosei Publishing Co., 1995 [4th pr.]), p. 222 ("A Happy Life").

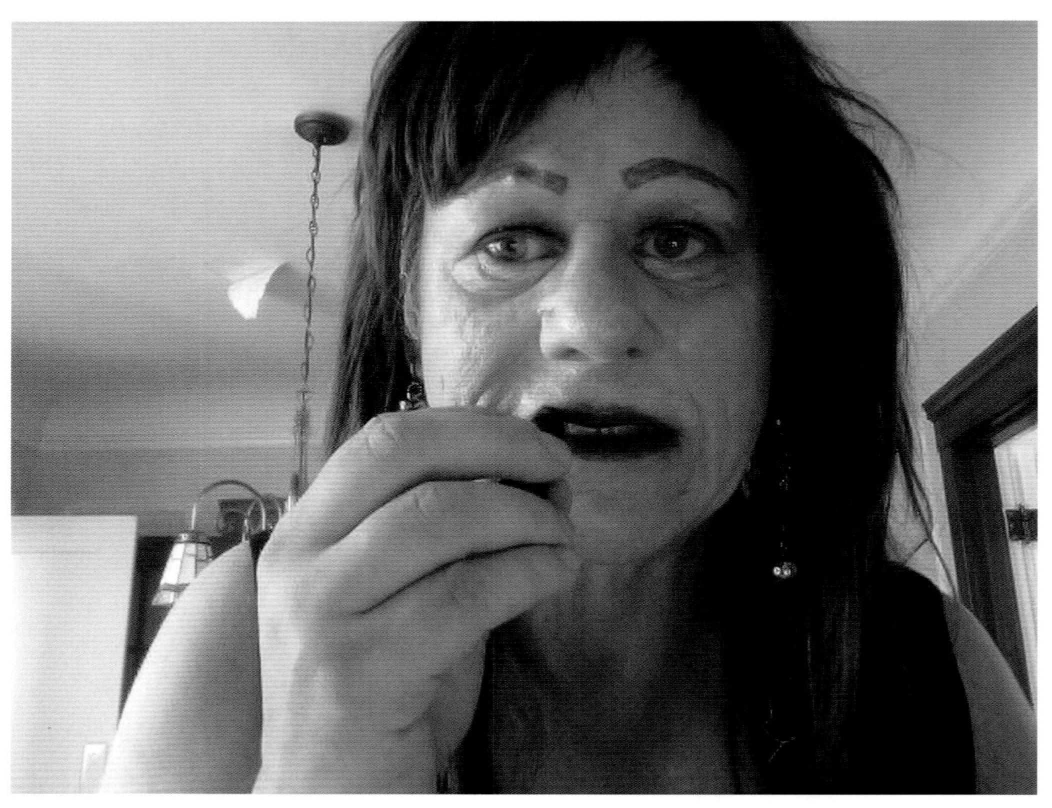

the "black lipstick" passage

The following passage was inserted into the novel almost a year after I had sup-
posedly finished it. Dolores was dressing up to go out with friends. It was a few
days short of Halloween, 2011. The laptop camera portrait which inspired these
words was accordingly taken a good four years after most of the others. In short, poor
Dolores had aged. I remember hurrying to get ready before my friends arrived, angling
the computer screen toward myself, and making a half dozen exposures for, let's say,
posterity. It wasn't until the end of the evening, when the guests went home, Dolores
washed off her makeup and I put on my glasses to inspect these photographs, that I
saw how old and worried, yet somehow natural, Dolores looked (this last might have
been the result of a new laptop which spared me the necessity of holding down the
shift key to suppress the flash). The portrait had nothing to do with my state of mind
at the time. Dolores was, in fact, happy. She had not come into existence for some
time, so she was concentrating, hoping her friends did not show up early and wondering what they would think of her, since they had never before seen her as a woman.
When I saw this picture, some words entered my mind, and here they are.

In the following scene, the Dolores of *How You Are* has just stolen money from a
drunken customer. *My* Dolores would never do such a thing.

> At the beginning of that evening, preparing for what had turned out to be her social
> triumph in the parking lot, her face whitely powdered and her long shiny earrings
> hopefully distracting attention from the rest of her, she gazed into the mirror, carefully
> outlining her mouth with black lipstick, and as she parted her lips to work the black-
> ness in deeper, she perceived the worry wrinkles at the corners of her mouth and the
> concentric wrinkles under her eyes; she could not tell at whom or what her greenish-
> blue eyes were looking, and as the lipstick rooted penis-like within the left underside
> of her upper lip, the right side hung crookedly down, so that instead of the fatuous,
> self-satisfied or screamingly gleeful appearance she so often possessed, or the fishy
> vacuousness of her early attempts to resemble the woman whom she had supposed
> she was, she seemed simply old, tremulous, a trifle hunted — which counted as a
> victory, for hadn't she achieved verisimilitude; wasn't she now an ordinary, homely
> woman, fit neighbor for Adelina upstairs? Pressing her long white fingers against the
> corner of her mouth, as if she were considering something, she rubbed the lipstick
> deeper and deeper, carefully keeping her lips away from her teeth. Admitting that she
> was not beautiful, she nonetheless loved herself. Her heart beat faster and faster;
> she could not tell why. Tomorrow she had better dye her hair again. Tonight she con-
> tented herself with brushing it, slowly, all the way down. The sparkly silver eyeshadow
> shone like sweat. Her wrinkled old throat trembled; she felt sorry for it. What was she
> thinking of? Quickly she smiled at herself, and discovered that she still looked *great*.
> Many other women let themselves go after fifty — not our Dolores! Here was a hun-
> dred pesos to prove it.

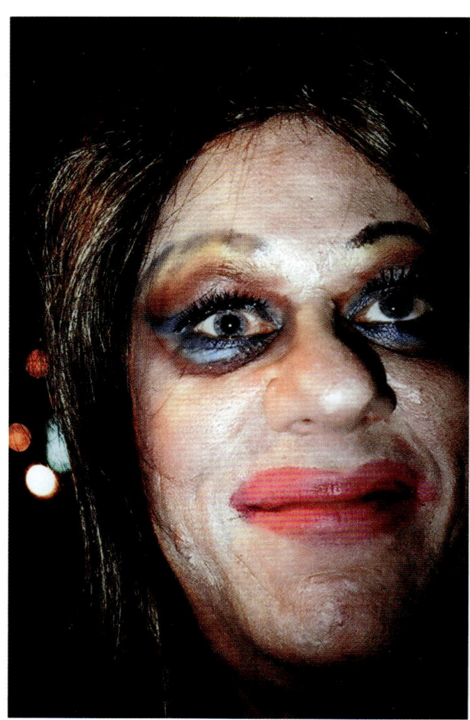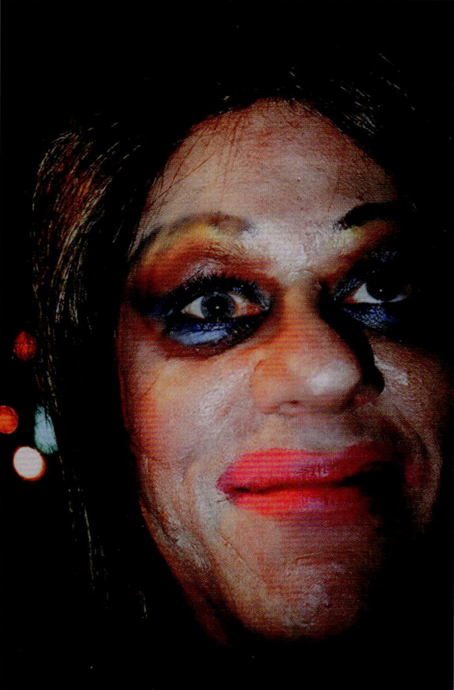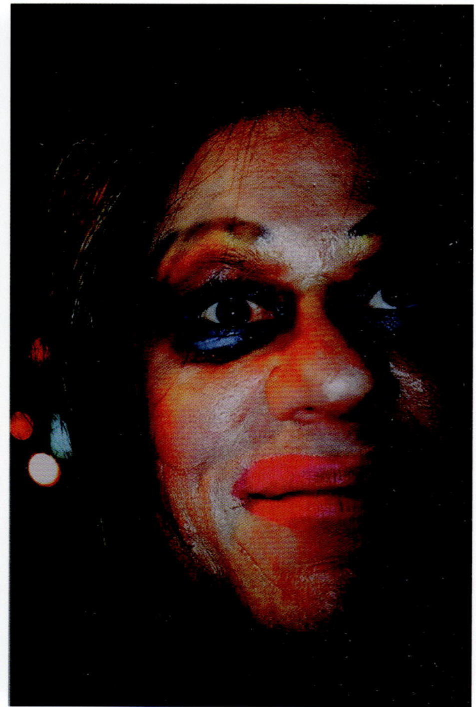

the "calliope" passage

The original version (left) of this portrait was made in Los Angeles, using my 35 millimeter Contax and drugstore color film, the two right-hand versions being progressively more digitally manipulated. I referred to the triptych when constructing the *How You Are*'s description of Dolores setting out for work as a transgender street prostitute in Veracruz, Mexico, where such sex workers are widely tolerated:

. . . so that Dolores, smiling like a happy, sickly middle-aged man as she combed her long coppery hair down around her face, offered the world fat pink lips, white-greased cheeks and rainbow bruises of eyeshadow as she emerged from her dark doorway, swimming into the darker street whose coins of white and orange light hung around her ears like parasites. The street darkened further as she went, so that craters got licked out of her cheekbones and the wattles of her many chins, her eyeshadow, and the bronzer along her nose both became more metallic, almost like electroplated jewelry, while the whites of her eyes, inflamed by the cosmetics, appeared bloodier. Proceeding another half-block, she arrived at the kindest, most murderous darkness of all, against which her makeup screamed like a calliope. The modestly silver-blue greasepaint around her eyes now proclaimed an iridescence superior to that of the wings of the loveliest houseflies. Her crimson lipstick insisted on itself all the way down to her first chin. Her eyes and nose were enclosed in red and yellow; her forehead was redder than autumn maple leaves. Still she smiled, but the shadow had eaten half of her smile away.

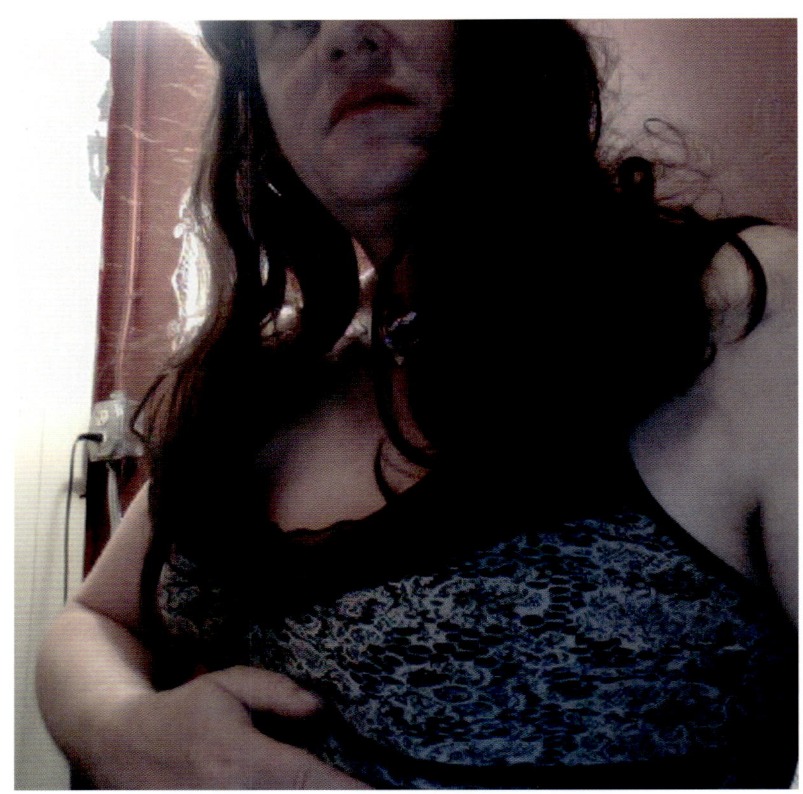

Dolores as prostitute

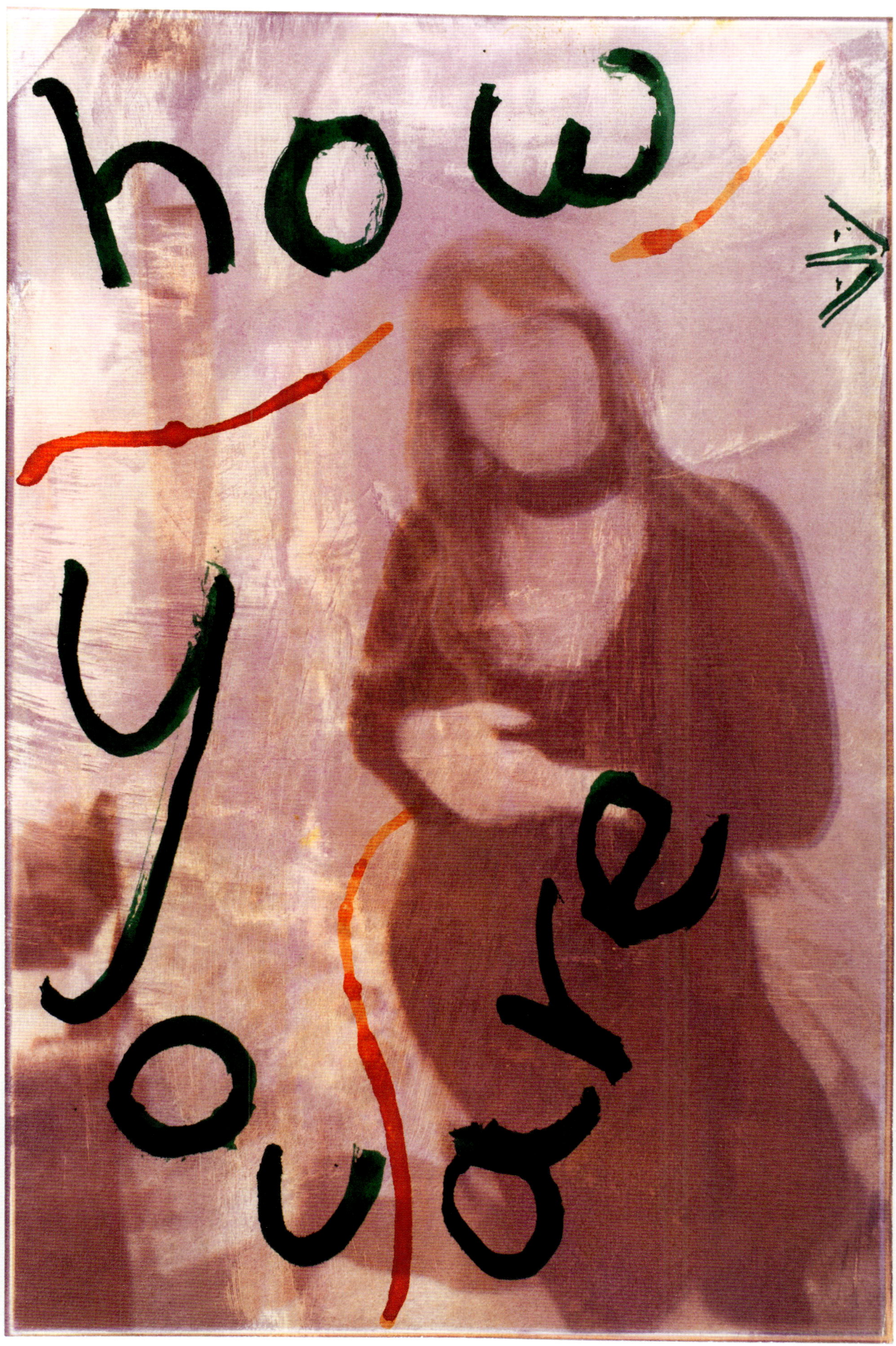

how
y
o
u
are
care

I n *How You Are* there is a chapter entitled "Grinning Cave," in the course of which the male protagonist sets out at twilight for an Indian birthing he knows about, and there magically transforms himself into Dolores. At this point in the novel the split between his male and female personas first becomes fully realized. The man looks upon Dolores in the cave, seeing her as an *other* who exists in her own right. To write

this section I required an ad hoc, empirical experi-ence. I also wished to scare myself slightly. Hence I did indeed proceed toward the birthing cave at twilight, with a wig, breast forms and makeup in my backpack, and my computer held out at arm's length so that I could photograph myself as I pro-ceeded. Stumbling up the desert ridge, trying not to get too much sand in the laptop, I made portrait after portrait, tripping once or twice. There was no path to the cave, but fortunately I knew its location by heart. When I arrived, I employed a miniature flashlight while transforming, eventually losing one false eyelash in the sand all the same. Then I pho-tographed myself as Dolores. For a long time I sat in the darkness writing and listening. Finally I shucked

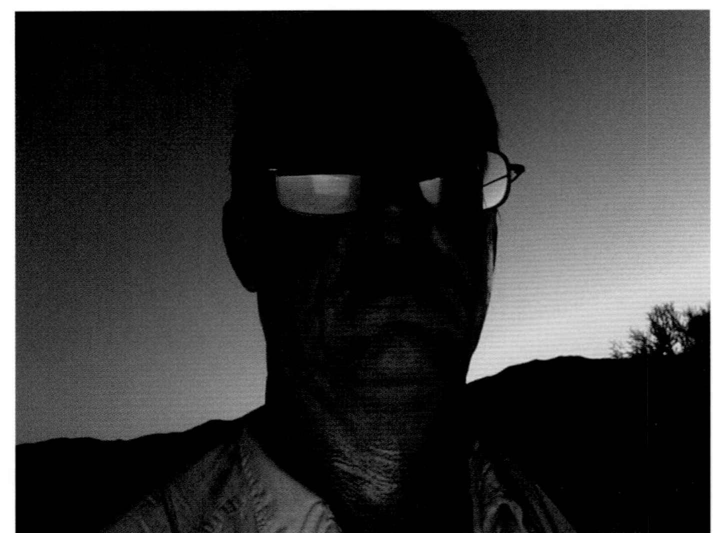

my femininity and descended back to the valley floor, extremely conscious of the cave mouth behind me and halfway convinced by now (for I have always been suggest-ible) that something was watching me up there. Upon arriving at my quarters, I began to organize the computer photos at once, throwing away the worst and arranging the rest into a slideshow of eighty-four images. The best two of these appear in the final gum print portfolio as "Cave Witch" and "Cave Woman" (the former appears here both as a gum print and in its original form). I certainly found it eerie to view the snap-shots for the first time, and stranger still to watch them fade in and out of each other, comprising a story whose elements I had constructed in advance but whose textures I could not have imagined. Few of them possess artistic merit, but composing and repeatedly viewing the story allowed me to observe the night visit to the birthing cave as if the two principals had nothing to do with me. While the slideshow played itself, I enjoyed the pleasures of a voyeur and a collage artist, resequencing any frames as I thought best, scribbling in my notebook, nearly believing that the mutation I had staged had occurred. The cave setting in combination with my still unfamiliar feminoid appearance did indeed convey the impression that somebody other than myself was their subject; why not call her Dolores?

On the following morning I returned to the birthing cave in order to obtain clear daylight portraits of Dolores (and find my lost eyelash). It took my several months to complete the chapter, which I did with the slideshow at hand. This being primarily a book of pictures and explanations, I cannot justify publishing that long episode here. But here are sixteen of the eighty-four laptop slides:

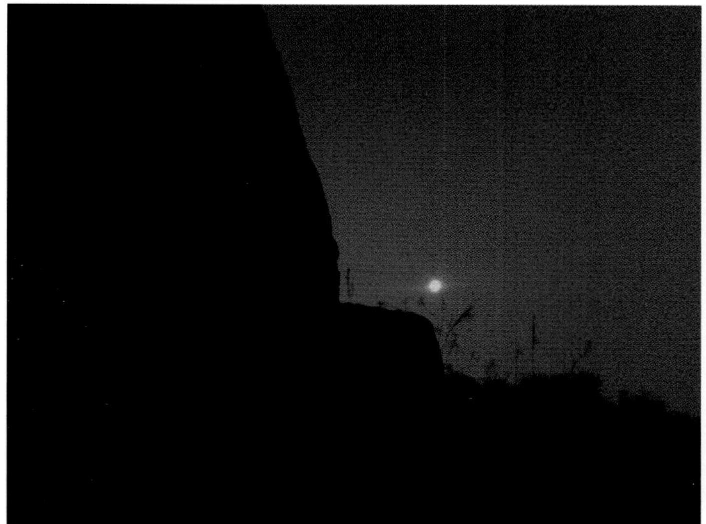 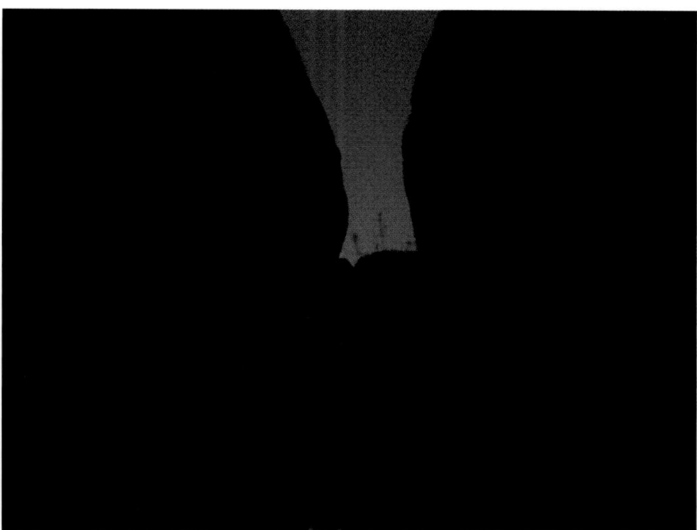

the birthing cave sequence

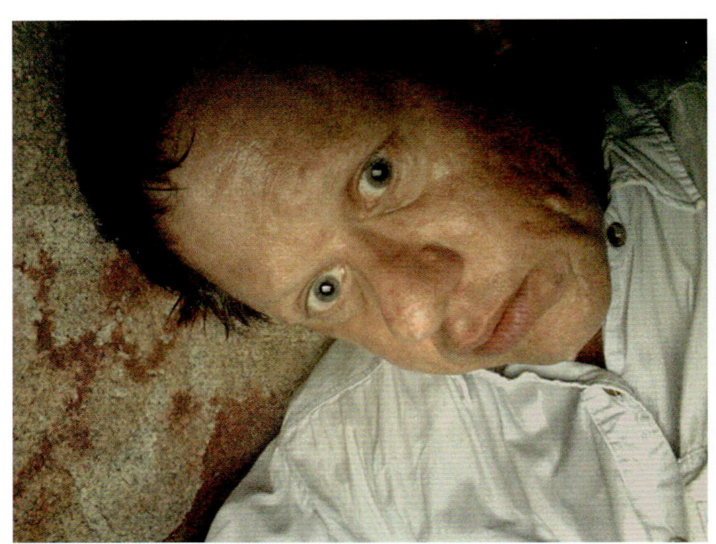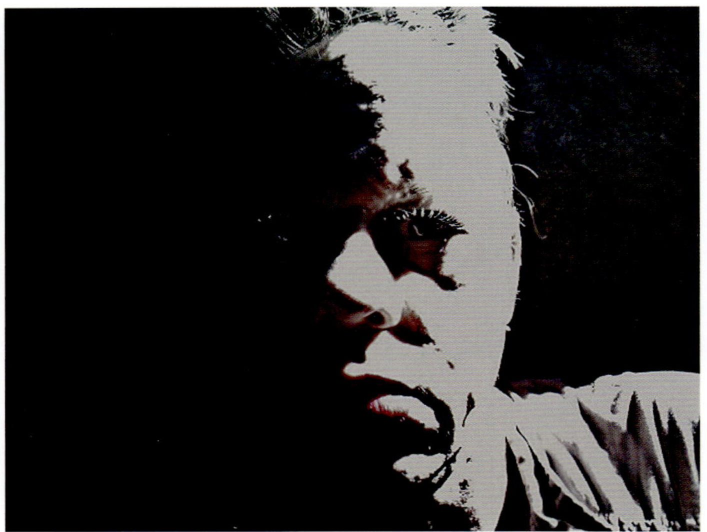

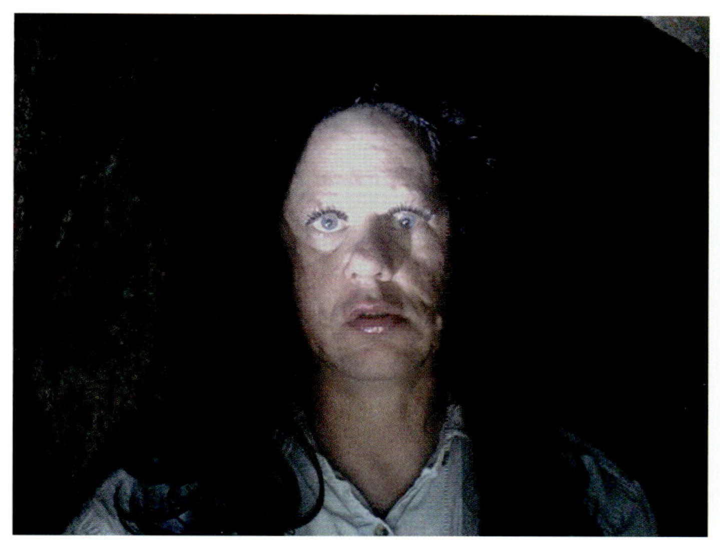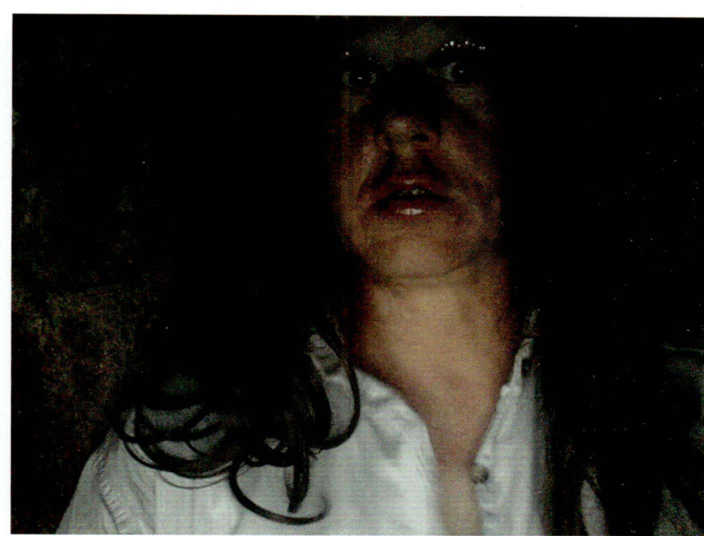

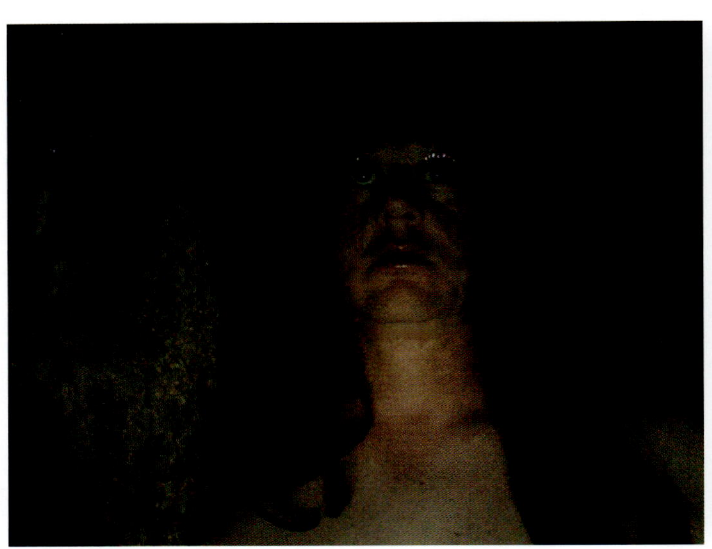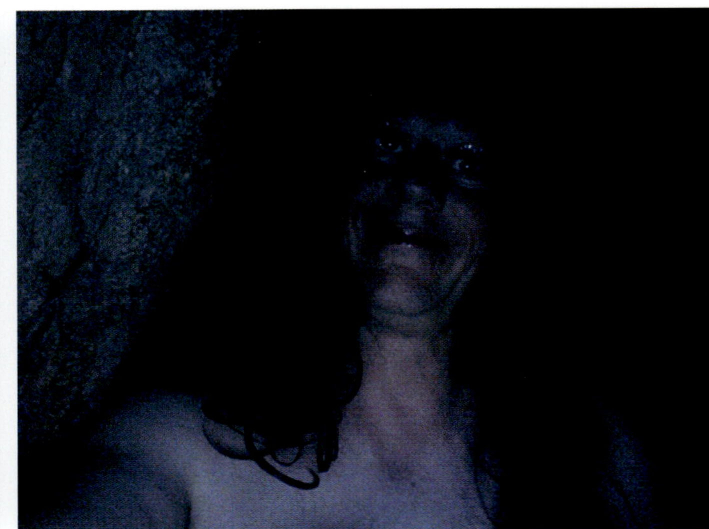

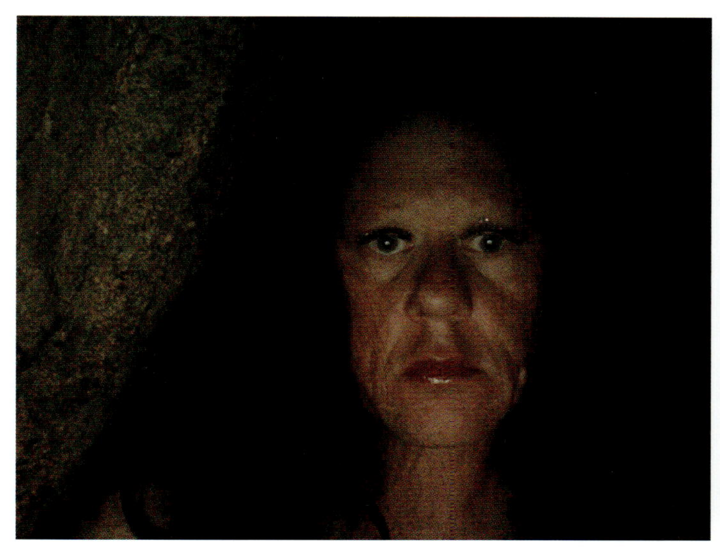 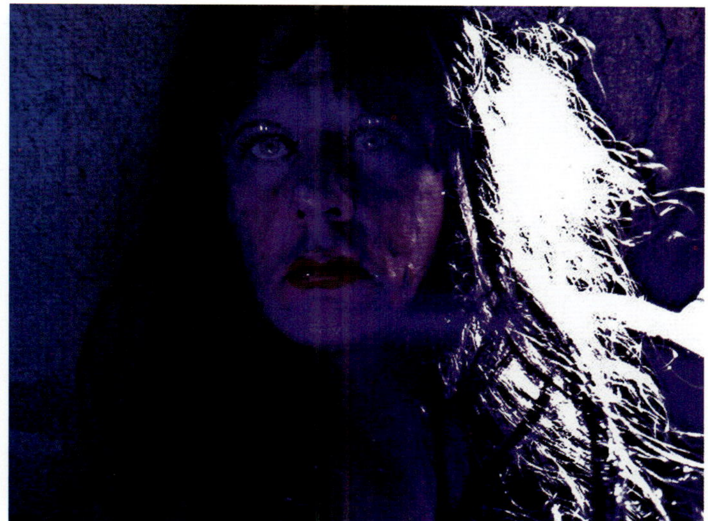

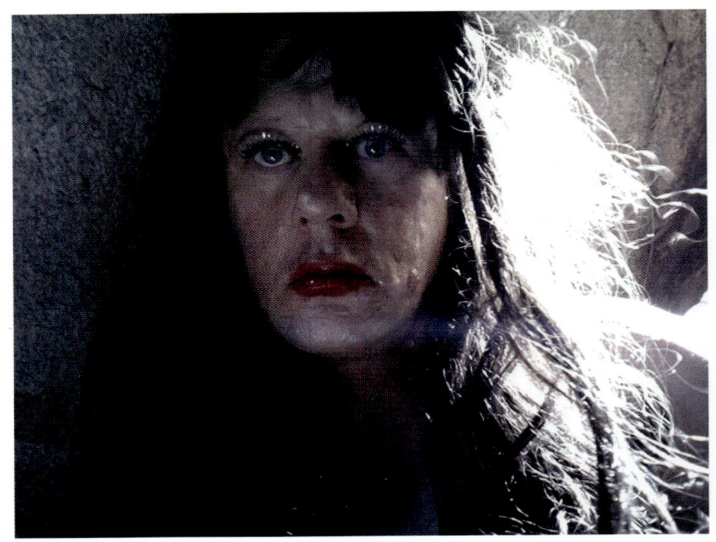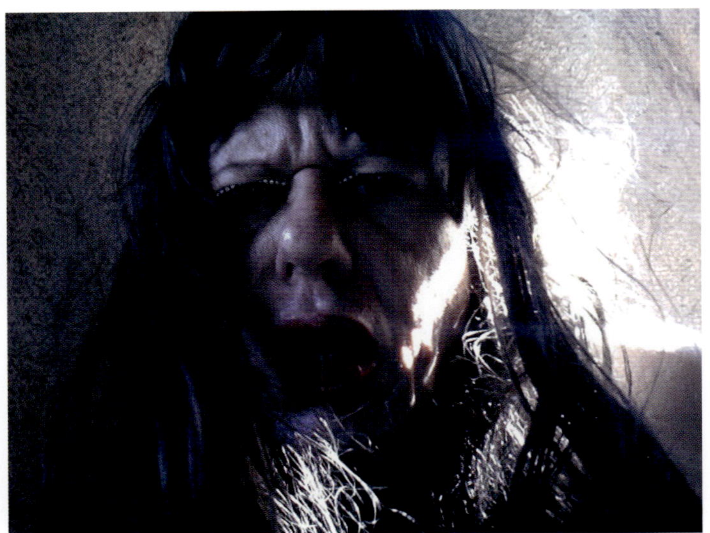

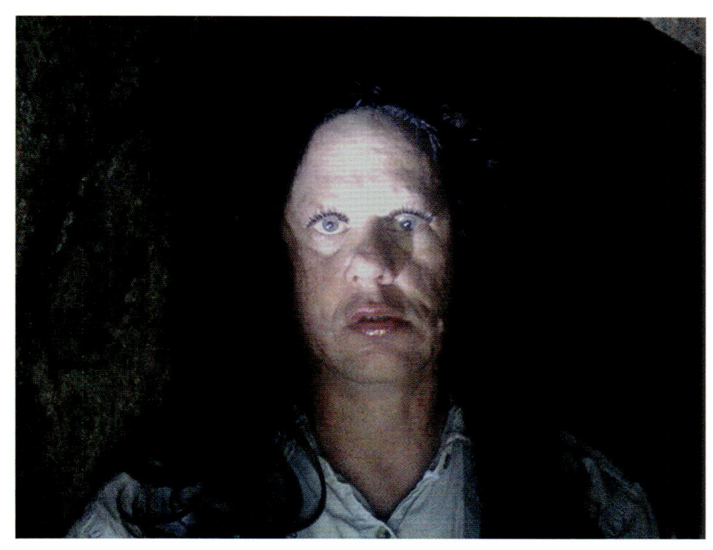

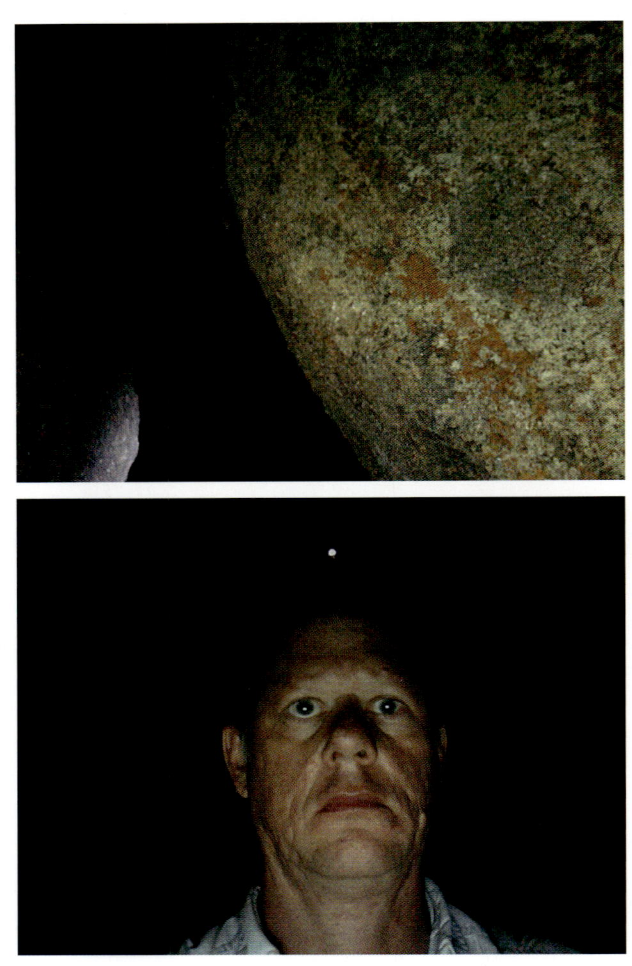

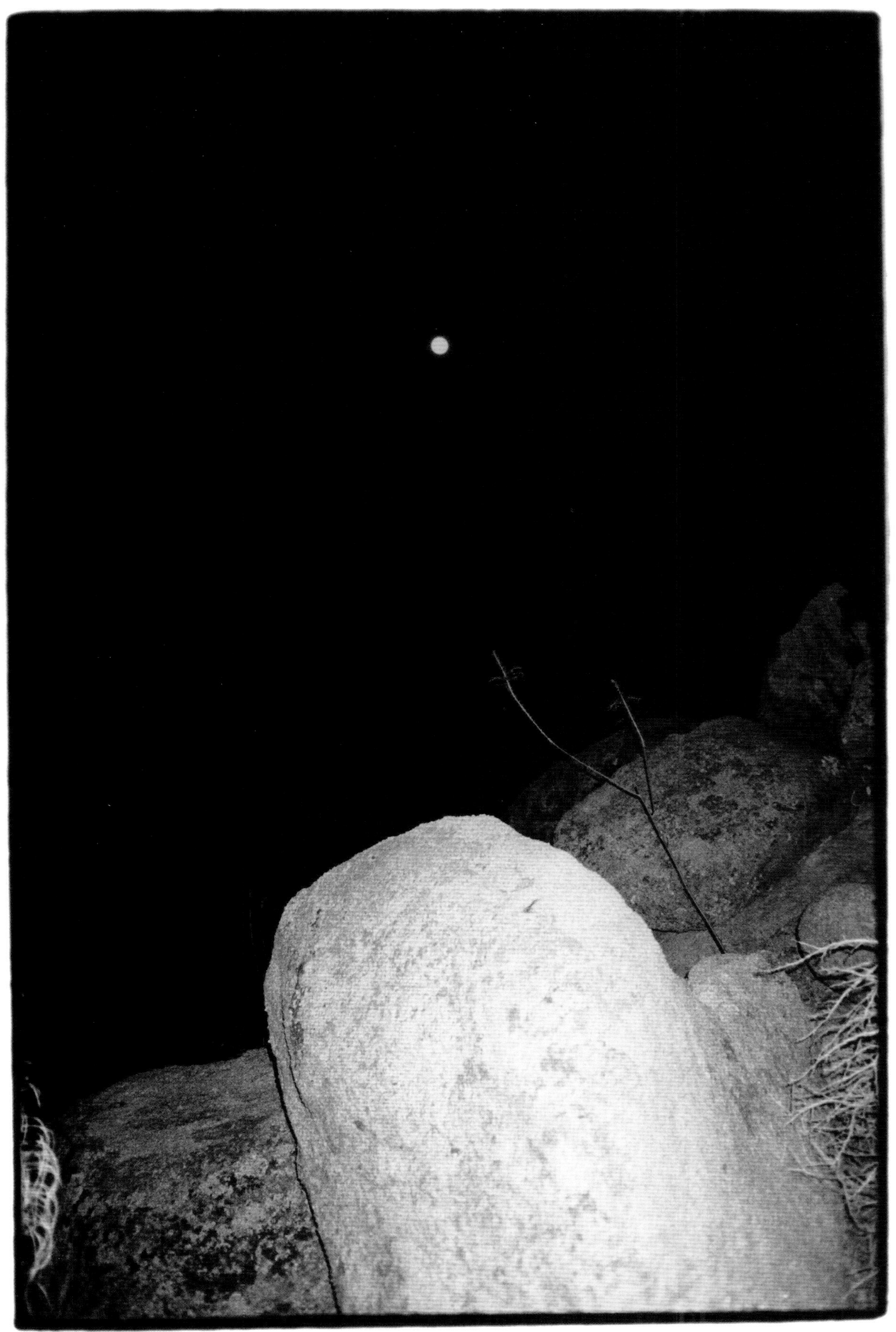

Night view from mouth of birthing cave

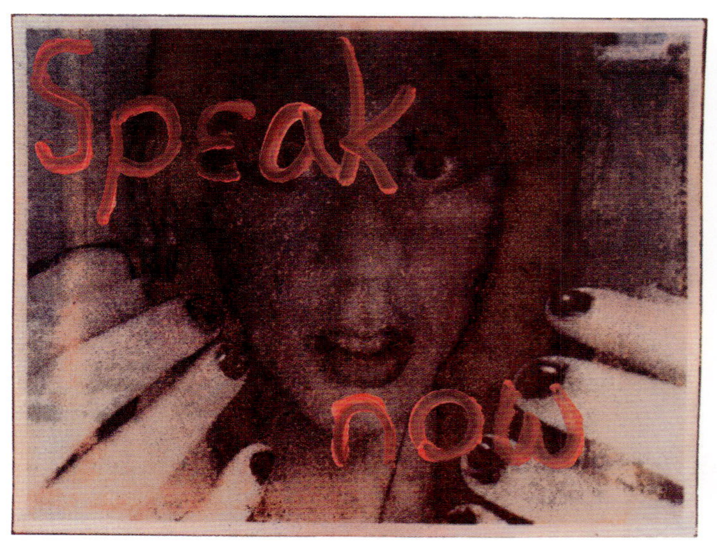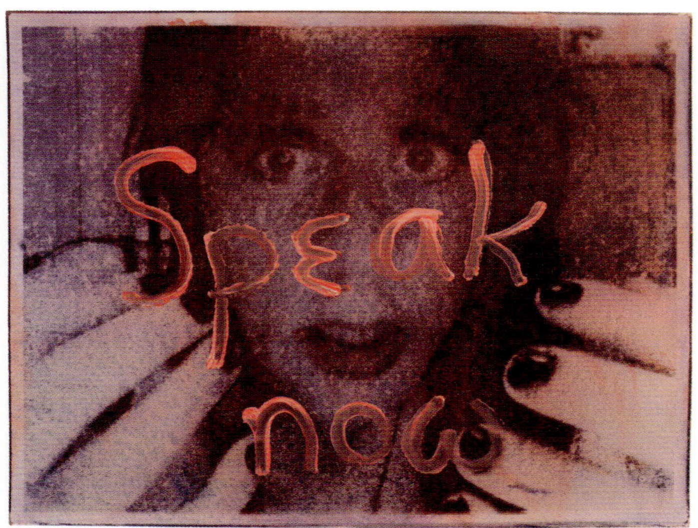

"speak now, my heart"

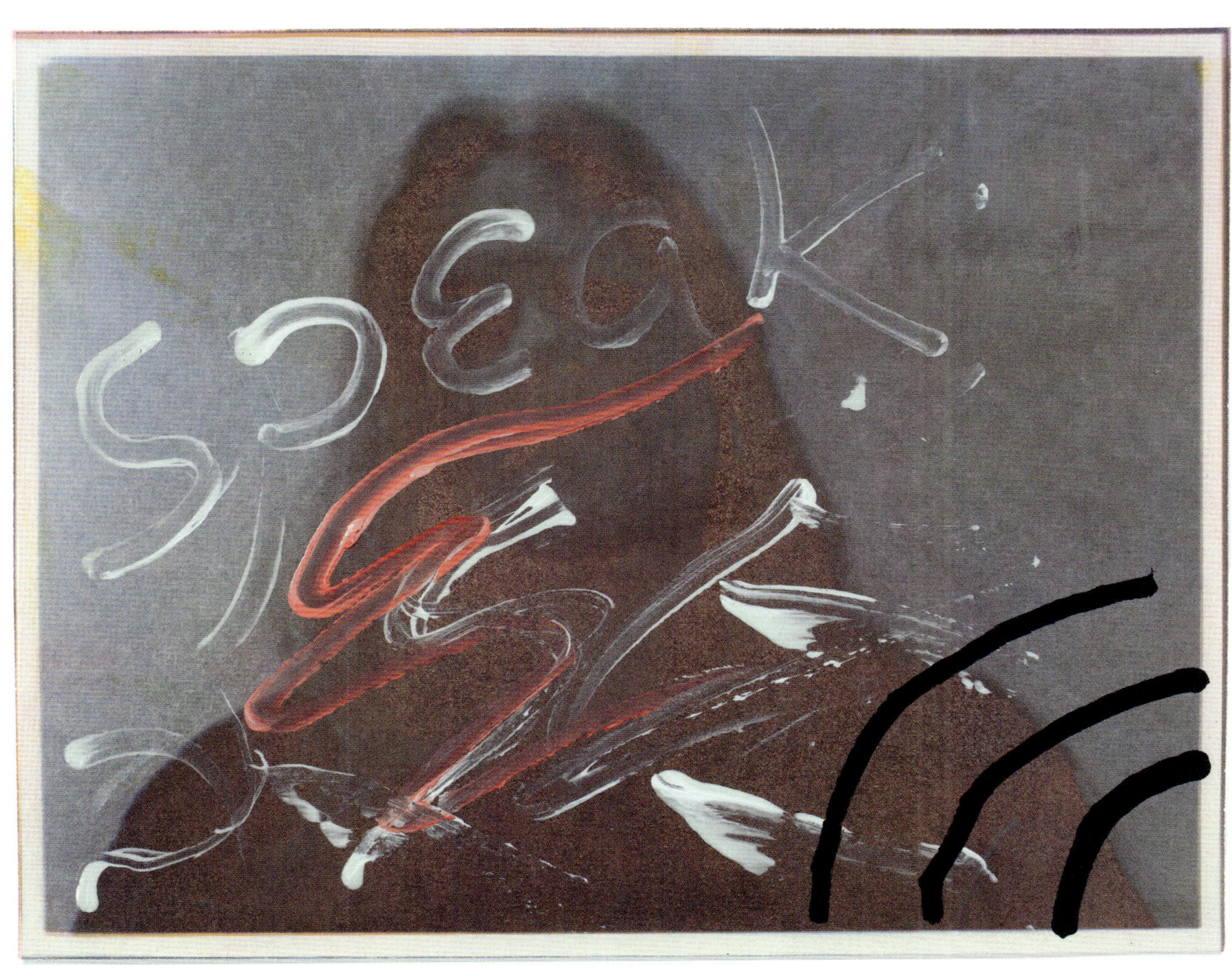

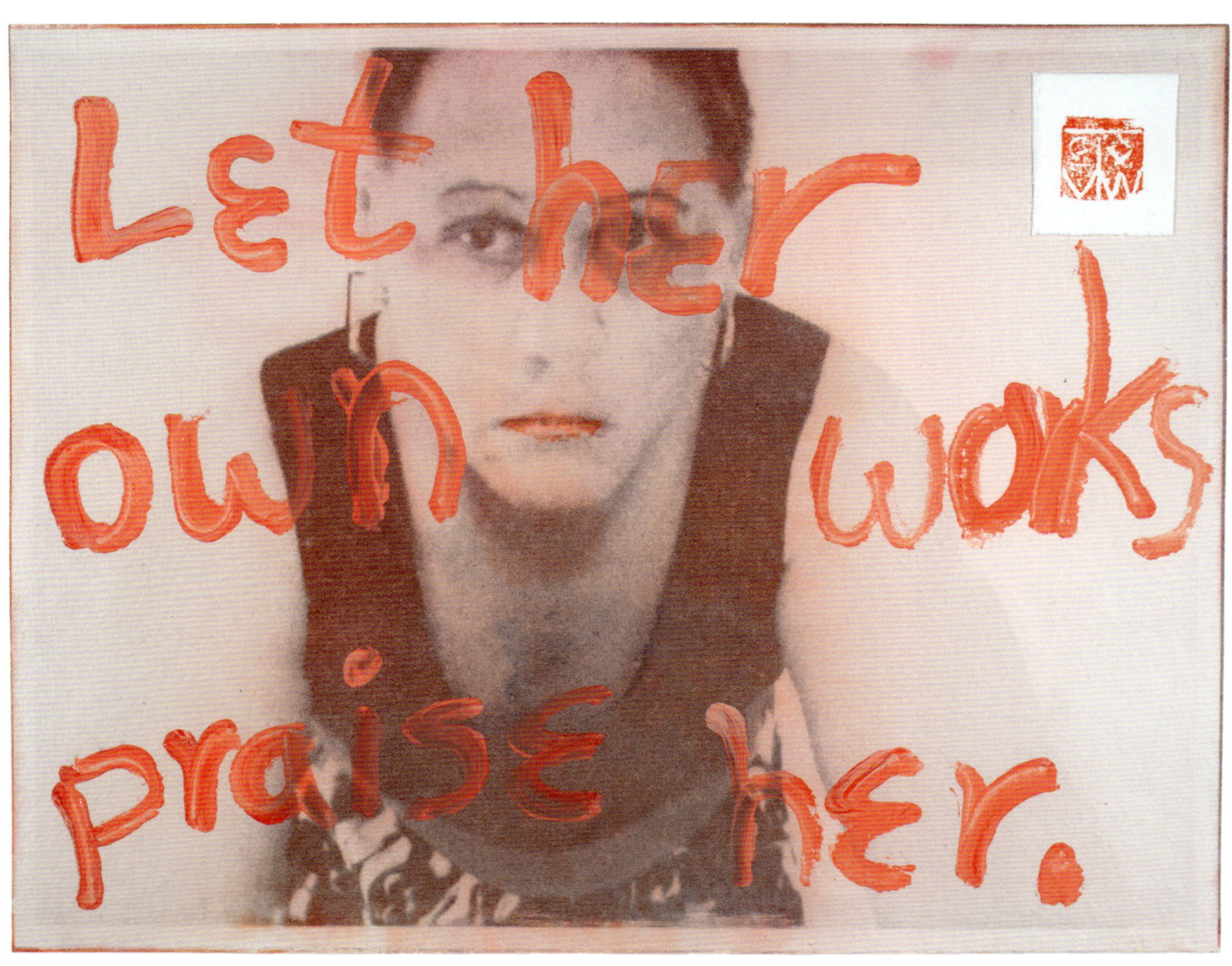

Let her
own works
praise her.

The four preceeding gum prints were some of many made to illustrate (and help me understand) two of the novel's most important phrases, which repeat throughout, with variations. Sometimes, "speak now" is "come now," just as it was in the original Egyptian papyrus from which I stole it. No final versions of the prints were ever made, and in the end I aborted my early experiment of using them as backing papers on the Dolores gum print portfolio. Following is *How You Are*'s opening.

Come now, my heart. Are you the crocodile or the donkey? Dolores's eyes keep teaching me the cold liquid glitter of diamond wedding rings. I want the blue dress and the red dress even though they might be jealous spirits who mean me ill. I promise to buy her a smooth chemise. Then I will lift the long glossy parallels of hair. I don't care that she will never be my sweet young wife.

Come now, my heart. Please let me bring the feeling back into my throat. Answer me my sayings. My heart, lovely heart, give me to drink of your pity. That feeling, how can I endure not to feel it?

* * * * *

They say that beauty is passing, but when he walked in the desert, the cocoa-colored sandcliffs topped with old cracking roots seemed so reliable that he could imagine them remaining more or less as they were for a thousand years, which naturally would require his continued presence. When we compose our funeral instructions, we know, never mind what great scientists promise, that we will see every bit of the show. The lilies will be over here, the coffin there on that dais; the minister will say *let her own works praise her*. Our children and theirs will weep obediently while we smile serenely down. I can see my bouquet right now! I want the casket with brass handles.

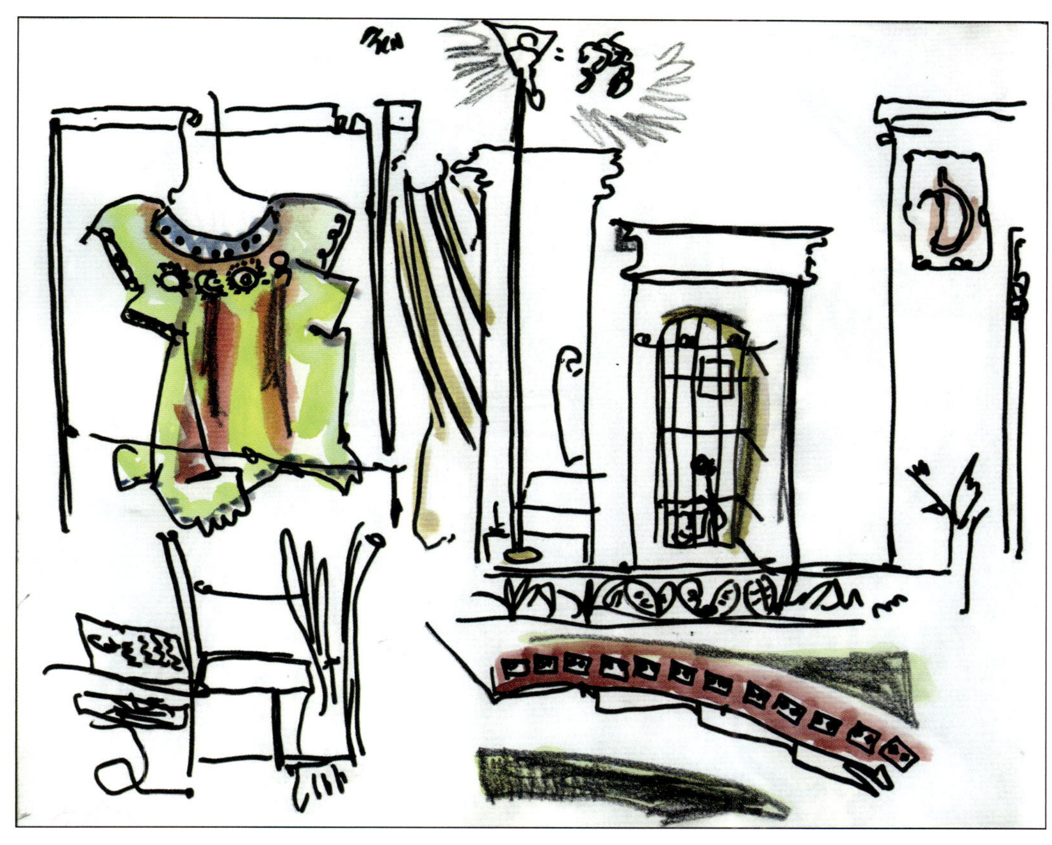

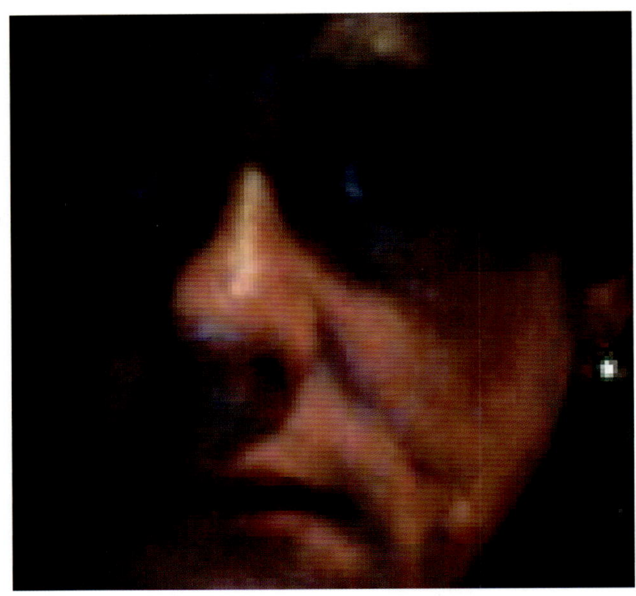

Detail of a laptop image

2.1: Laptop Photographs

All photographs in this section are among the forty-three which I selected for gum bichromate printing. As mentioned earlier, some of them, such as "Cave witch" and "Melissa's work," may be found in this book in both gum and laptop versions.

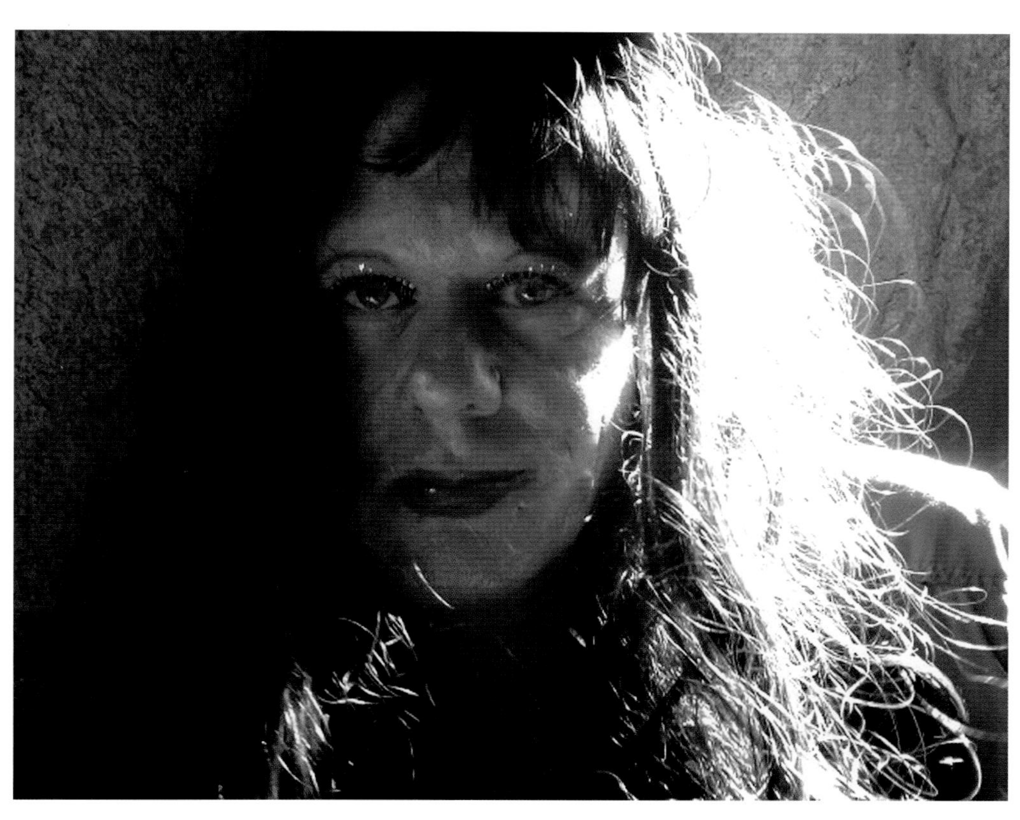

Cave witch (see p. 179)

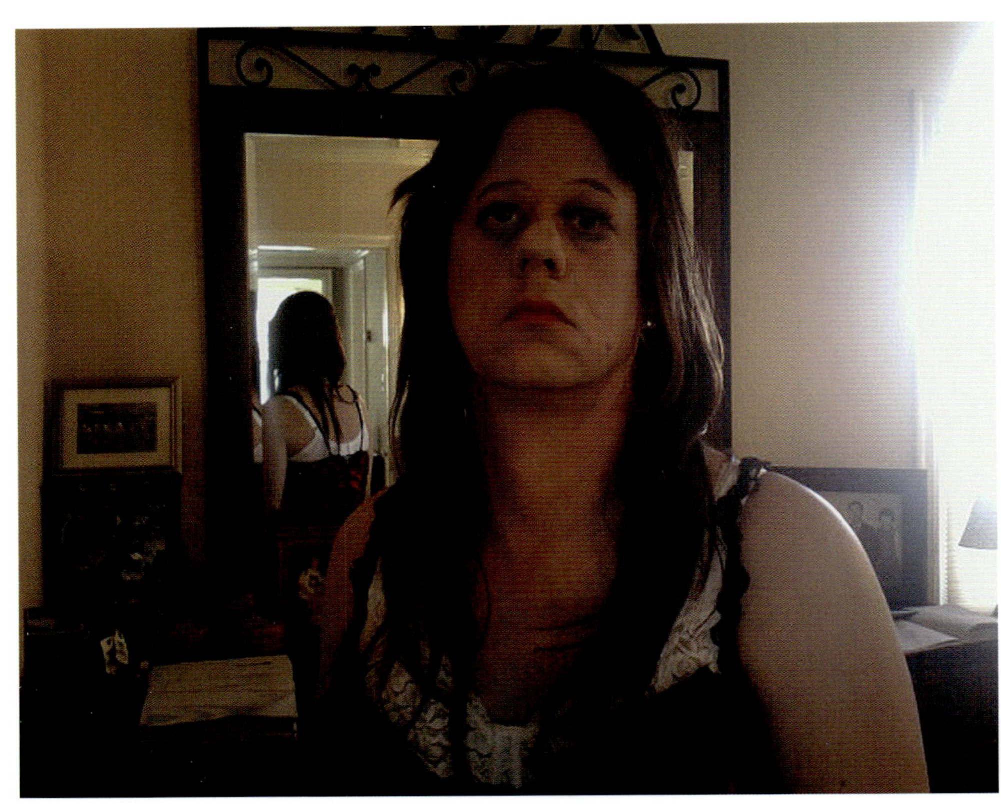

Red corset

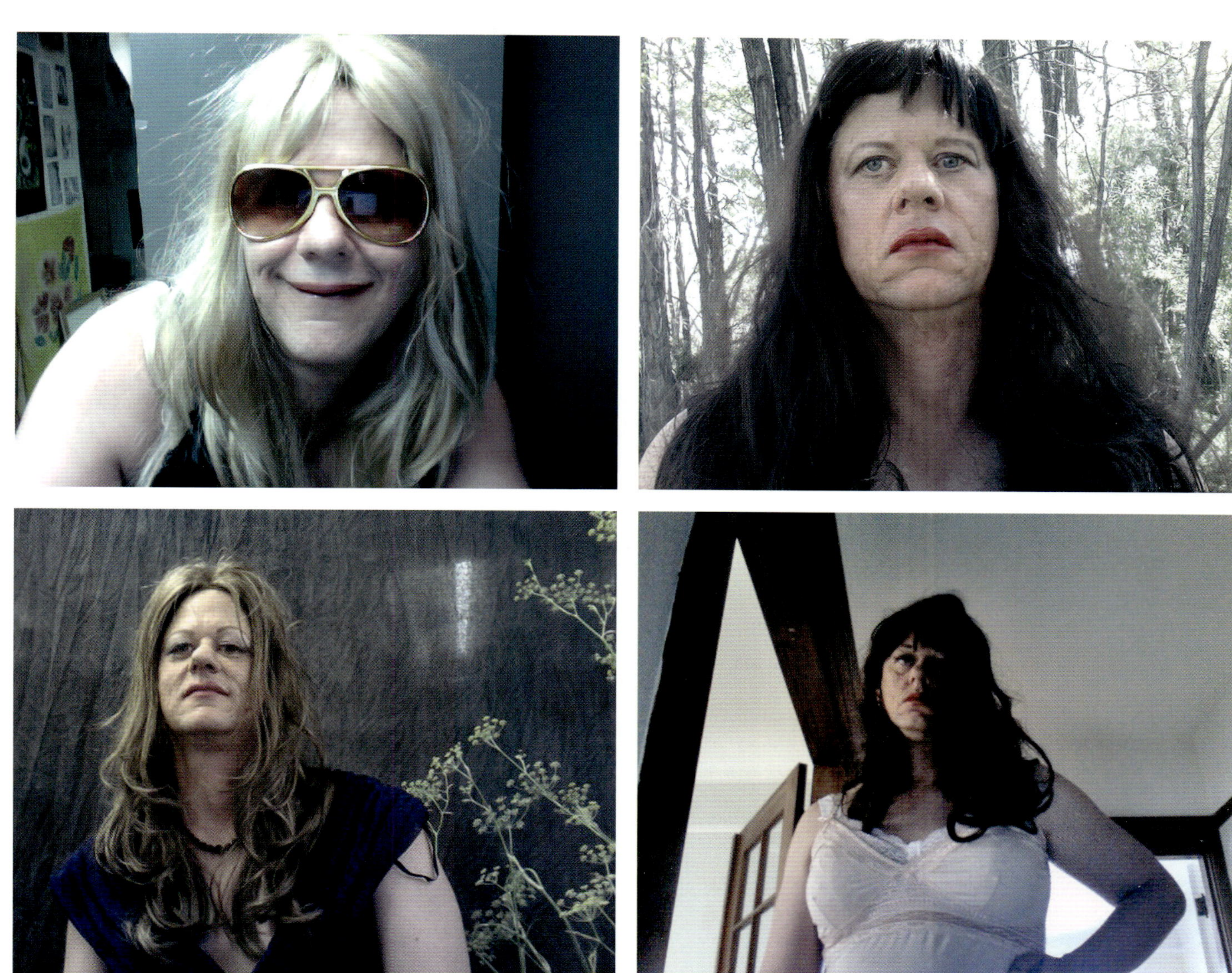

Top left: Valley girl; top right: Forest (see pp.180–181);
bottom left: Blonde (homage to my sister Sarah); bottom right: White dress

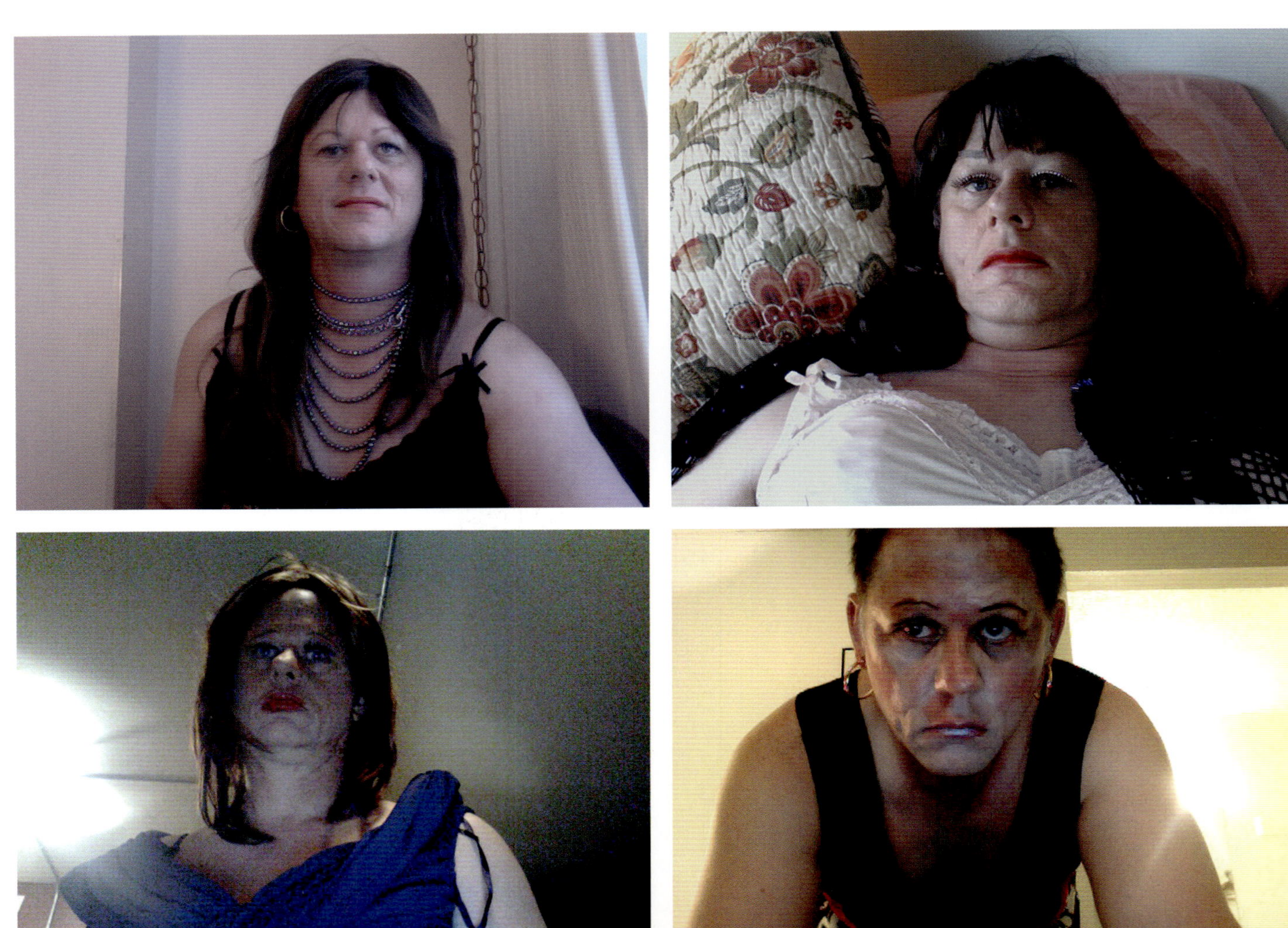

*Top left: Necklaces (see p. 182); top right: Bedtime;
bottom left: Prostitute; bottom right: Desert motel*

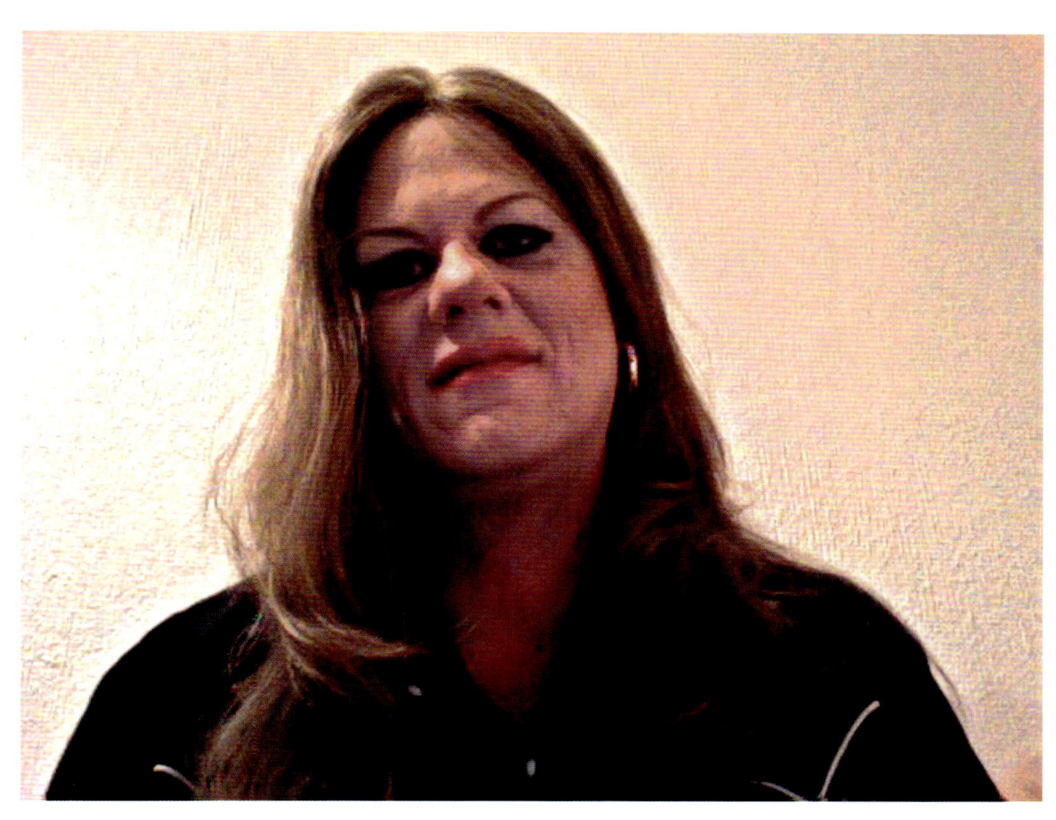

Melissa's work (see p. 125)

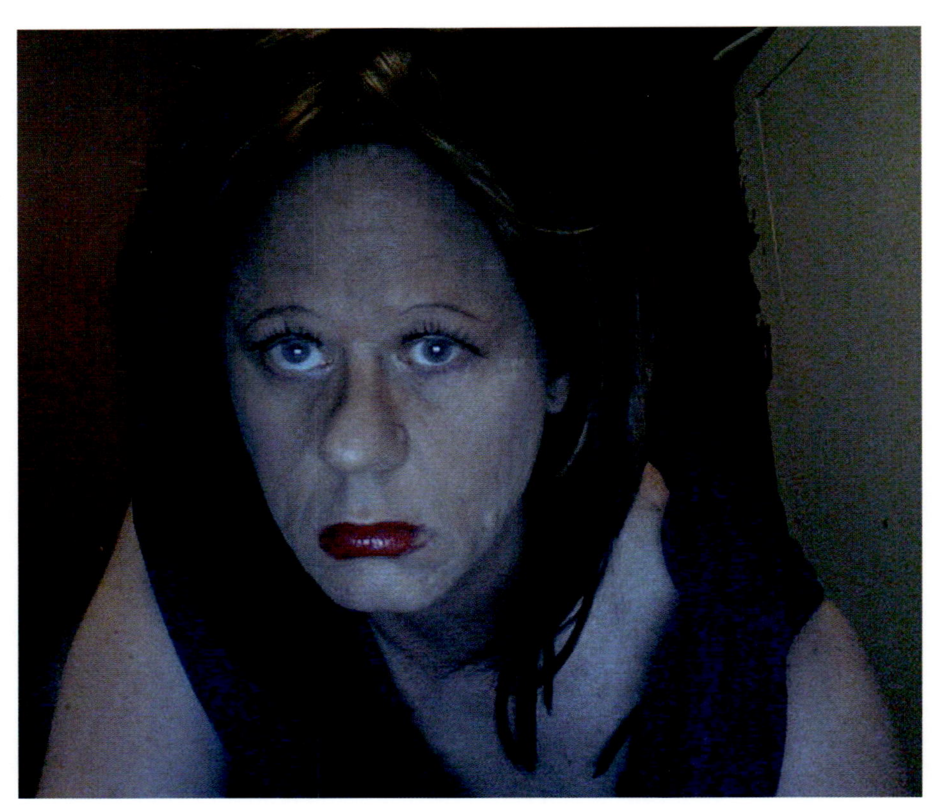

Meat locker woman (see p. 178)

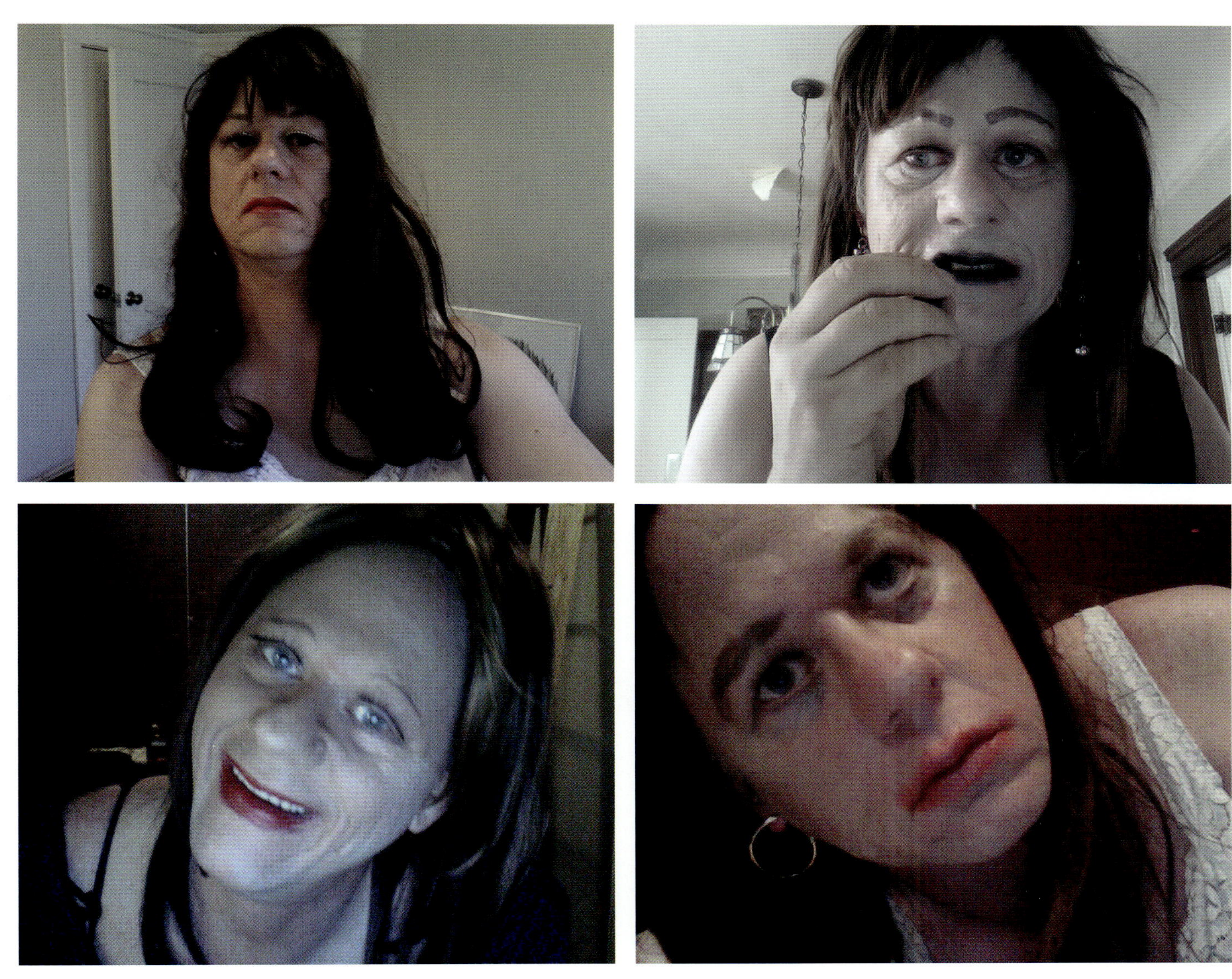

*Top left: By the white door; top right: Black lipstick;
bottom left: Ecstasy; bottom right: Hoop earring (see p. 177)*

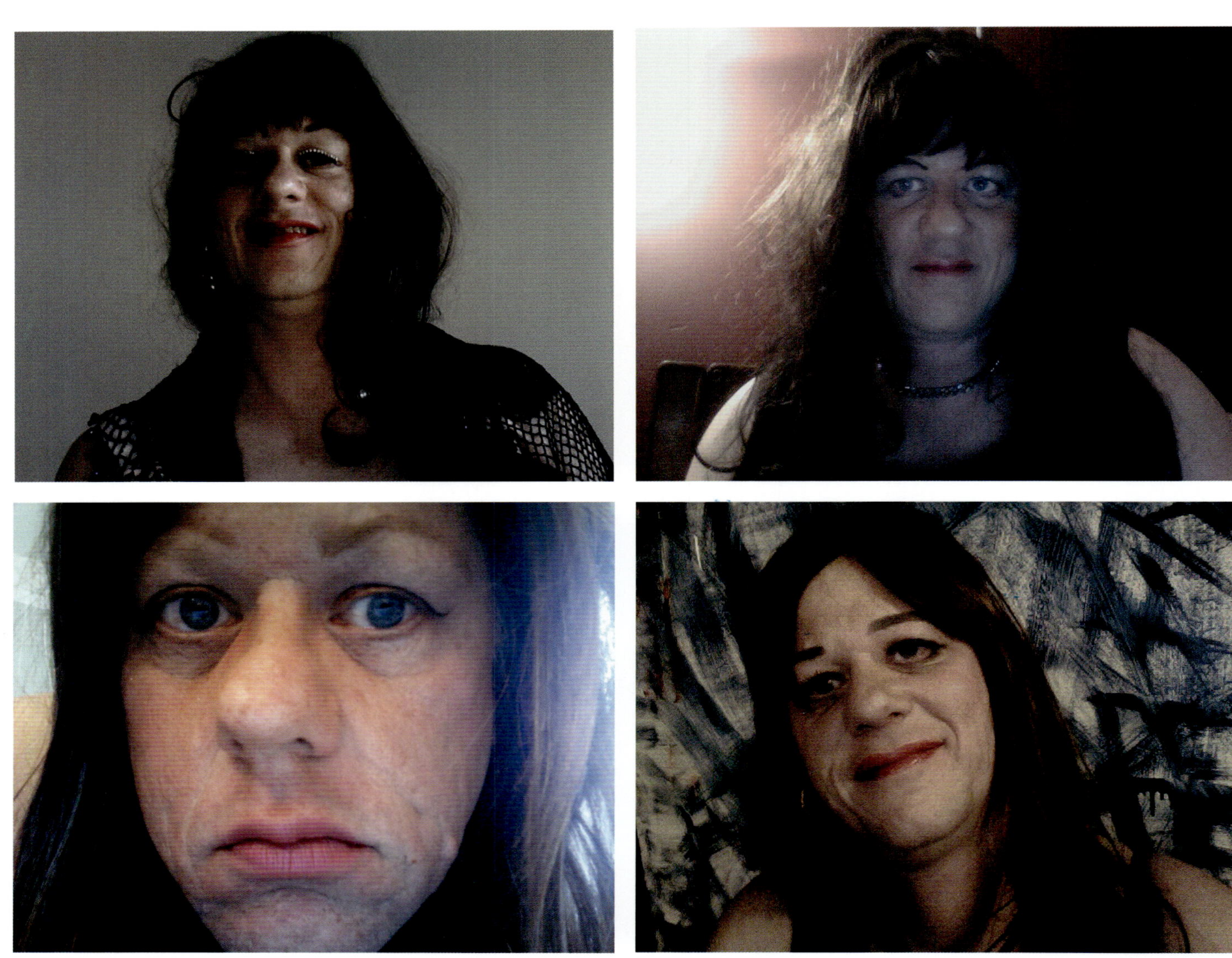

*Top left: Kurdish shawl (see p. 121); top right: Shy girl;
bottom left: Blue eyes (see p. 184); bottom right: Smile*

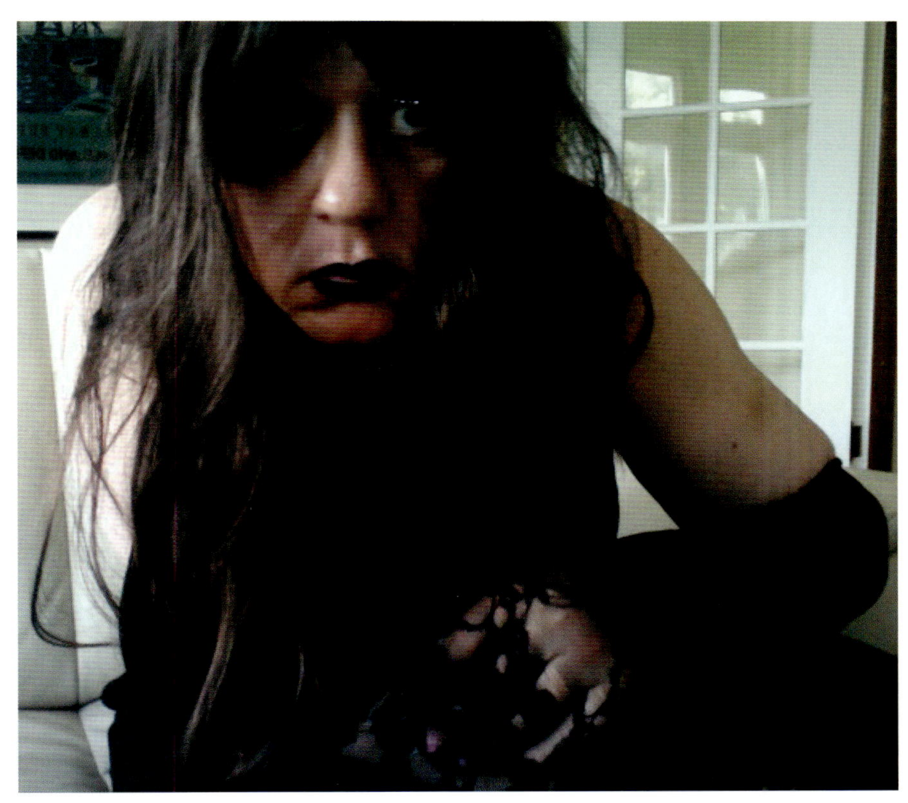

Black gloves

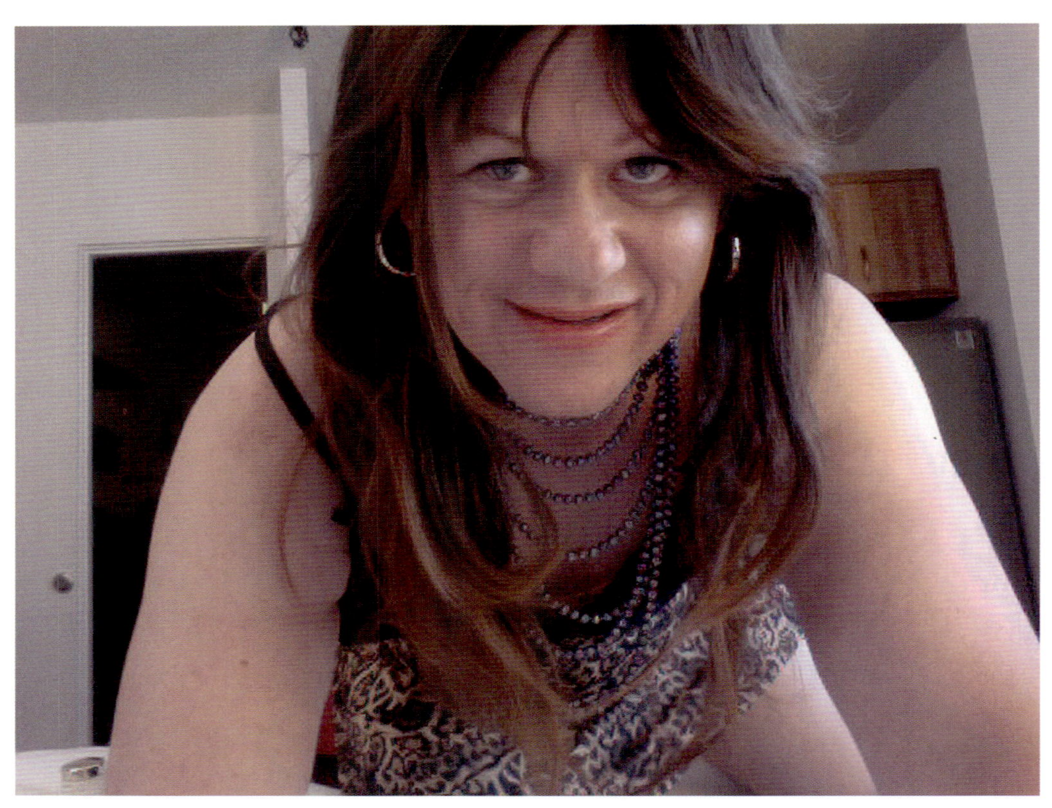

Nasty girl

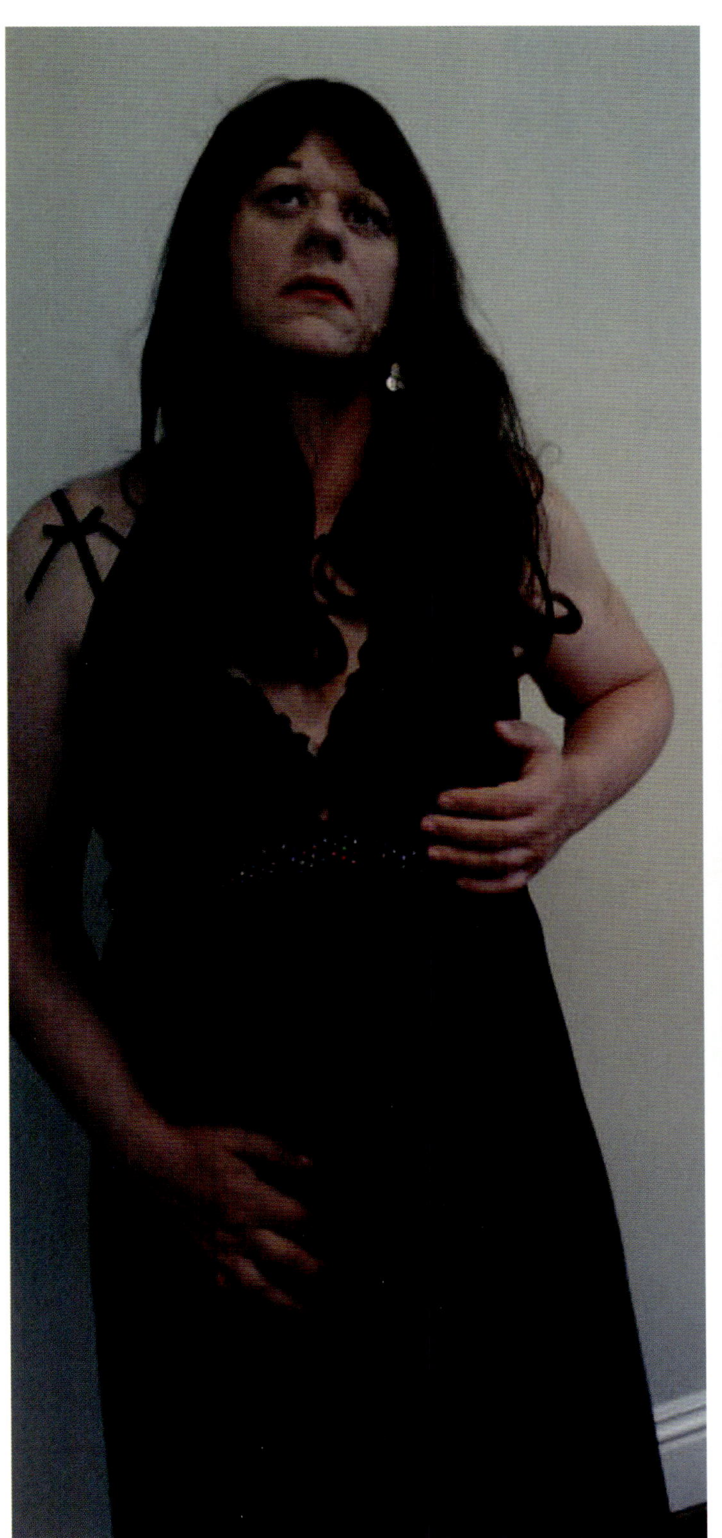
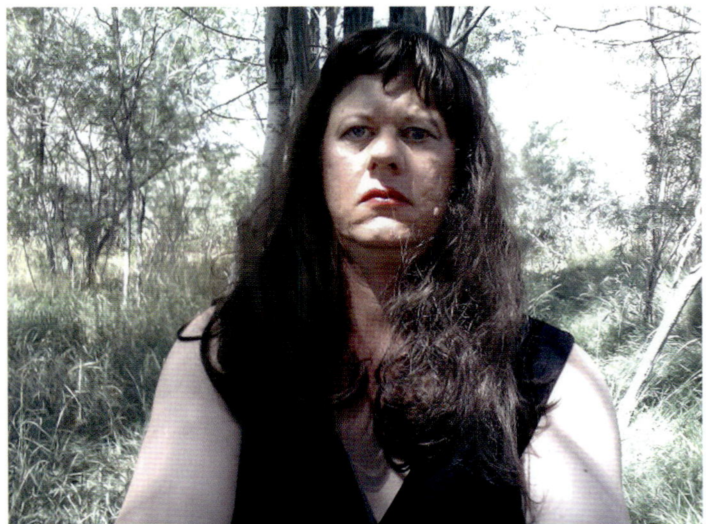
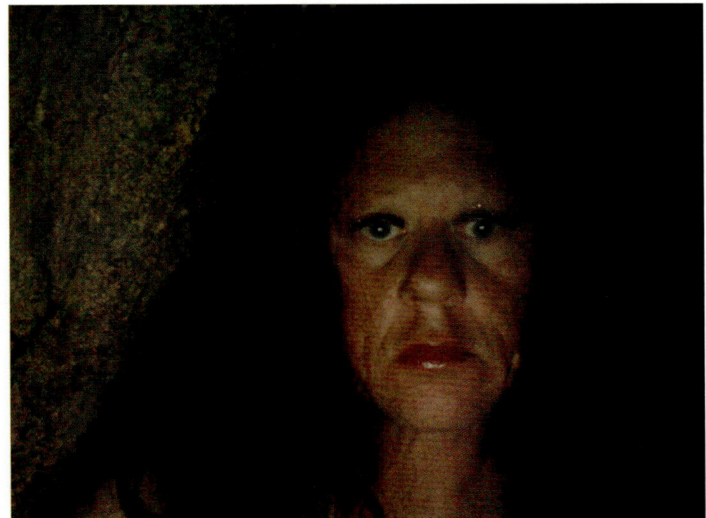

Above: Evening dress (see p. 172);
top right: Desert oasis; middle right: Cave woman

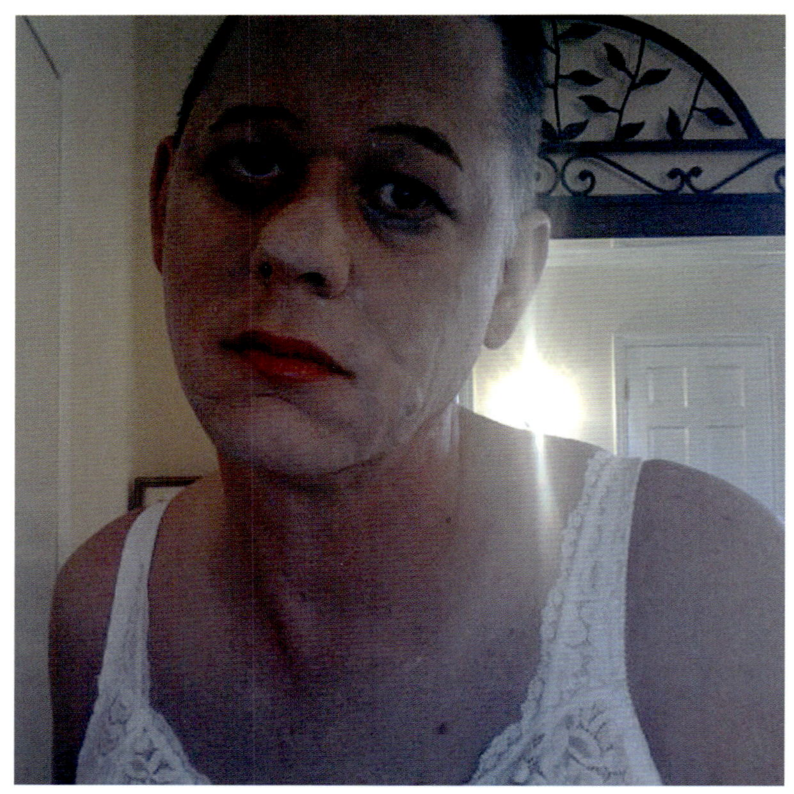

White brassiere

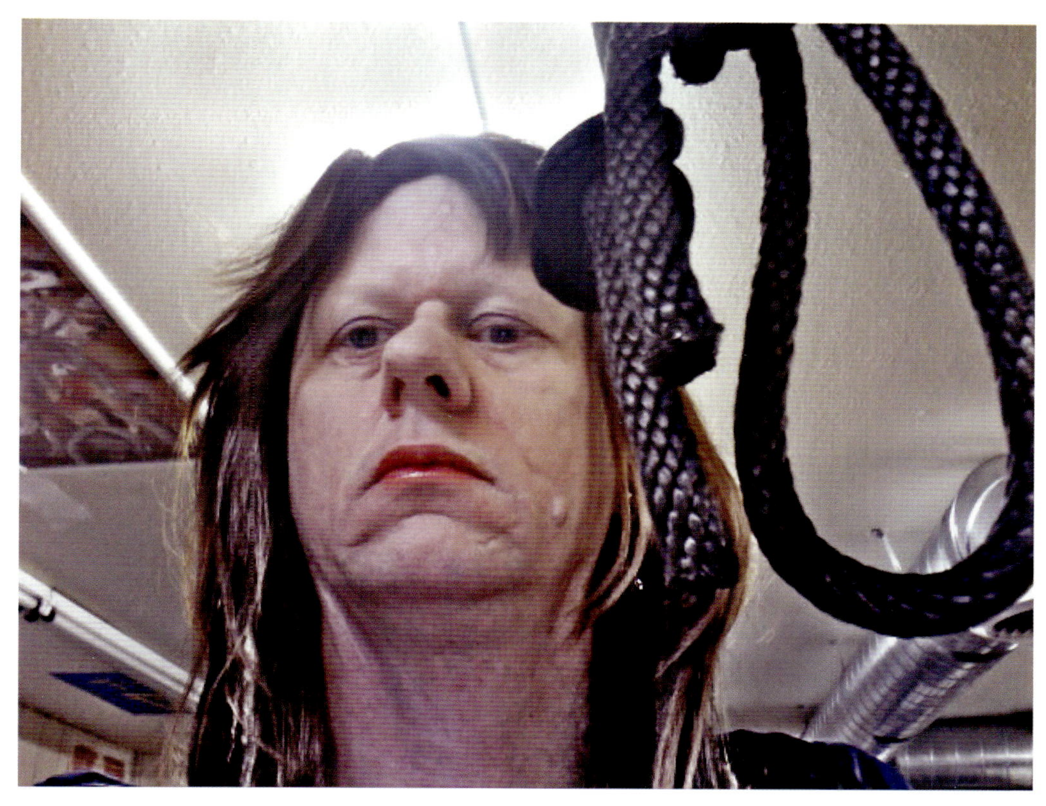

Bad end

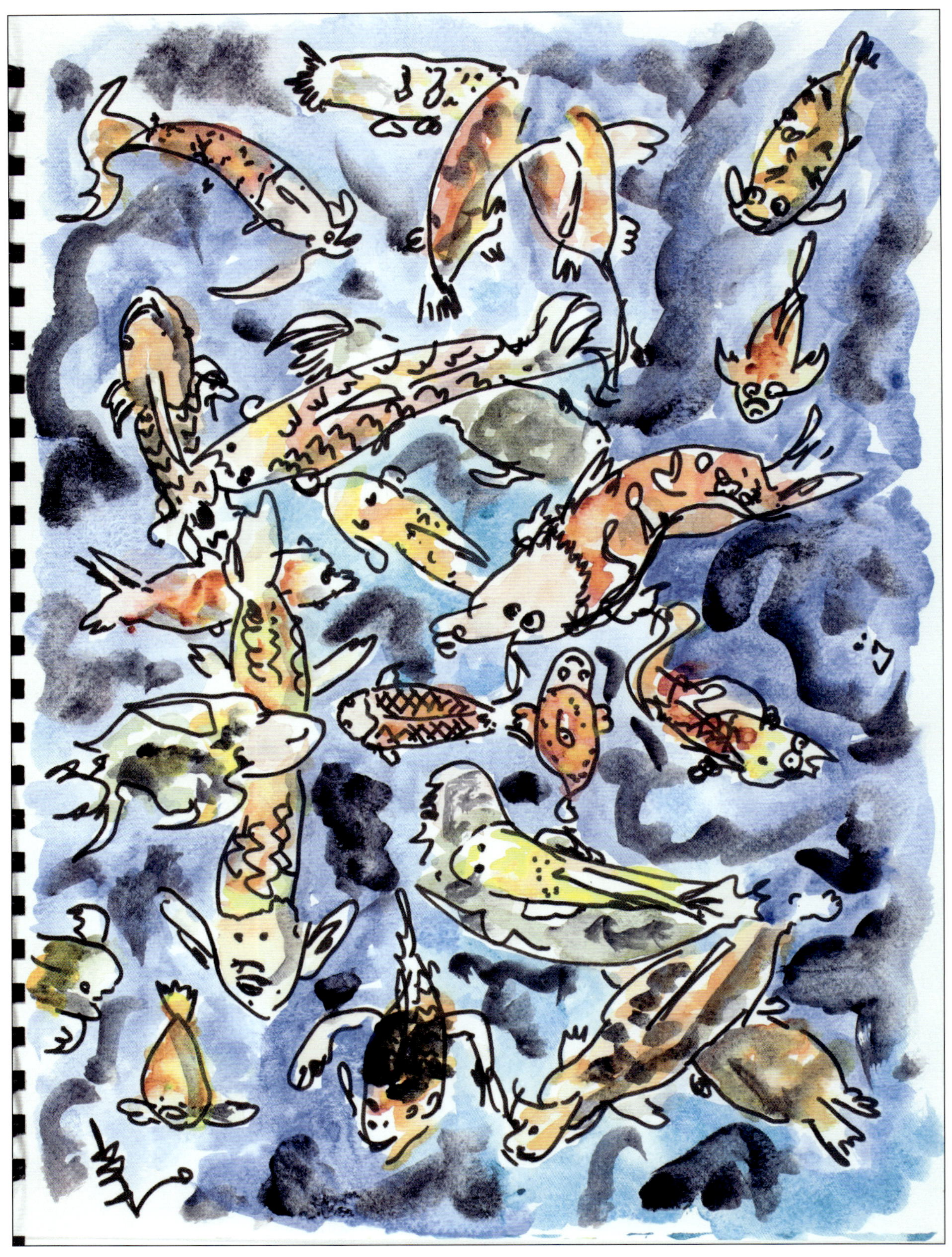

Carp

2.2: Mexican Watercolor Drawings

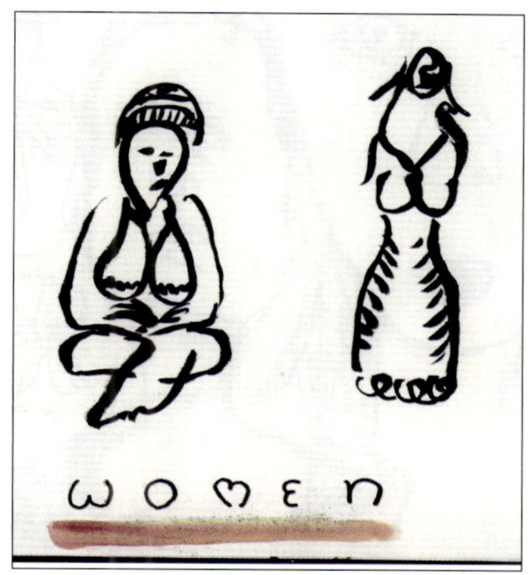

In Mexico I drew myself not merely as I wanted to be, but also as I seemed to see myself. The fact that these meetings with myself sometimes surprised me may be evidence of a lack of self-knowledge, of the unconscious content of psychological projection, or, as I prefer to believe, that anything is worth studying. On occasion I felt lonely when Dolores modeled for me; sometimes I feared that I was wasting a portion of my life, and that rather than dwelling on myself, which I could have done anywhere, I should have gone out into the Mexico of other people, as in the past I would certainly have done. But I had now come to believe in the existence of a Mexican Dolores, and it was only here that I could find her.

When I encountered myself instead, this entity likewise began to take on a faintly Mexican appearance. But no matter whom I saw, my half-blindness continued to be convenient.

For example, the sketch called "Dolores's *novio*" [p. 96] is a likeness of the man whom I perceived in the mirror. The details which without my spectacles I could not see consisted of rough-pored, age-spotted skin, unskillful bouts of shaving, my new double chin, etcetera. Hence the man in the portrait looked younger and smoother-skinned. In the next picture, "Debutante" [same page], I added long hair, eyebrows, earrings and mascara as I pleased. Dolores might not have been beautiful even then, but at least she was the way she saw herself.

I never saw the astigmatism of my left eye, evidently because it is the one I use for the closeup vision entailed in drawing. Hence in these sketches, as is far from the case in the photographs, Dolores's eyes appear to track.

The Oaxaca portraits were all done in a sketchbook. As they accrued, it became a thrill to page through them and observe how protean Dolores could be, and yet how much she remained very much herself. Since the little book was always with me, whether I sat down for an ice cream at the *zócalo* or wandered up a desert hill, I could pencil in whatever I pleased on any leaf, before or after the fact. Thus the two "earring and pyramid" drawings were each begun on an ancient archaeological site; later on I whisked a bit of paint onto them, and in place of a moon I finally hung one of Dolores's first earrings in the sky. In "Public offering" [p. 100] the man in the hat was sketched first; and after Dolores posed for me, I added in the tilework pattern at the very last. It was as a result of these Mexican drawings that I began more vividly to imagine the Dolores of *How You Are* becoming, or trying to become, a Mexicana.

By the time of my visits to Xalapa and Veracruz, that aspiration was a settled matter — in the novel, anyhow. The respective sketchbooks were larger and less portable than the one I had taken to Oaxaca. Accordingly, I often worked in the hotel room or on the balcony. These portraits took on a semiformal character; but I continued to feel free to imagine myself in anywhere I liked — for instance, in an candy store with carp swimming through the air.

"First Jadeite Dolores," so called not only because there was more than one such composition but also because the main watercolor pigment was jadeite — and jade rock occurs in the province of Veracruz — was begun from two sketches of figures in the Anthropology Museum in Xalapa. Returning to the hotel I then, as usual, sketched myself posing in imitation of one of the statues. (It is easy to tell Dolores from her exemplars by her narrower nose and fuller eyelids; she is in the center of the trio.)

In "Dolores as an indigenous giantess," I narrowed my eyes, widened my eyes and tilted back my head in an attempt to resemble the woman in the foreground, whom I had sketched in the park.

 "Dolores as a young Mexicana" modeled herself after the hotel chambermaid, who posed for me after work. In this latter case, once Dolores was alone I parted her imaginary hair in the chambermaid's style, added imaginary squiggles of earrings, and left her essential facial features alone as always. She looked fresher than usual since I somehow neglected to draw the wrinkles in. Here she is wearing the one dress she had with her in Xalapa, a black one with a red stripe across the breast; it struts itself again in the gum print "Desert light."

By the time of the final sketching trip, to Veracruz, I felt more willing to alter the contours of my body (excepting my face) as if my flesh were another fantasy garment. The girl on the left in "Blue devil" was an outdoor waitress. After she had posed, I returned to the hotel room, stripped, and modeled, giving myself breasts and hips similar to hers, painting in hair and earrings of my own invention, and coloring Dolores blue. The differential between my height and the waitress's is shown accurately.

In "Banana crown" I was feeling my age. One can see in Dolores's eyes that she has begun wondering when it will all come to an end.

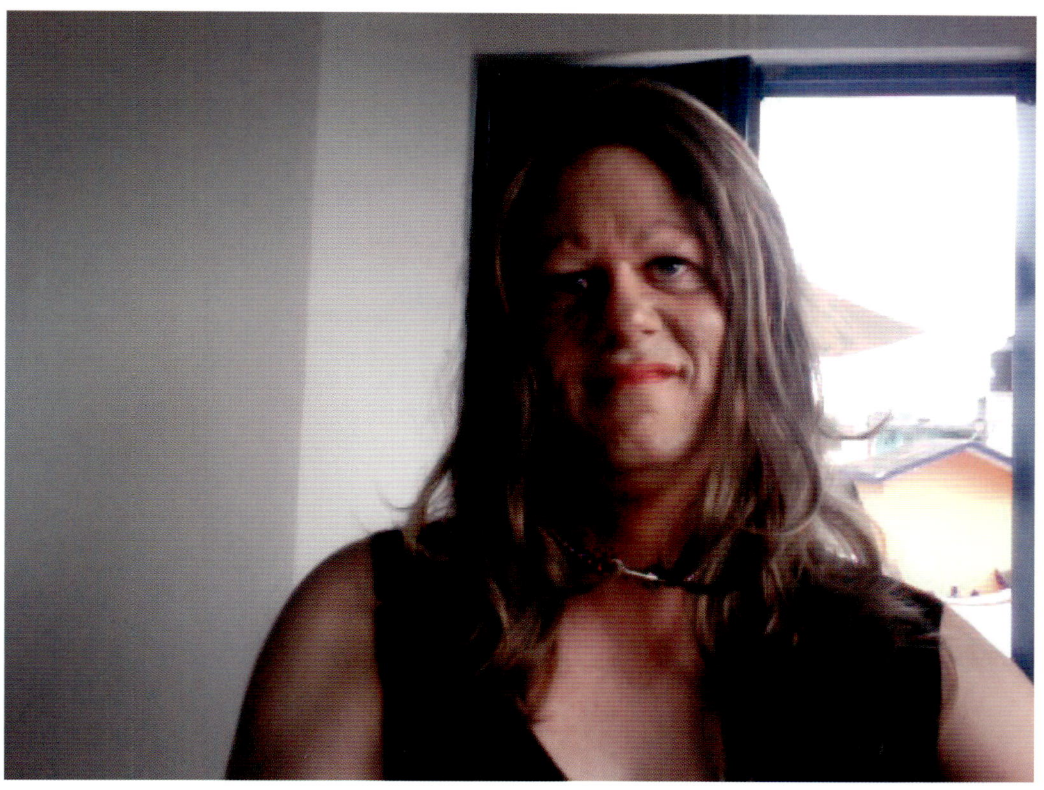

Dolores in Xalapa

Oaxaca, 2008

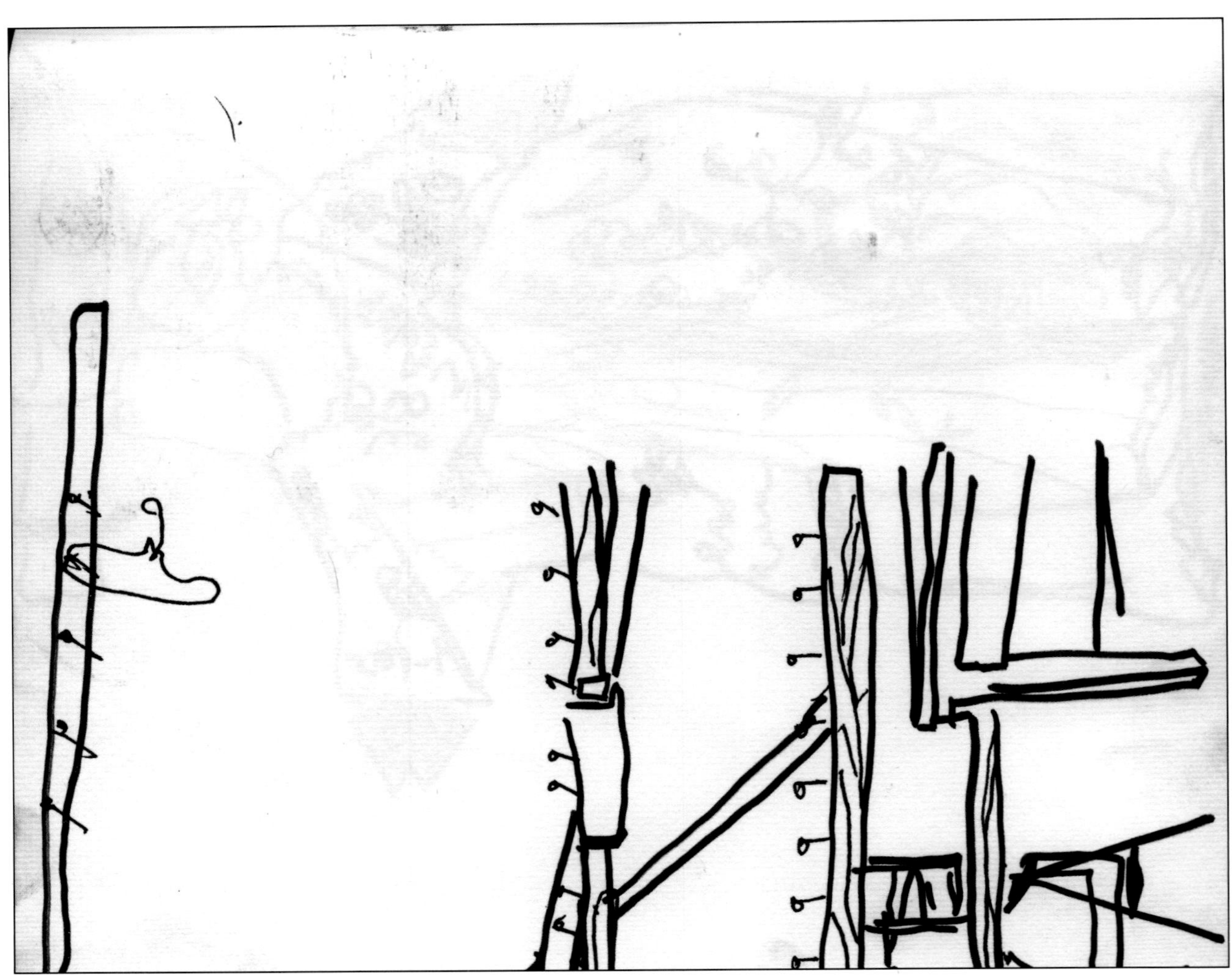

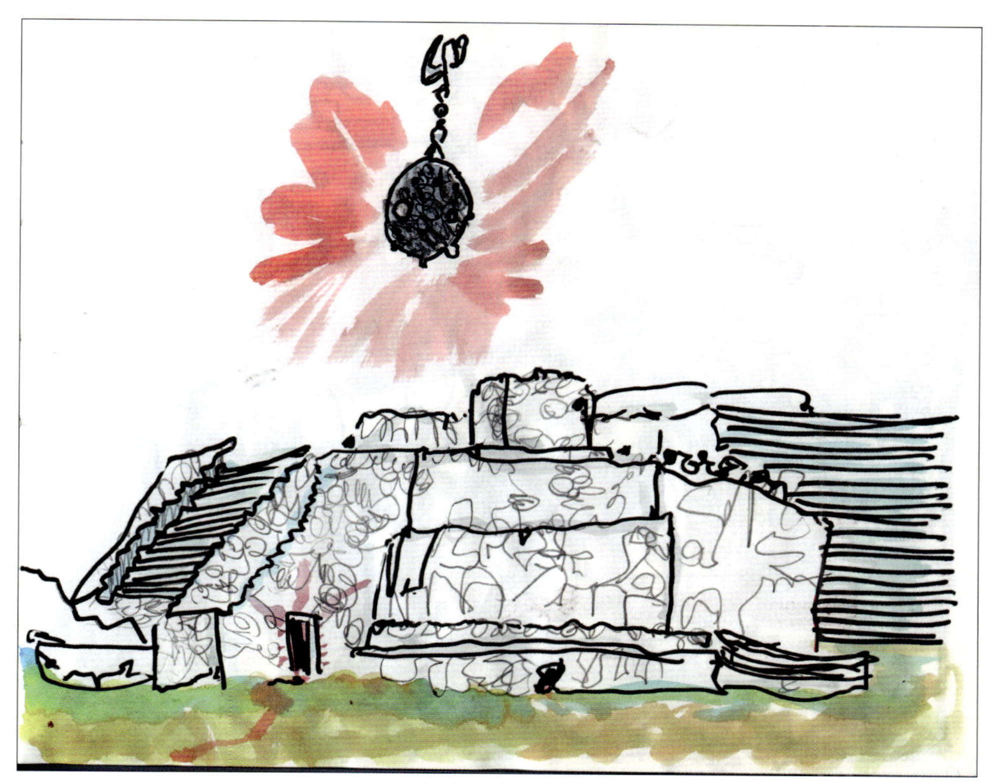

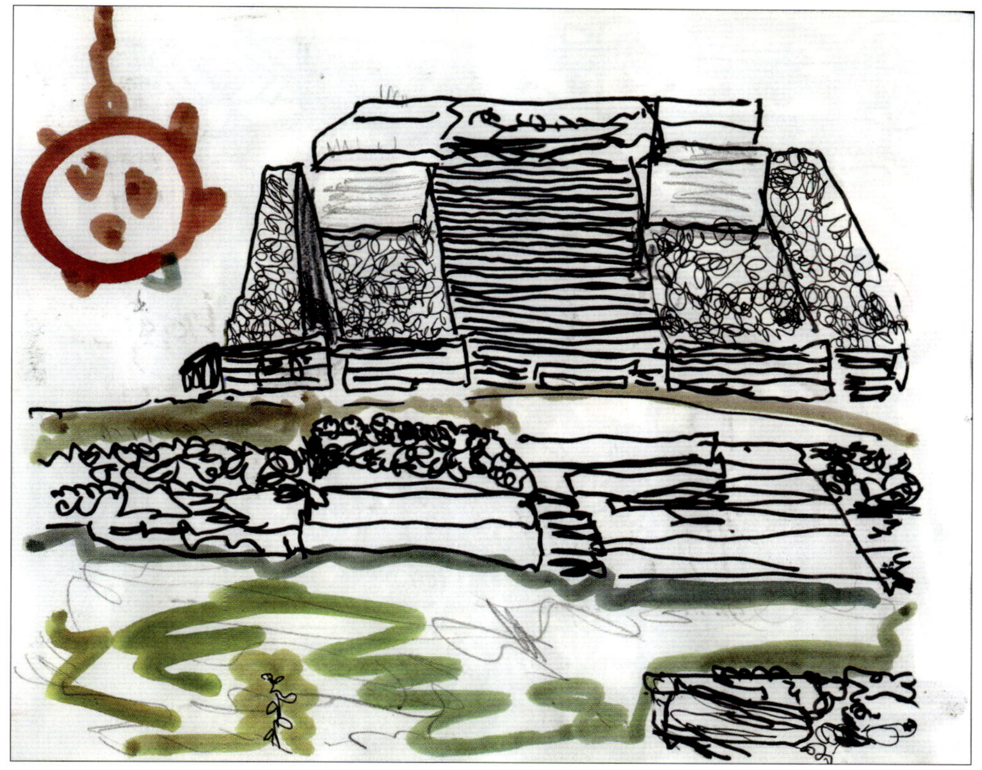

Dolores's earrings

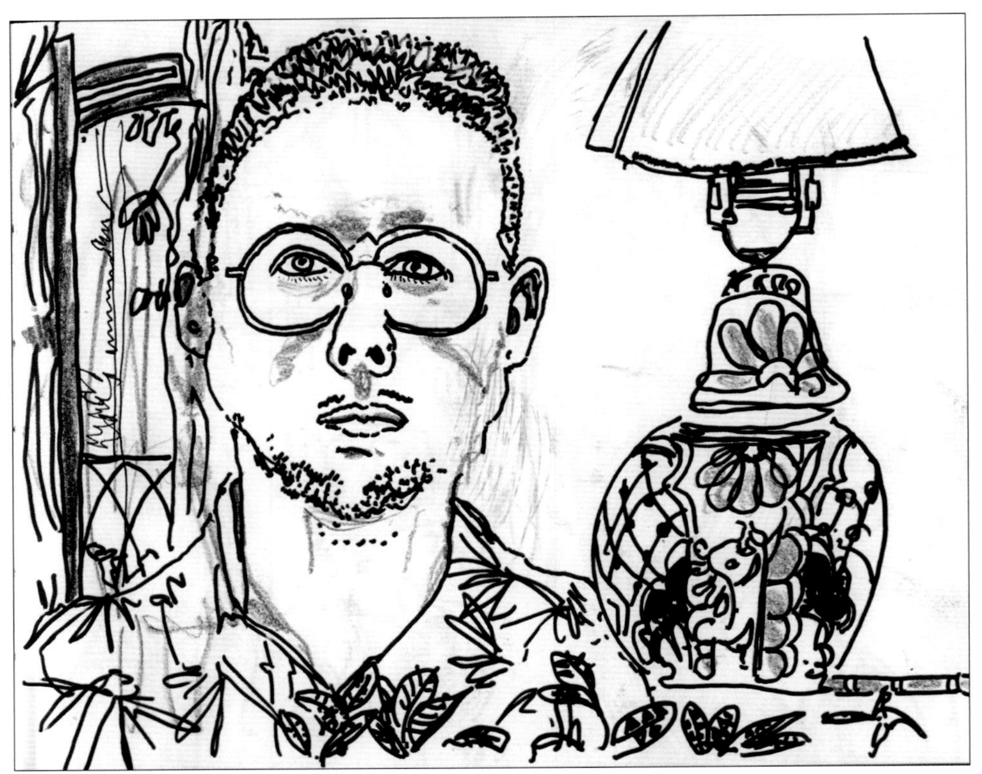

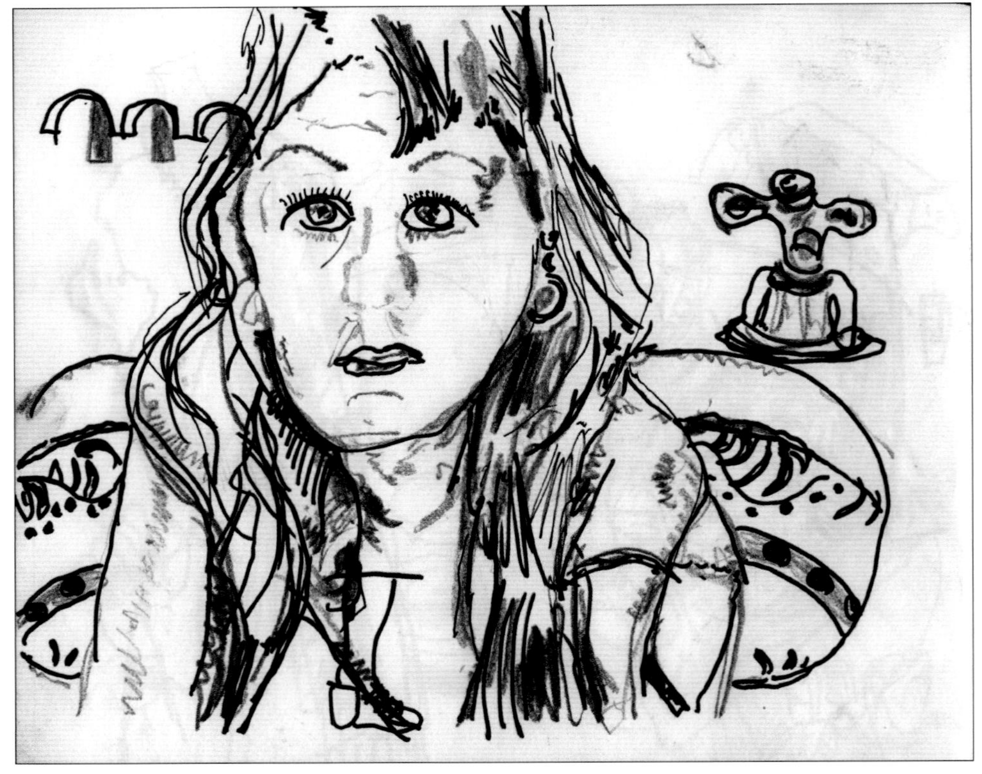

Top: Dolores's novio; *bottom: Debutante*

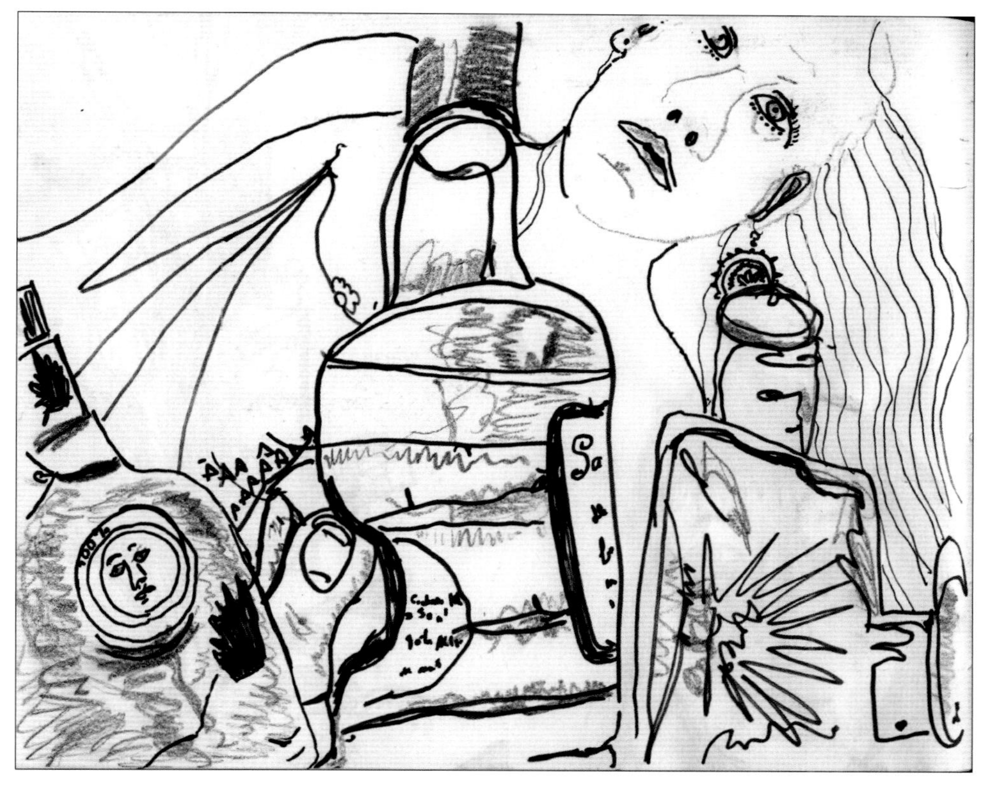

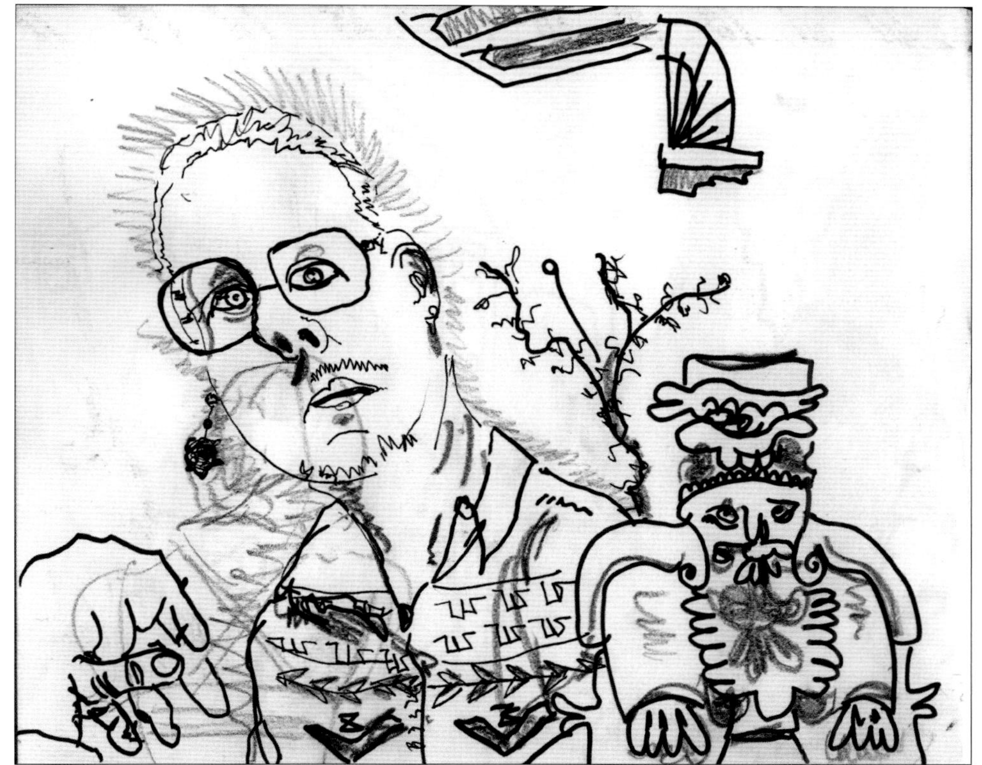

Top: Dolores Mescalita; bottom: Man with earring

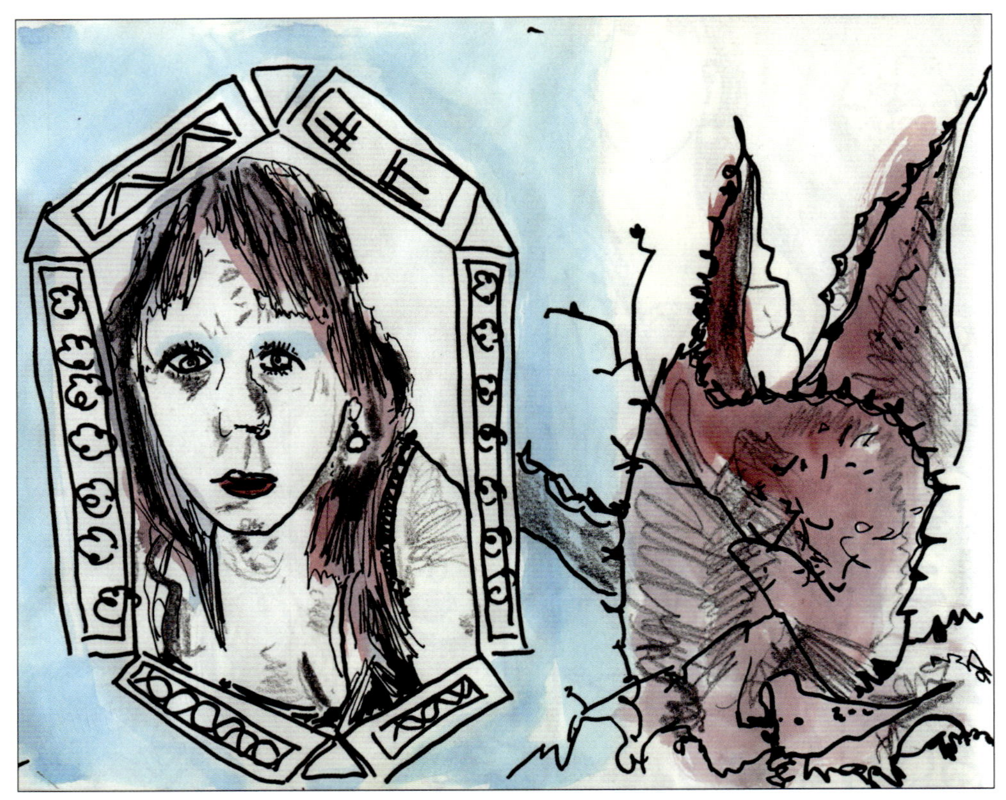

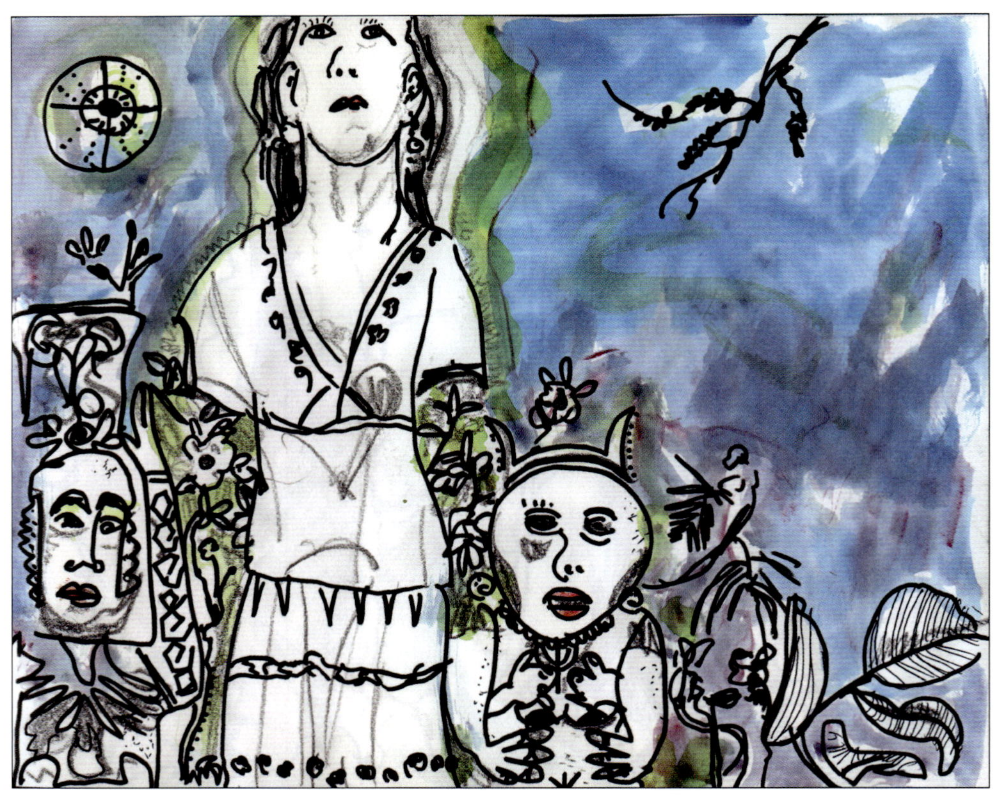

Top: Princess of the Red Cactus; bottom: With her familiars

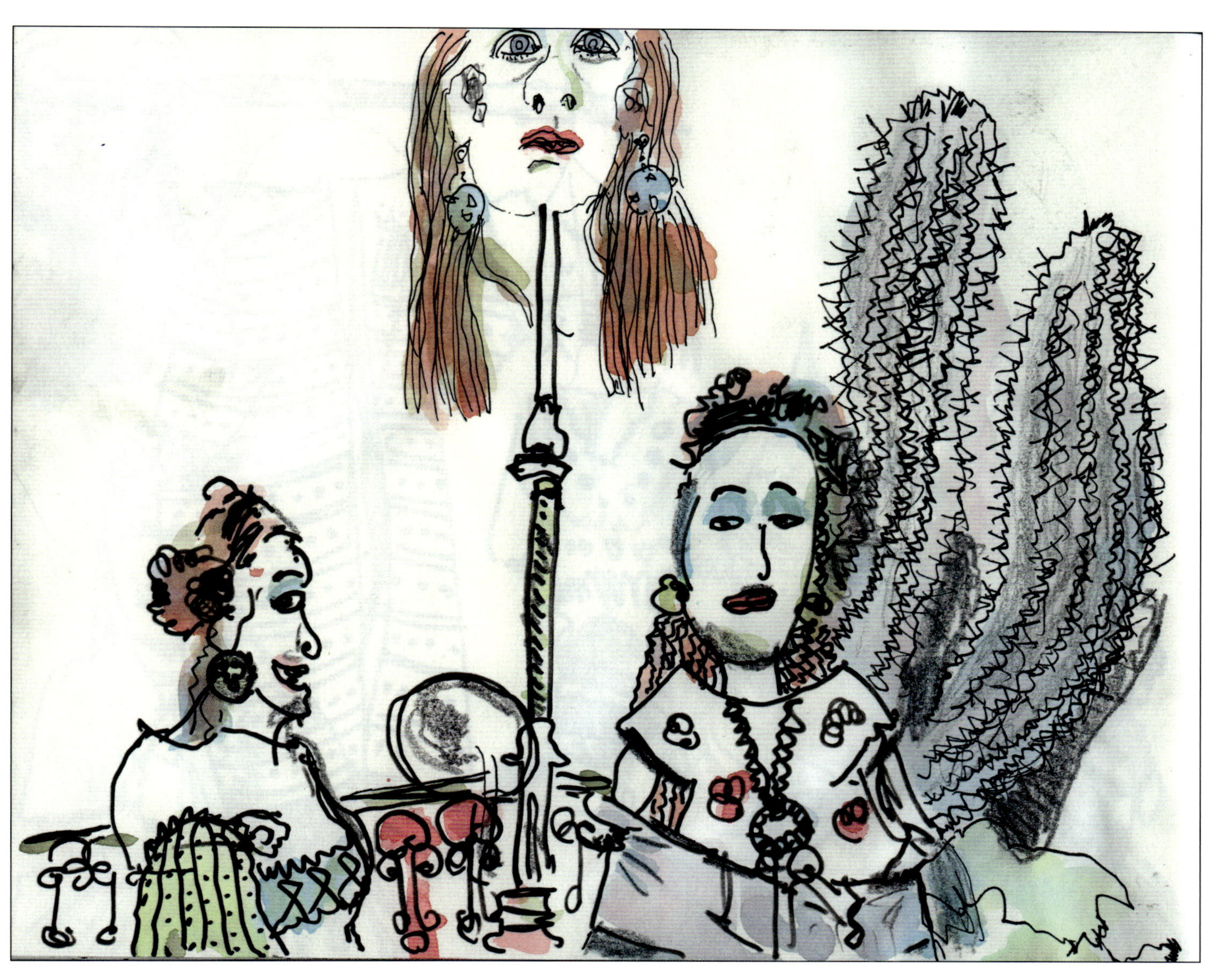

Dolores as a decapitated head

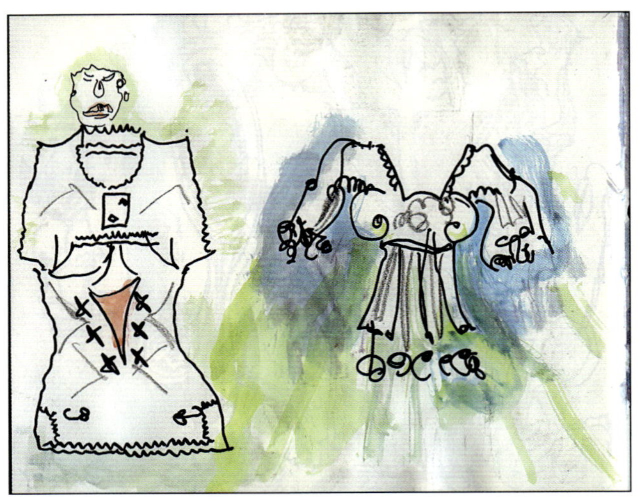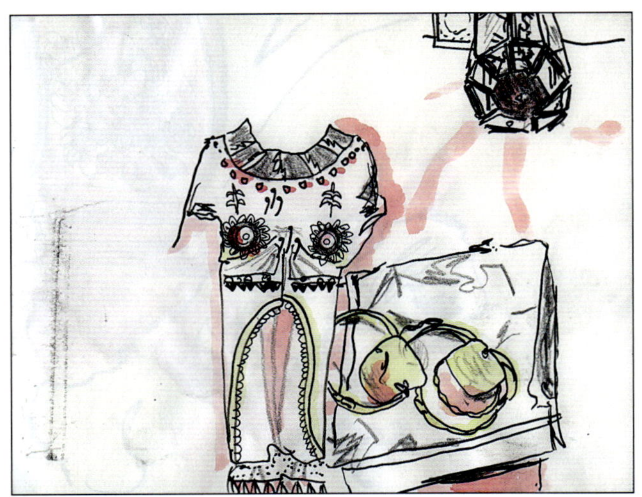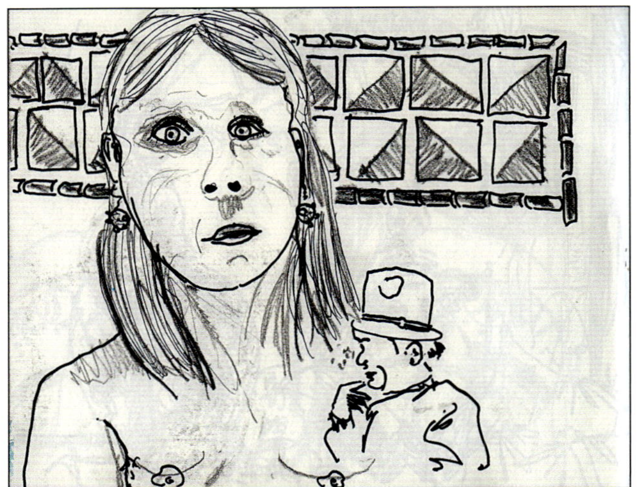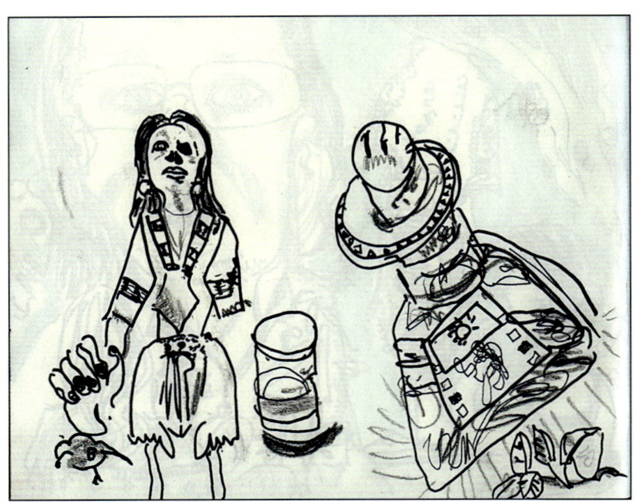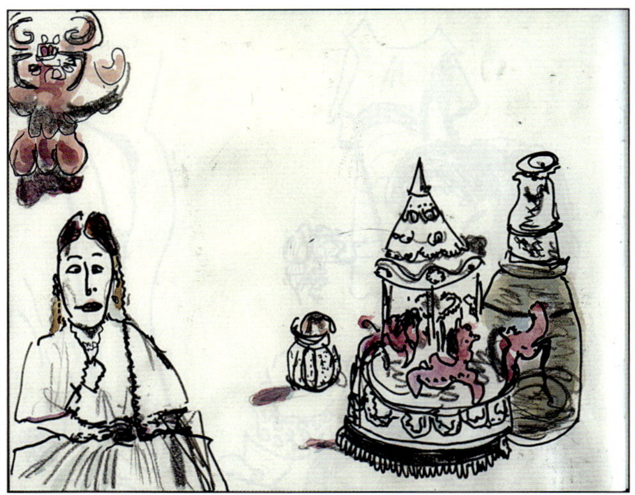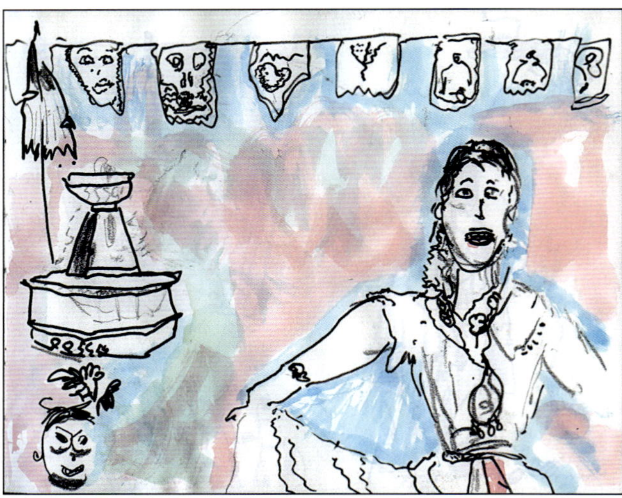

Top left: Mask-dress and breast-skin; top right: Breast-dress; middle left: Public offering; middle right: Woman and bottle-man; bottom: Mexicanas

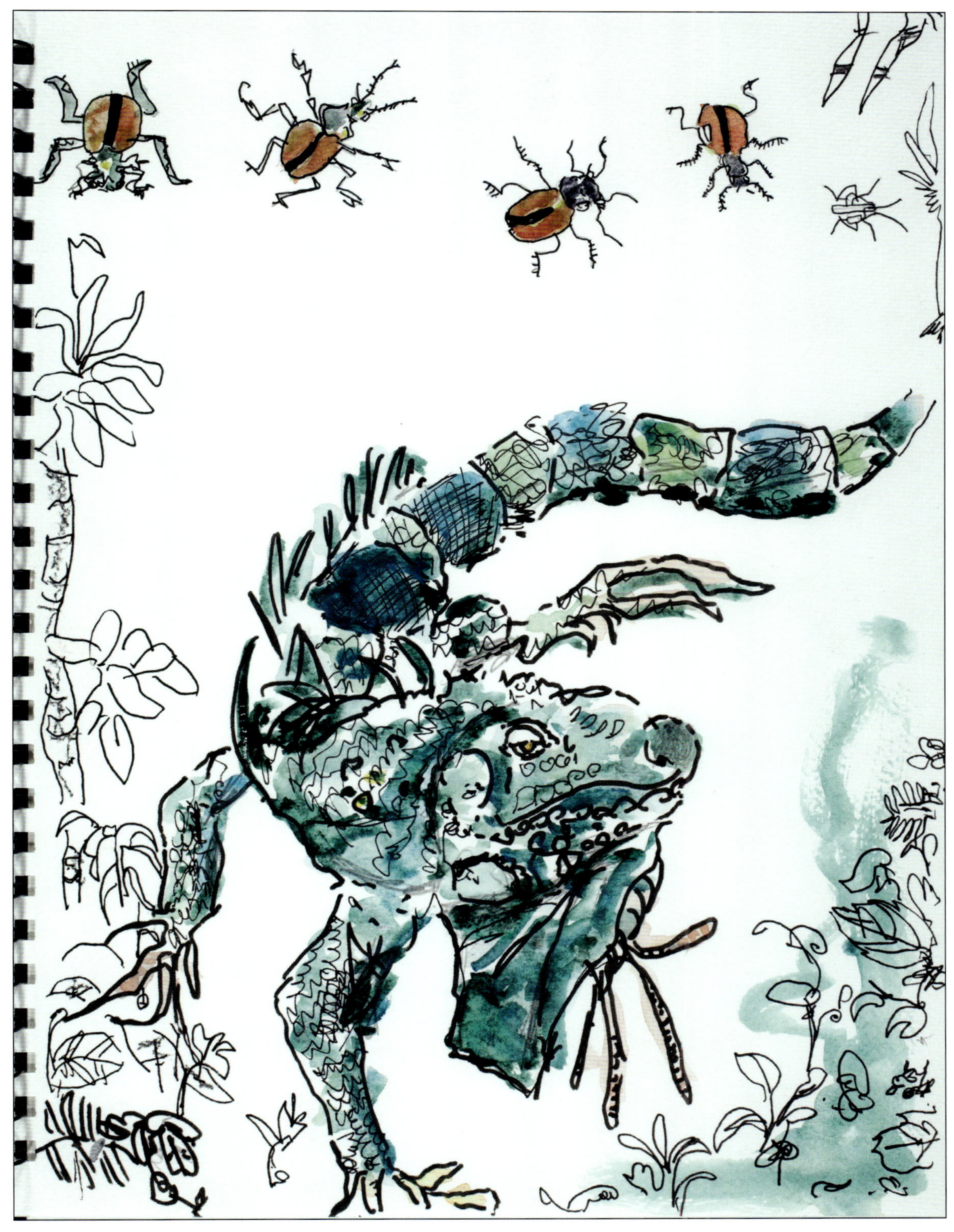

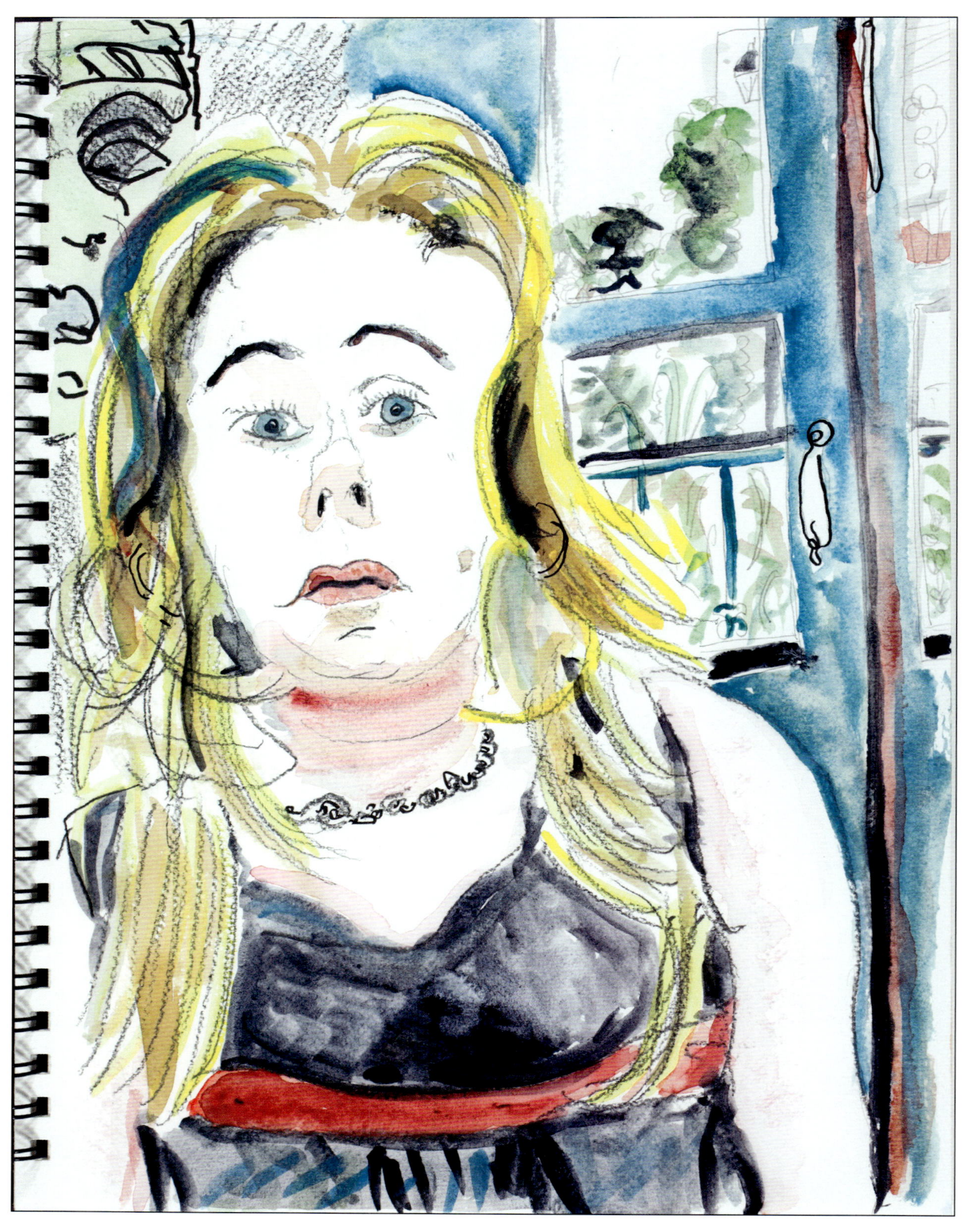

Blonde and blue door

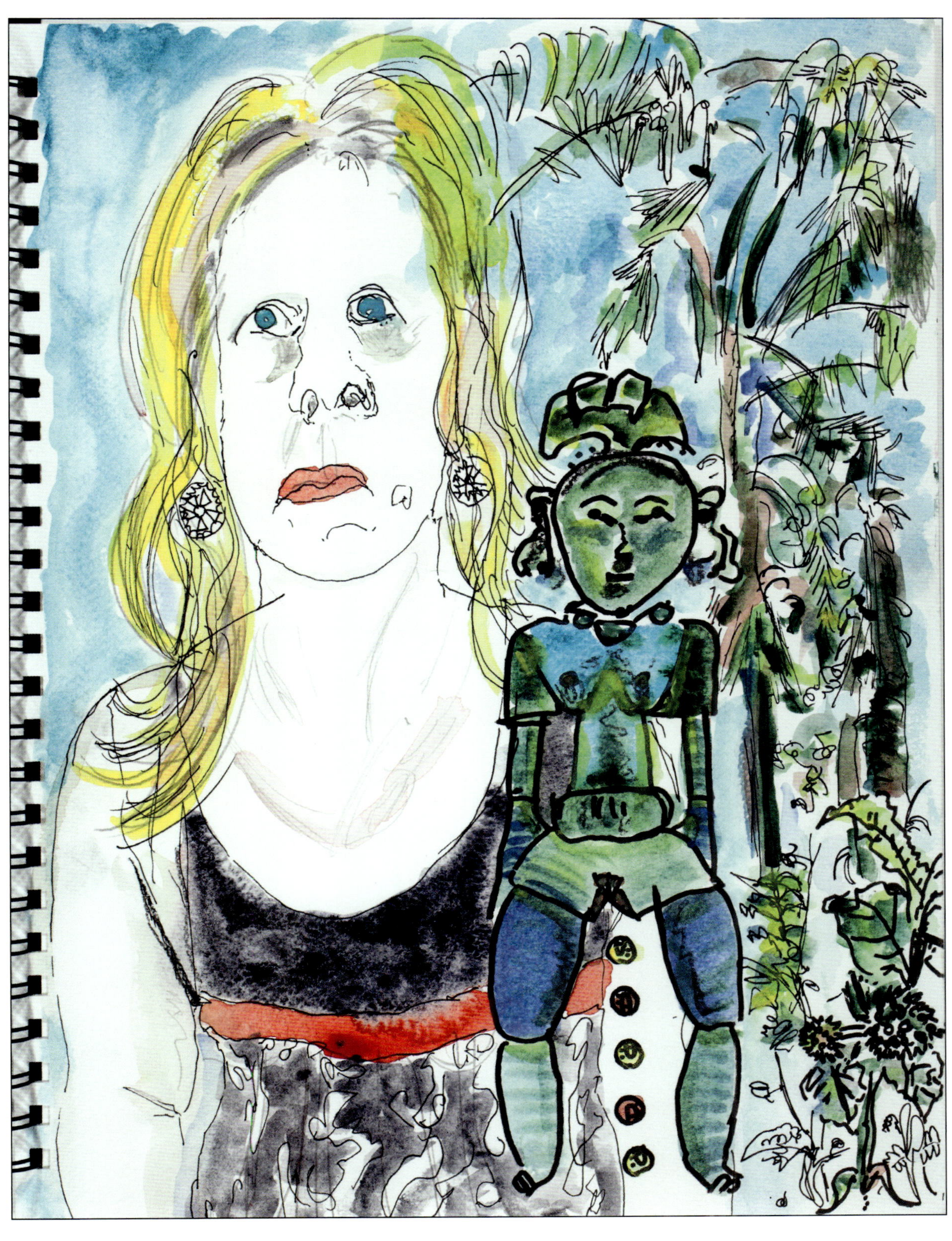

Inner child

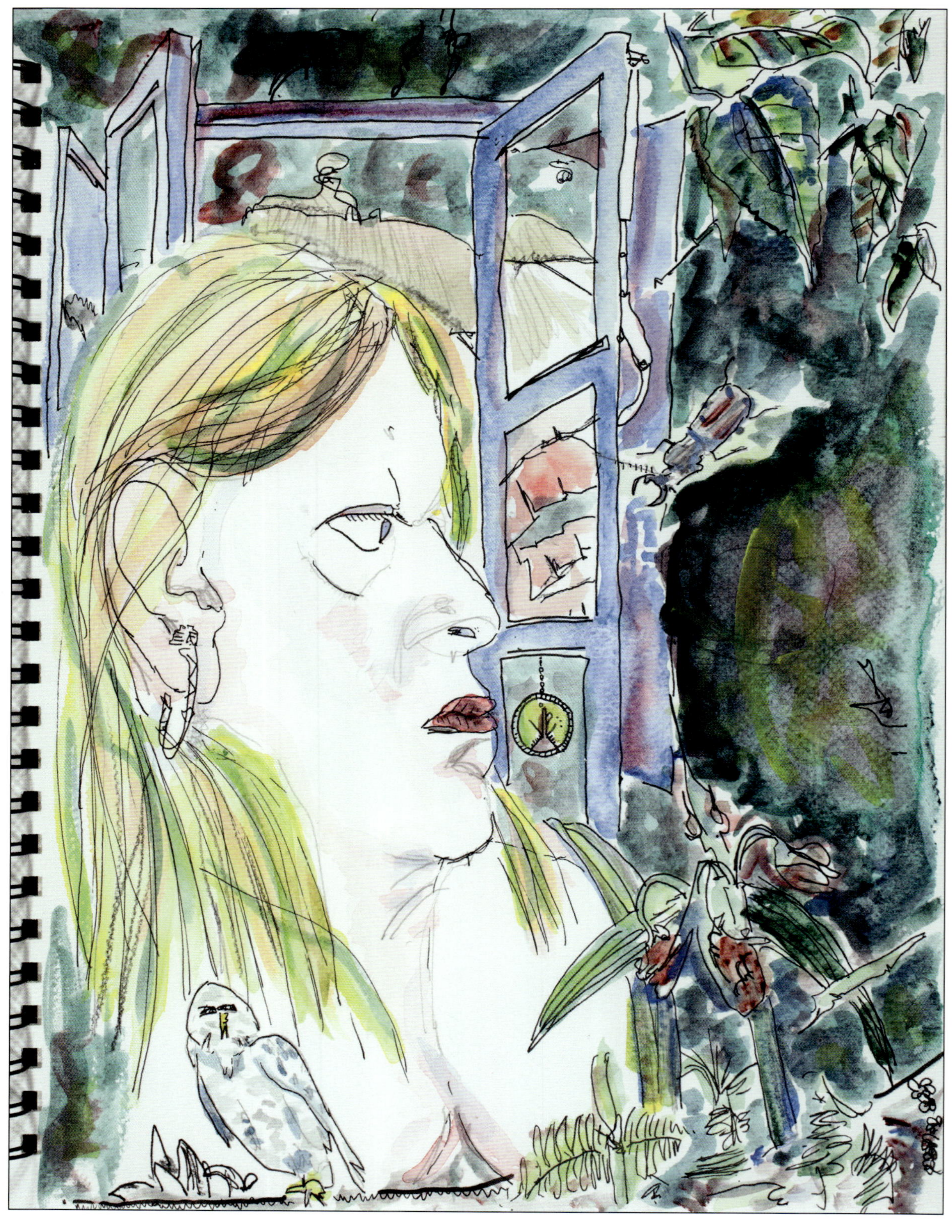

Profile

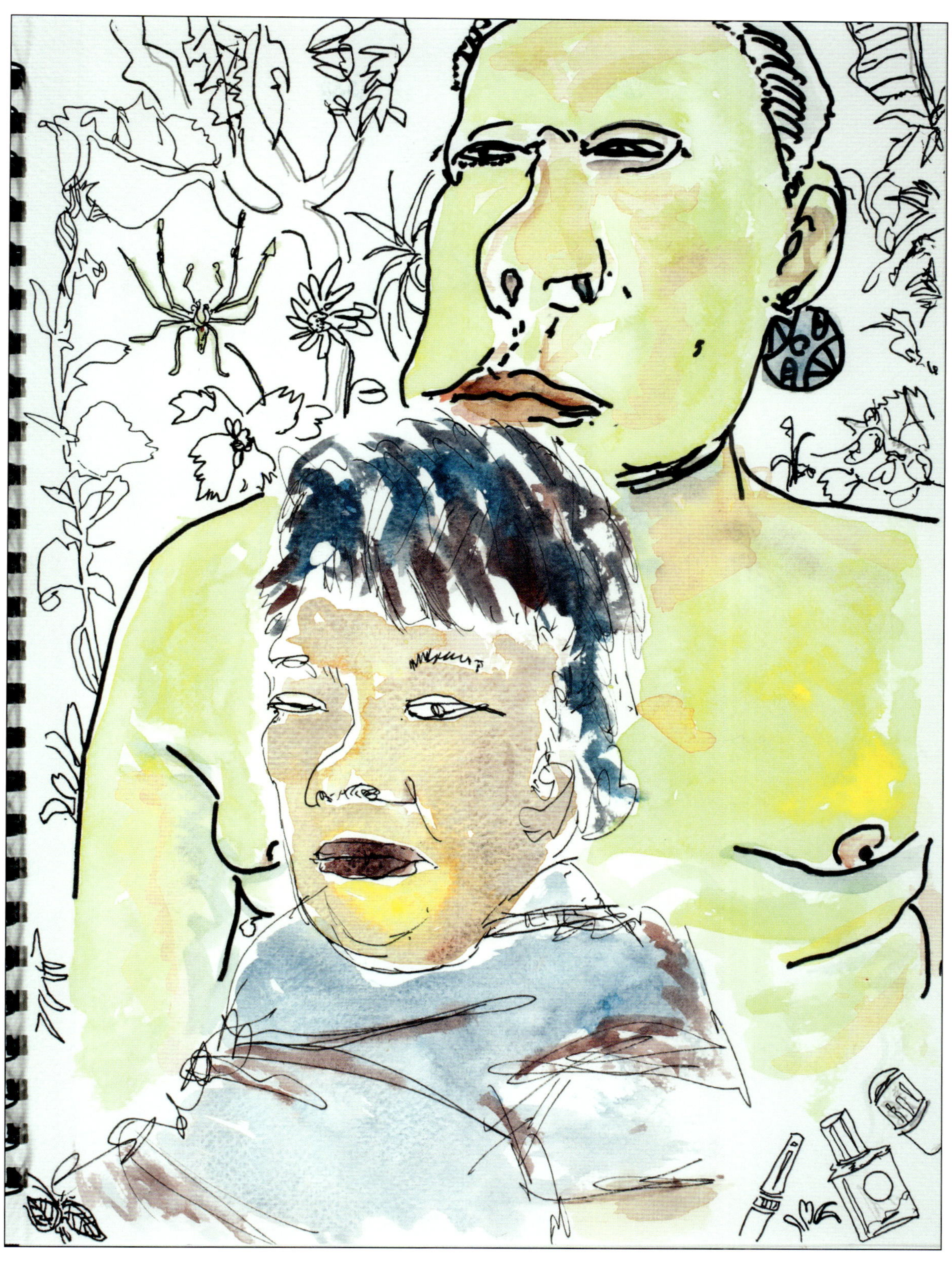

Dolores as an indigenous giantess

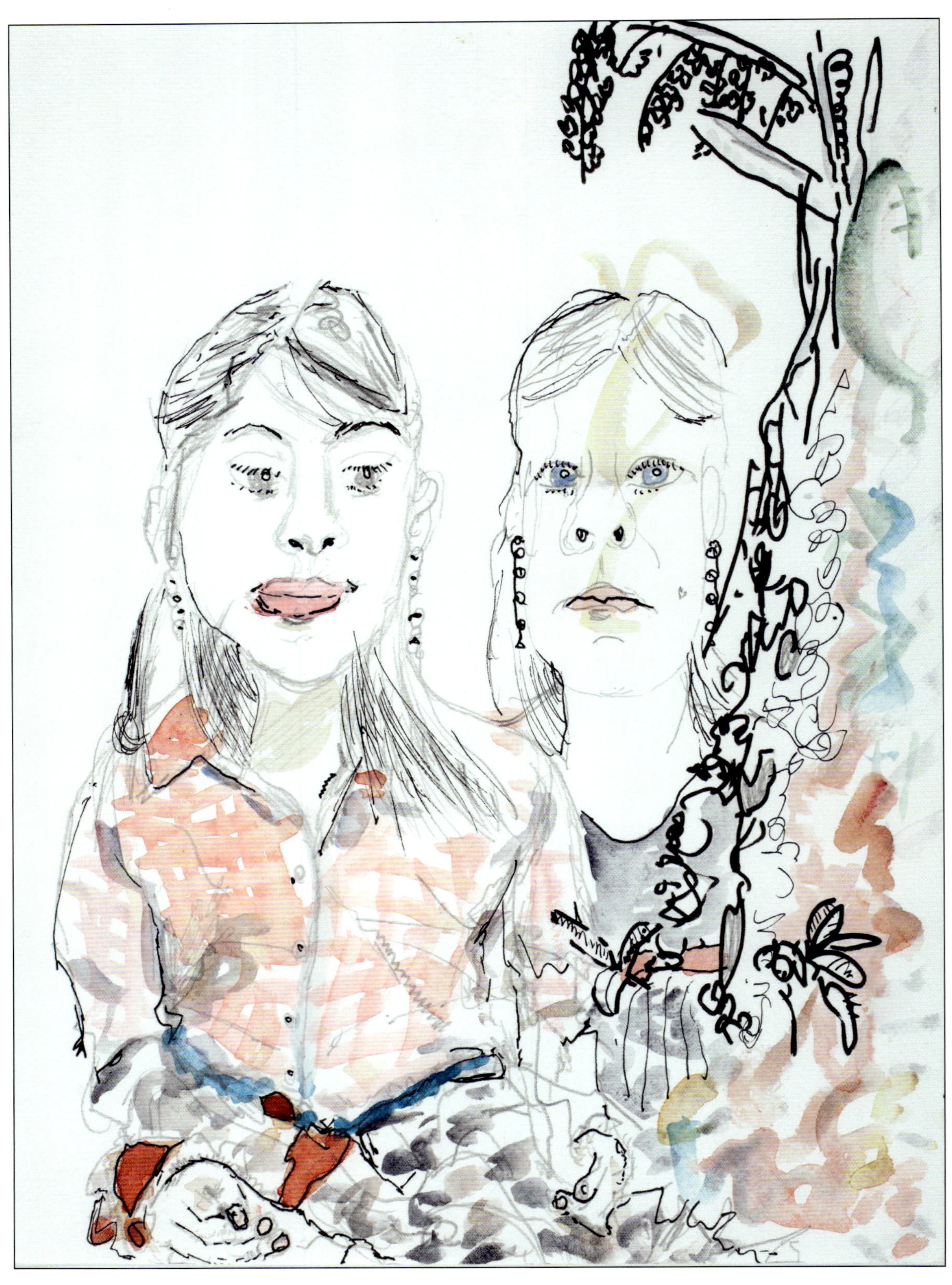

Dolores as a young Mexicana

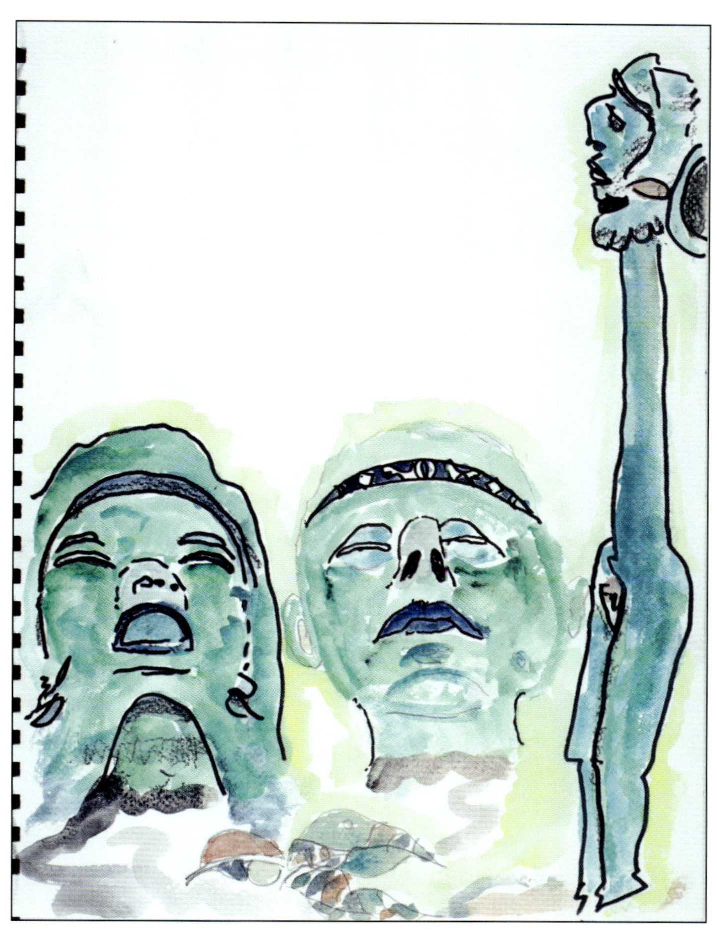

First jadeite Dolores

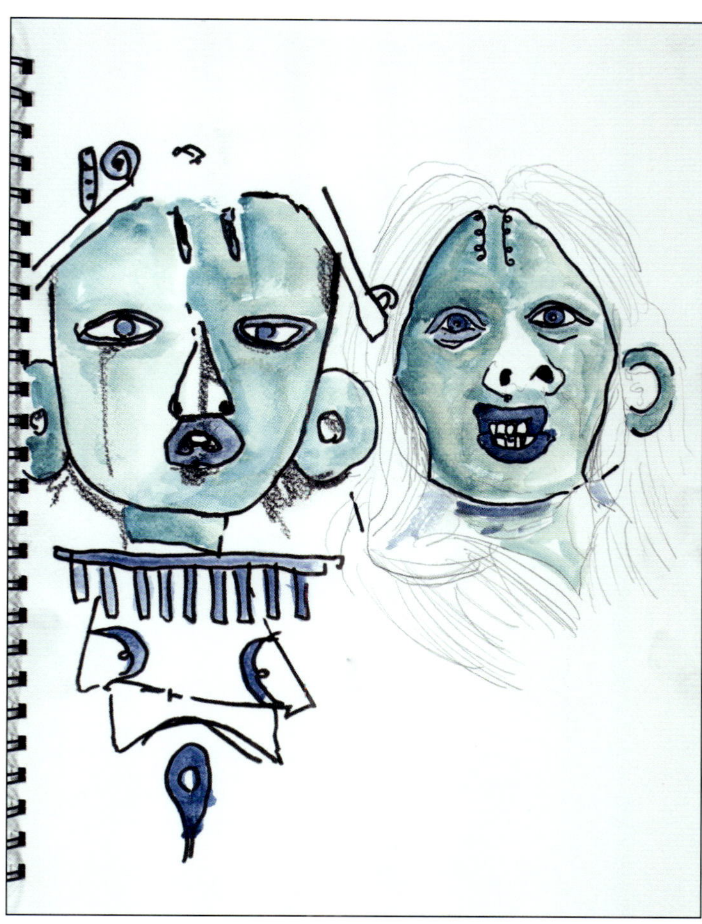

Second jadeite Dolores

Veracruz, Veracruz, 2011

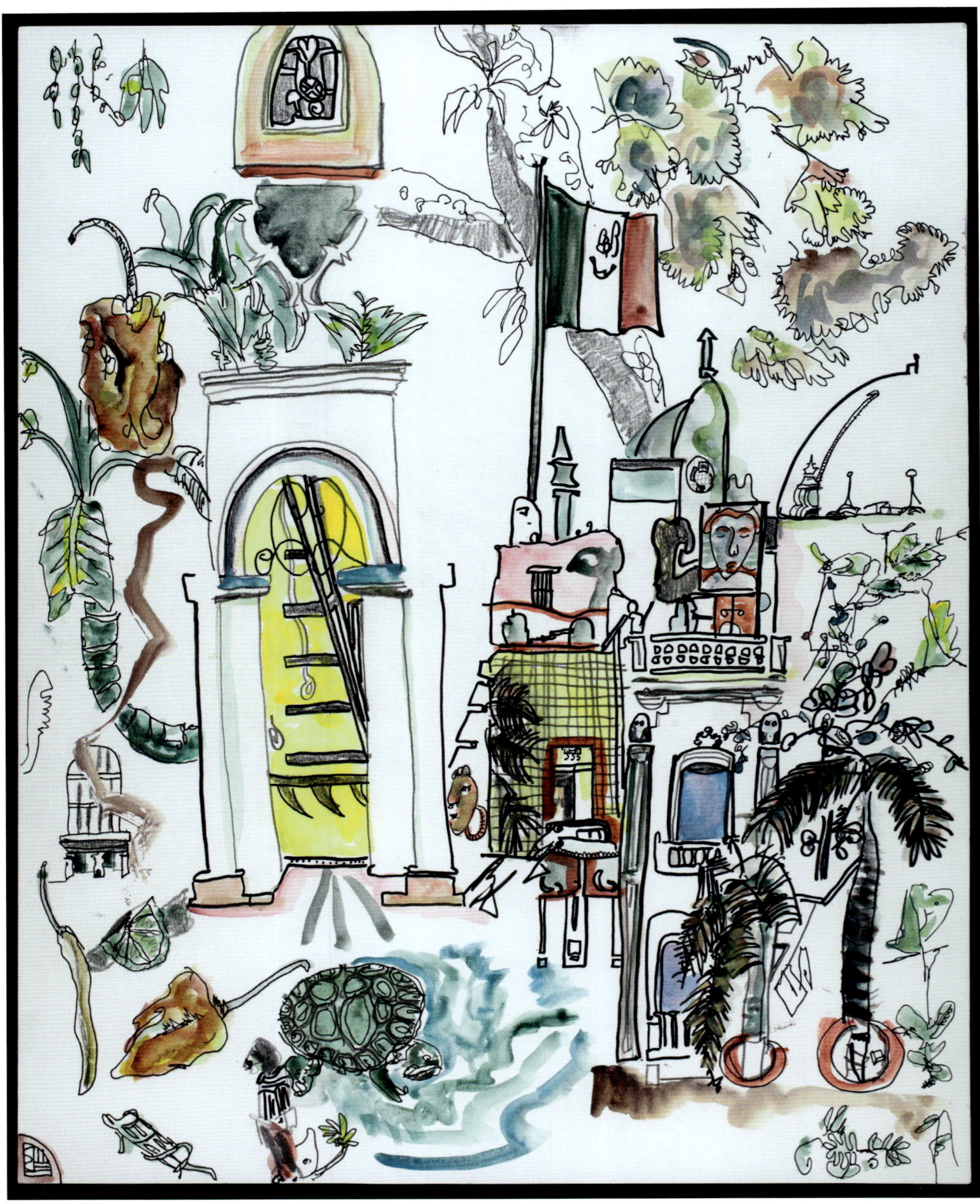

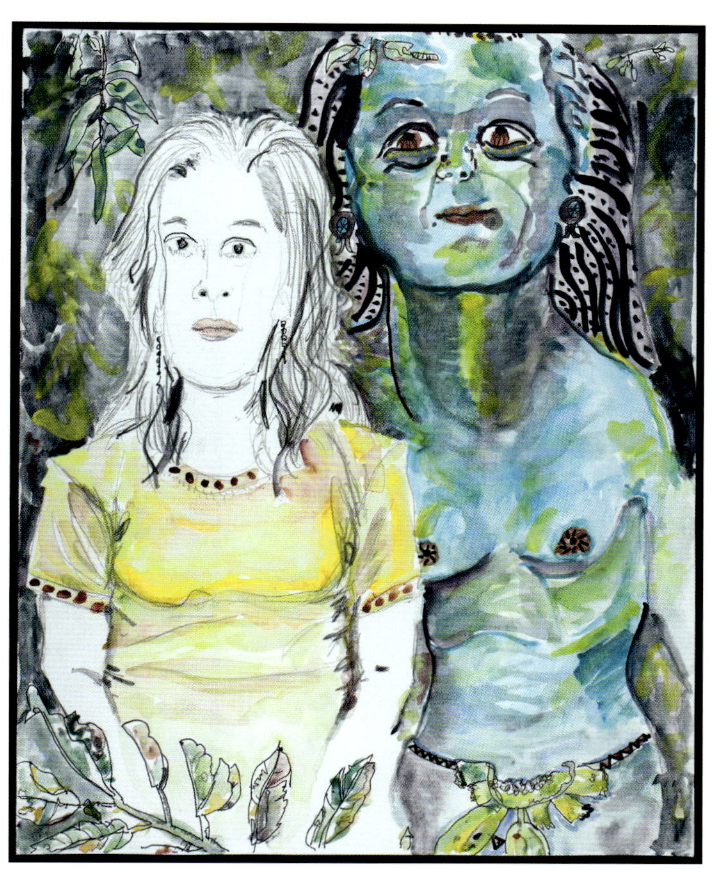

Dolores as a blue devil

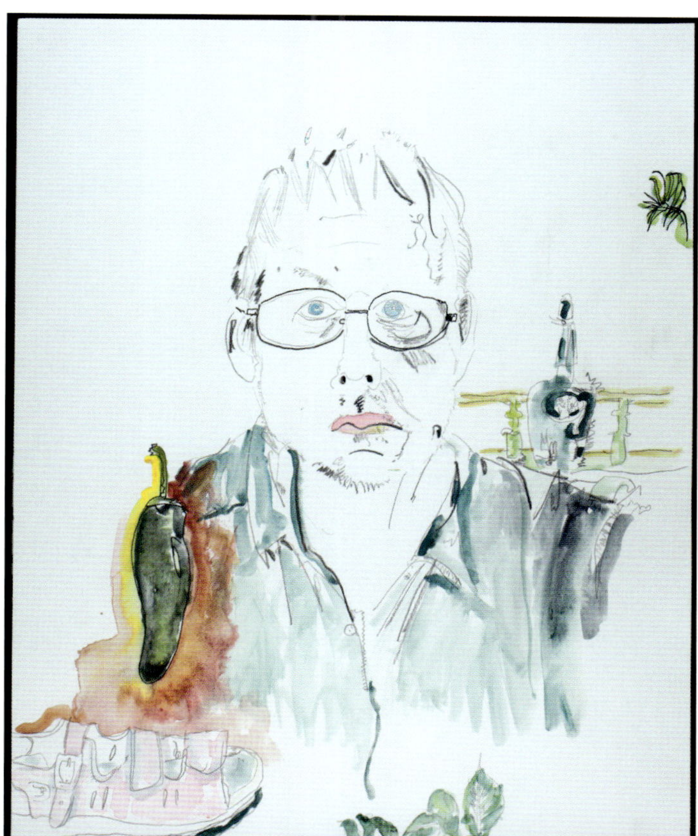

Man with serrano chili

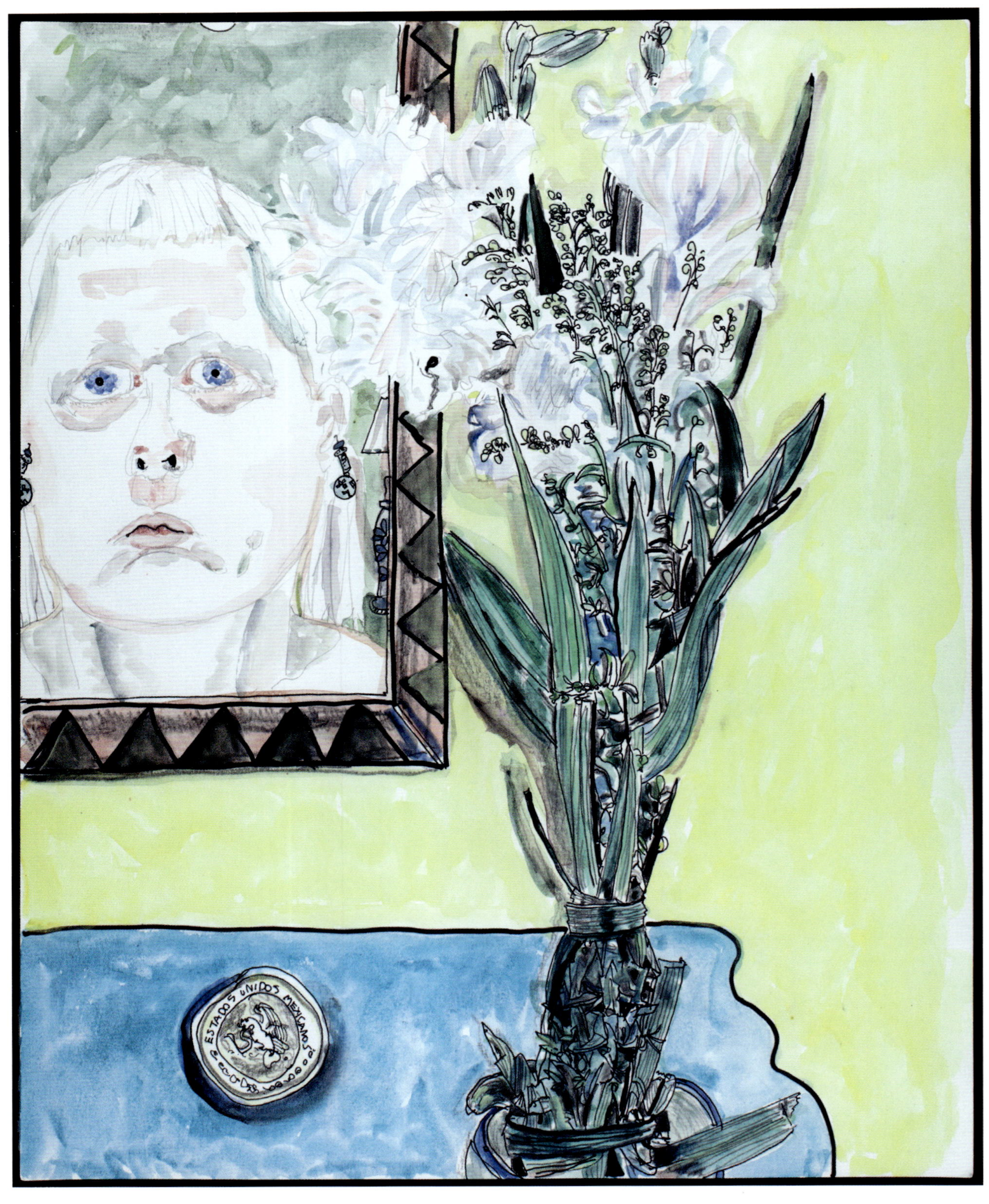

Blonde with flowers

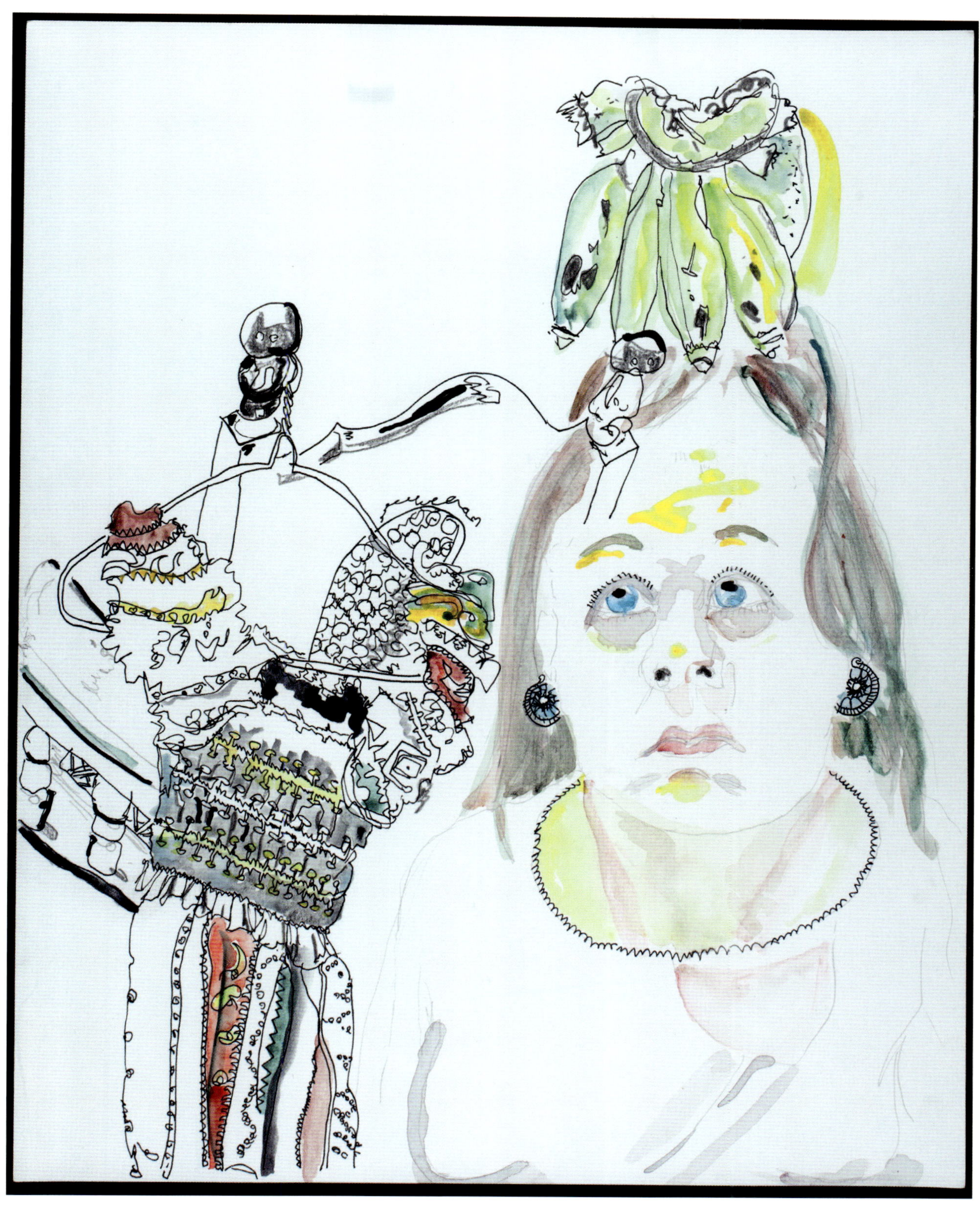

Banana crown

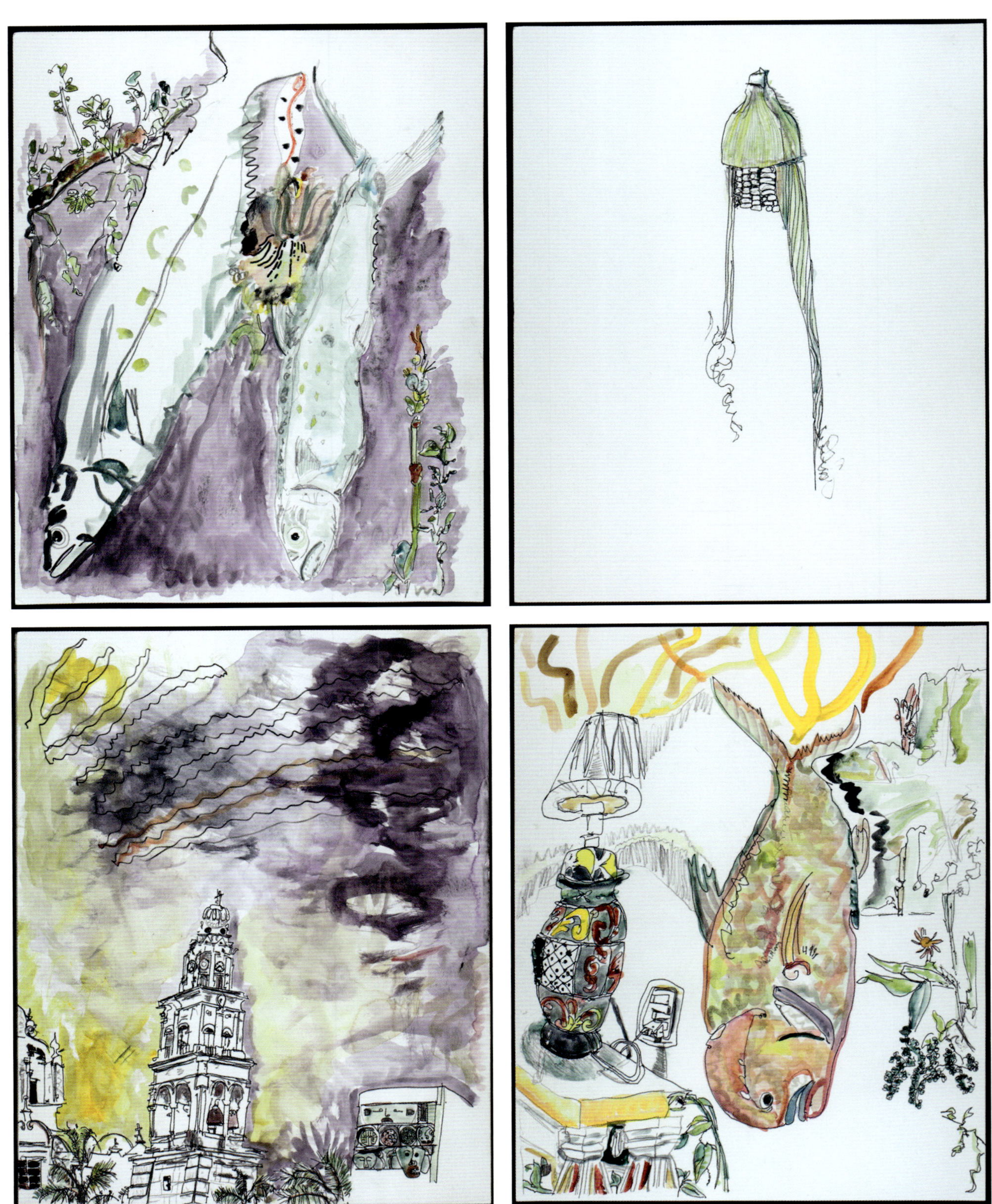

Top left: Fish leg; top right: Corn; bottom left: Zócalo; bottom right: Fish and lamp

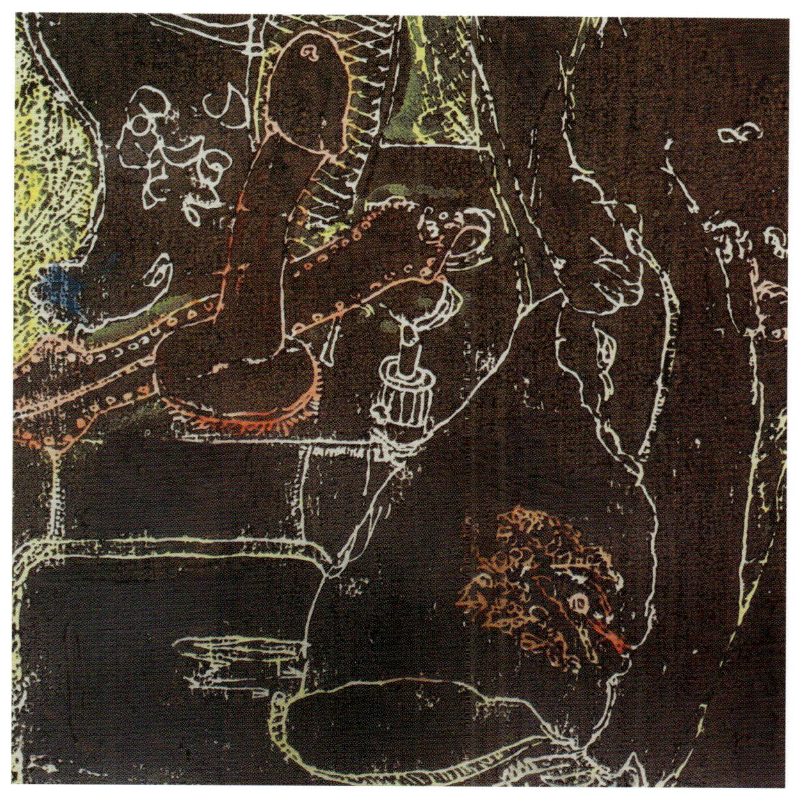

Detail from "Dolores with Isabel . . ."

Since Dolores likes women near about as much as I do, we might as well call her a lesbian. So in these woodblock prints we see her both alone and with her lesbian lover Isabel. What they do together I can't imagine.

When I travel to other countries, I frequently buy the local wood, hire models and start drawing straight onto my blocks. If I have time, I carve them on the spot. Thai *ulo* wood is crispy-soft and comes in tall, narrow, thin lengths — nearly too thin in my opinion, since it can break. Japanese cherry, the traditional choice for *ukiyo-e* printing, is hard and nearly grainless. American pine and redwood can offer knots and grain for

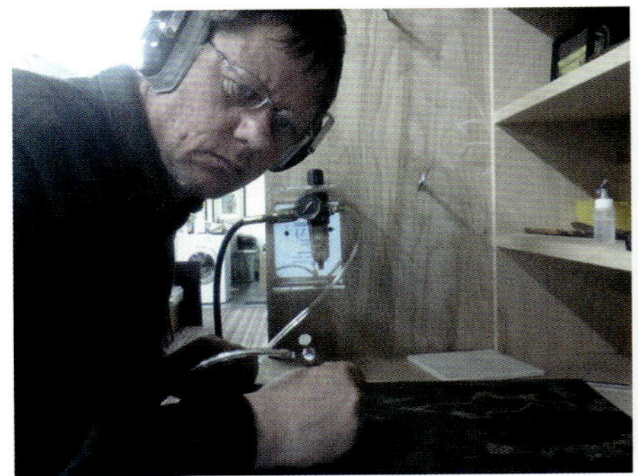
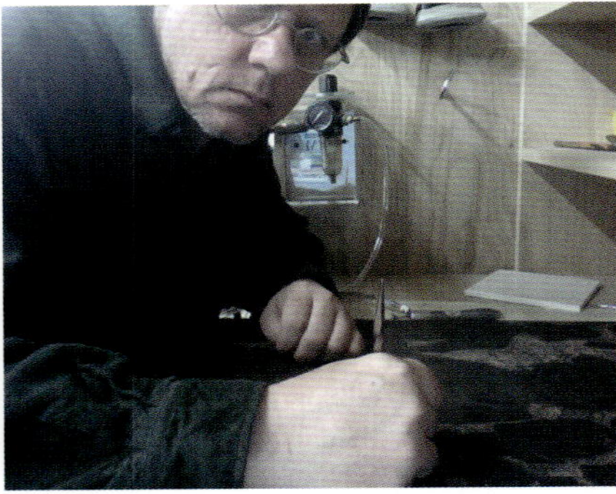
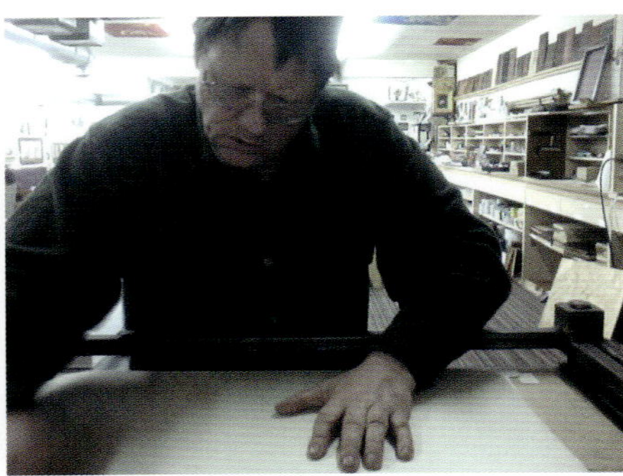

special occasions. I like Norwegian pine better. American oak is a bit like cherry, while poplar and birch are easy to work and somewhat featureless. Malaysian *datang* is so extremely soft that it can be incised with a fingernail. Therefore it comes thick and

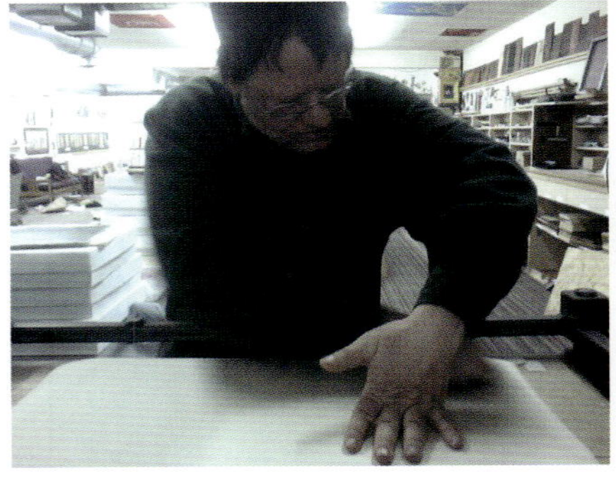
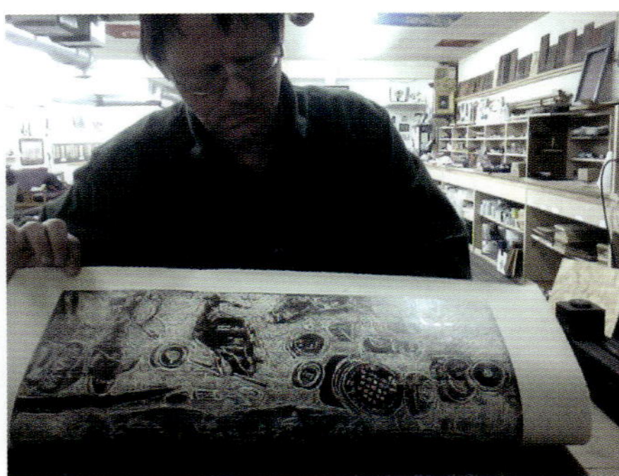

heavy — a joy to carve, but unnerving to print, since too vigorous a rubbing can ruin an image. Its strangely globular grain enhances certain images.

I carry cheap gouges in my suitcase. In the studio, however, I make increasing use of an air-compressor-powered engraver which cuts nearly as easily as a felt-tipped pen draws on smooth paper. Most of the figure-lines in the Dolores blocks were cut with this tool, although I widened some grooves with a gouge or two, and much of the crosshatching was accomplished with a steel comb.

I have always preferred the bold effects of relief printing over the greater detail of intaglio, which requires a press. My favorite printing tool is a spoon. For larger blocks such as these Dolores prints, I first employ a round Japanese barren, establishing the block's edges through the paper, and then passing rapidly over its entire surface in a series of circular motions, before the ink can dry. After that I pick up my spoon

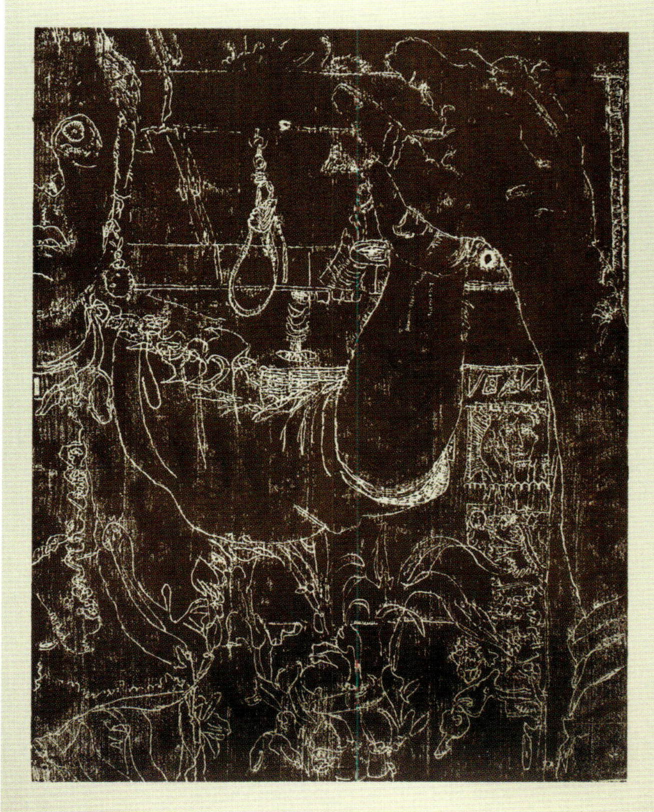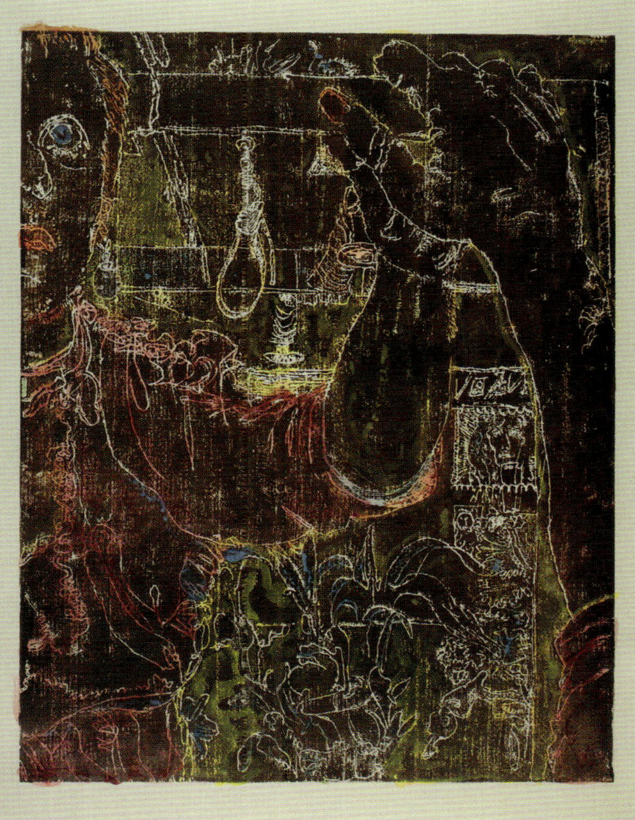

"Happy landings," first and second states of block

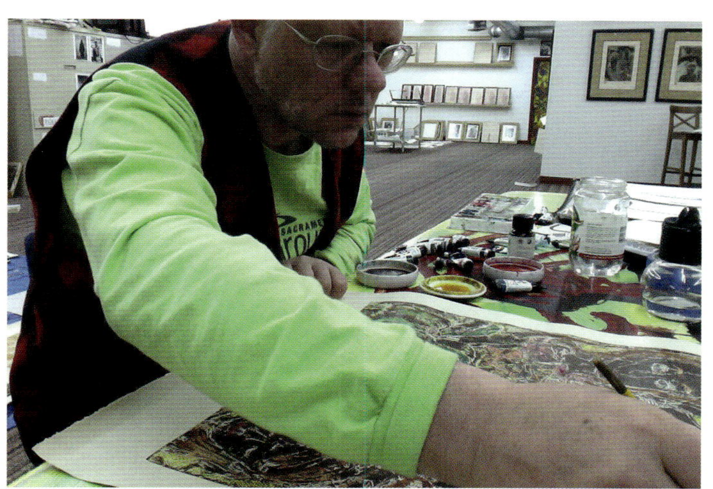

and cover the area again, this time in slow, careful rows of to-and-fro motions. Whenever I like, I can hold down part of the paper with one hand, while with the other I can lift up a corner or edge to study how the print is coming along. Should I wish to add emphasis to a face or some other element, I'll swirl the spoon more forcefully over that one spot, darkening it. Or I can print a background extra lightly. In effect, I can dodge and burn with more ease and leisure than in the darkroom.

Once upon a time there was a gruff old man named Leonard, whose cigarette smoker's voice would answer the phone: "Action Machine." In those days he was investing in gold and silver. I asked him to build me a hinged table to ensure registration for my relief printing. My idea was that the woodblock would rest on the bed, the paper would attach to the underside of the hinged top, and then I would close the top, and the paper would drop onto the block — somehow. Leonard said he would think about it. But it would have to be metal, because "I can't even build a doghouse out of wood." He made it good and strong. I had to hire a truck and two helpers to move it. I am still using it twenty years later. Leonard's solution to the matter of maintaining the paper in place was a shop vacuum cleaner, which sucks air through holes in the tabletop. I position my paper, turn on the vacuum, close the lid, turn off the vacuum, and wait a couple of seconds for the paper to fall. The system is precise enough to print multiple blocks in register. Thank you, Leonard. As a bonus I gave him a three-block hand-colored print of my favorite Cambodian prostitute. He looked at it and said that his wife might be interested. I hope she was.

Dolores being a good old American girl, I asked the neighborhood lumberyard to prepare me some 16 x 20" blocks of American cherry. All of our big cherry trees had been cut down long ago, so they sold me strips of wood glued together and then milled gorgeously smooth. I went to work, drawing and carving.

Speaking for myself (not for Dolores, who is not the manual type), I would like to assert the pleasures of squeezing ink onto a marble slab, rolling it out, enjoying its odor, which reminds me of some sort of food — the stuff is made from linseed oil — inking my block, sometimes first with a large brayer and then a little one, establishing it on the bed of Leonard's machine, registering the paper, and rubbing a spoon around until my shoulders tire. On a good day I can make ten prints in three hours. The first two prints are no good because the wood is still thirsty or the ink is too thick. Sometimes my weary or careless spoon misses a patch, but if there are no carving-lines in it I can recoup at the end by smearing ink over it with a balled-up scrap of rag — which I often drag around even on good prints, painting concentric volumetric arcs on flat-inked limbs and torsos.

I leave the prints to dry for two or three days and then tint them with inks and water-colors. When the image dissatisfies me, I cut the block some more.

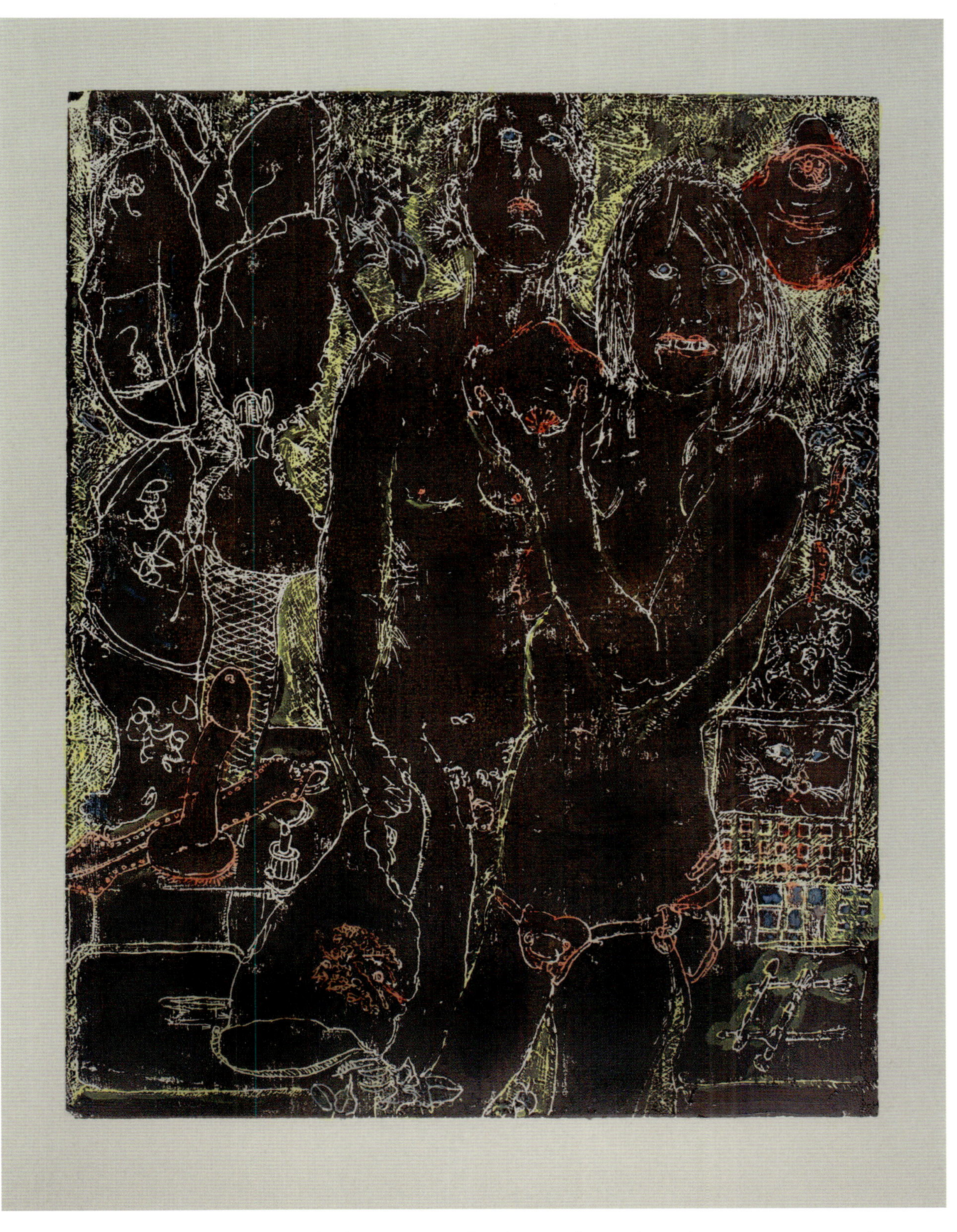

*Dolores with Isabel, cat, dildo, harness, merkin, breast forms, brassieres, cosmetics, mirror,
chili plant, "devil tongue" paddle, earrings and enema syringe*

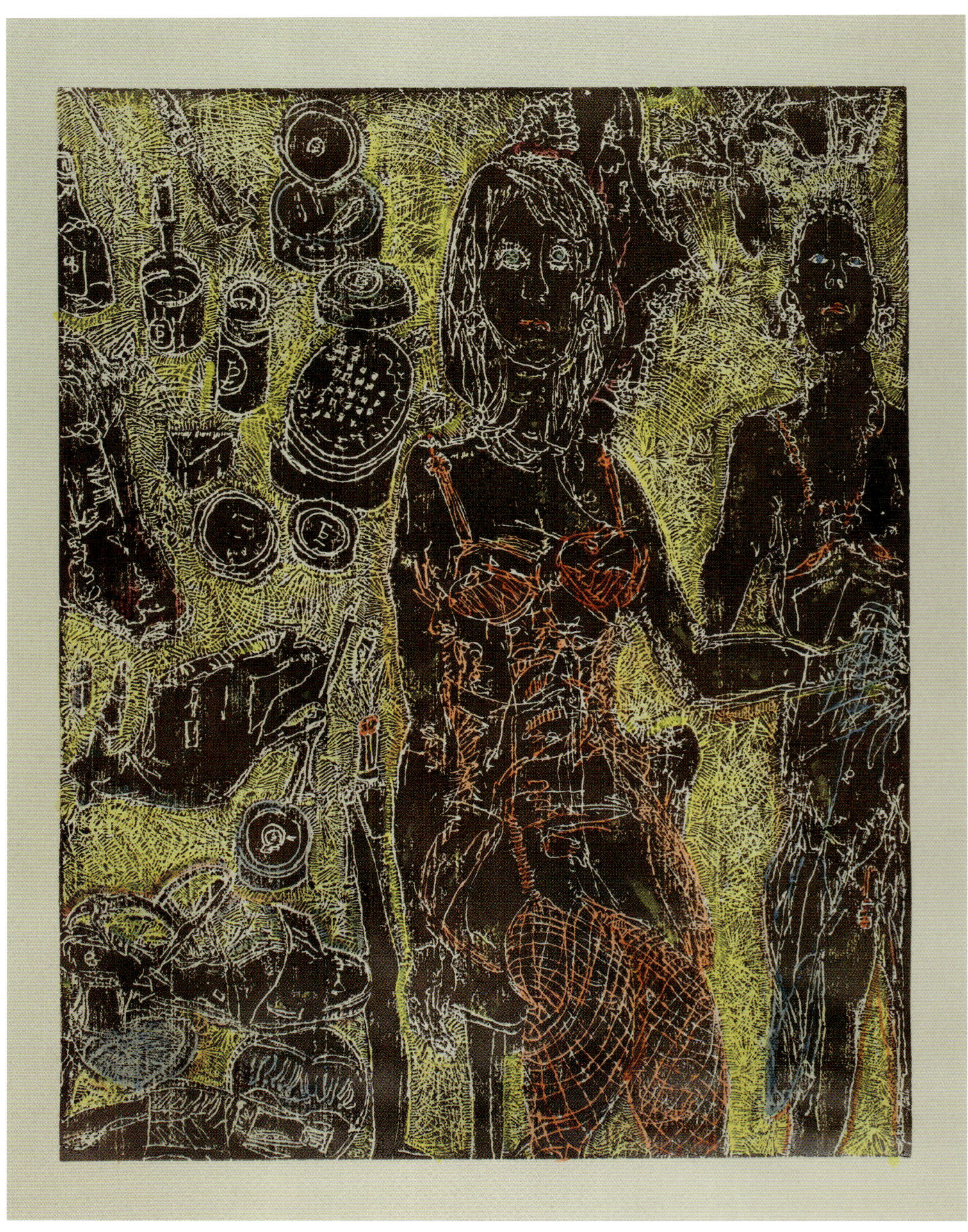

Isabel protecting Dolores from the material world

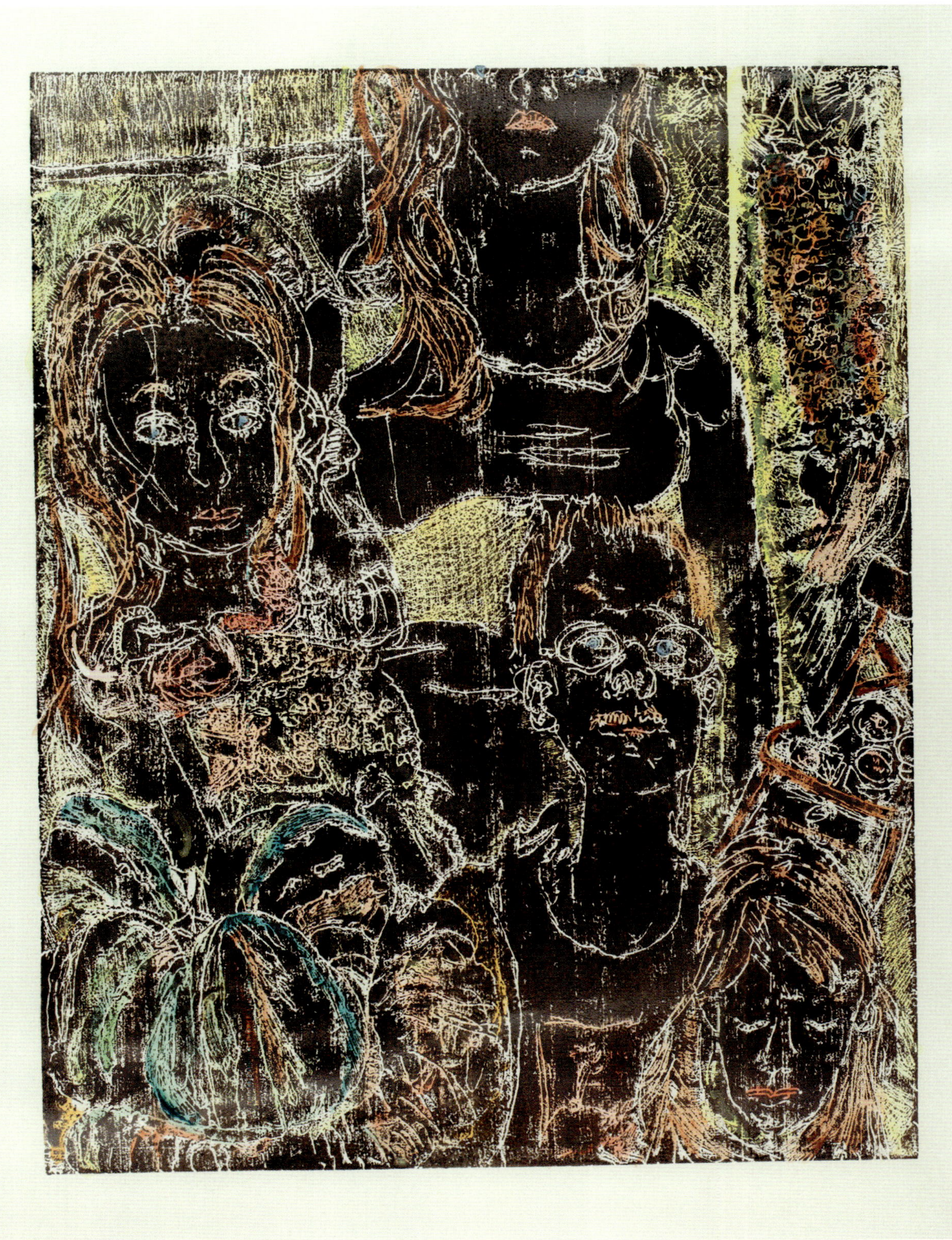

The artist with Dolores, wig head, Indian corn, feminine accessories and girl-child

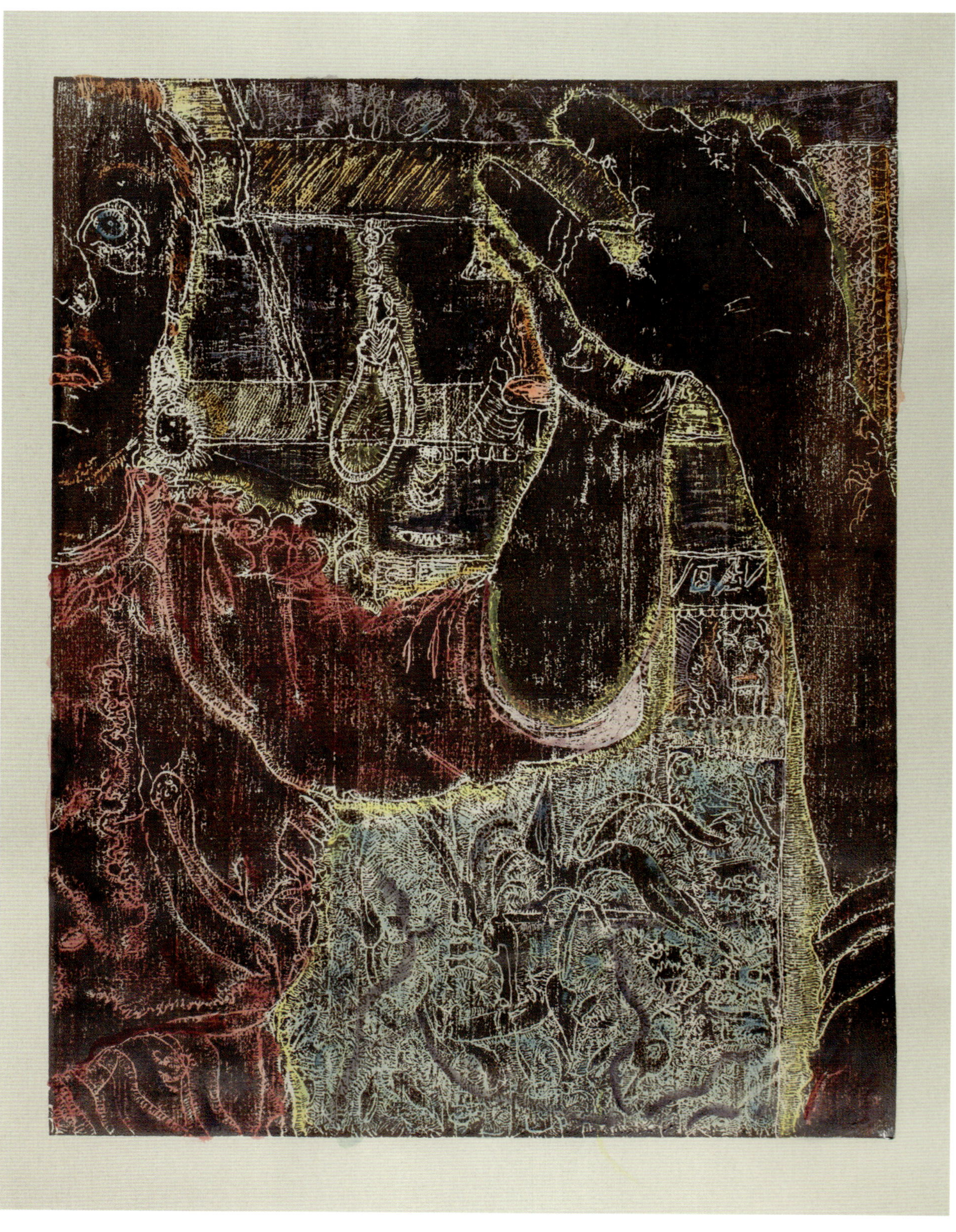

Happy landings (dildo, noose and mirror)

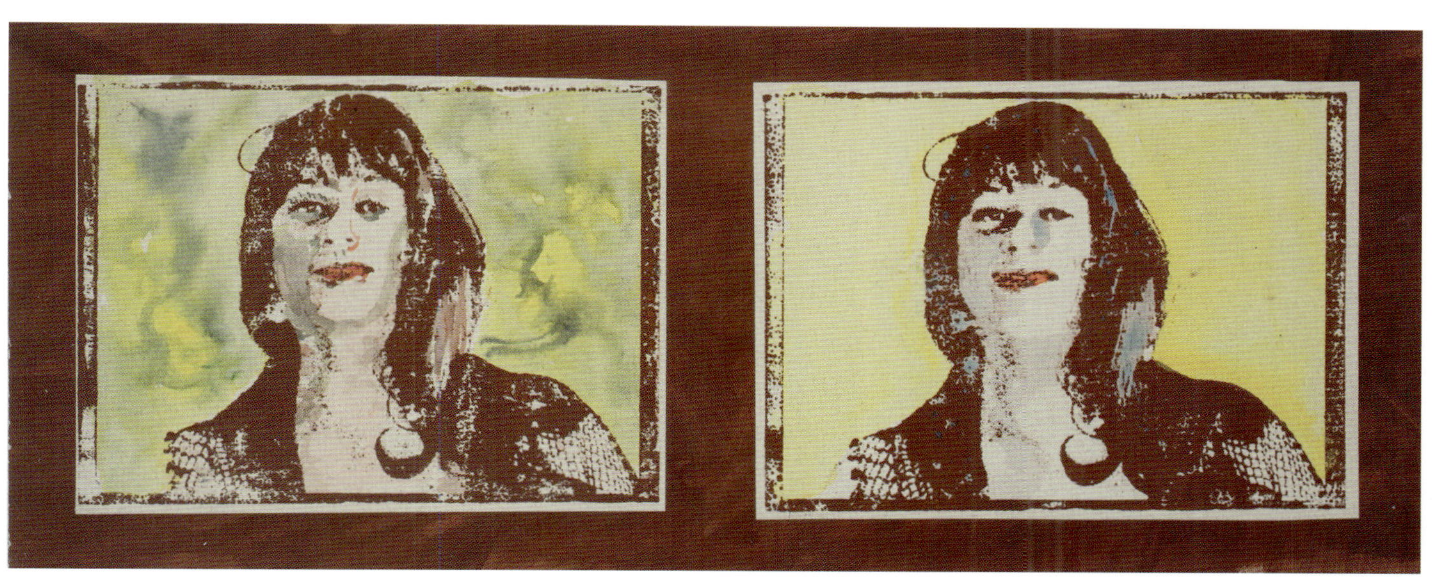

Laser engraved diptych from JPEG laptop original "Kurdish shawl"

2.4: Paper Negatives

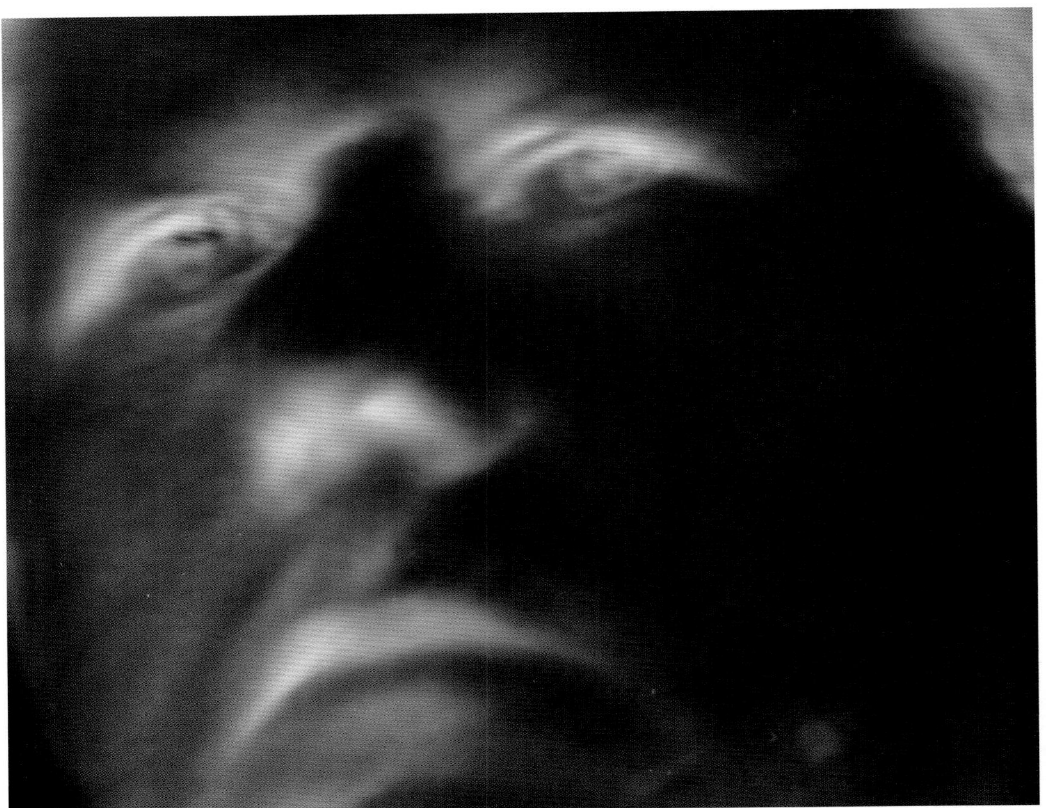

Detail from untitled 8 x 10" portrait

I have heard that there is a speculative field of human endeavor called digital photography, which allows somebody to capture an image and see it instantly. It is hard for me to understand the use of that, when I can wander into any smidgeon of total darkness I like, load a sheet of Bergger cold tone developing-out paper in the holder (an indefinite loan from my friend Roger Vail, who has renounced analogue processes), stride grandly into the light, insert the holder in my 11 x 14" camera (a gift from my equally famous photographic colleague, Mr. William Linne, who last I heard, so in fashion are his skills, was applying to be a bouncer at an adult bookstore), verify that the ancient lens, which lacks click settings or even gauge-marks, remains stopped down to f/16 for a reasonable compromise between depth of field and speed,* pull out the dark slide, remove the lens cap, start my kitchen timer, direct obedient Dolores to run and instantaneously compose herself upon that chair over there on which I previously focused, encourage her to remain still for the two to four minutes of the exposure, whisk her out of the picture once the timer sounds, close the lens, re-insert

---

* Empirical tests indicate that this aperture contracts to at least f/200.

the dark slide, withdraw the holder, carry it into the darkroom, shut the door, pull out the paper, convey it into my ruby-lit inner paradise, which invariably exalts my spirits and expands around me in an infinity of unborn pictures and deliciously poisonous fumes, place the paper glossy side down in the developer bath (HC110, dilution B), rock the tray four times, grasp it with tongs sufficiently tenderly to avoid crimping and just tight enough to preserve it in my clutches, turn it over, release it and continue agitating gently and nicely, developing by inspection, my hopes as pleasantly blank as the sheet itself, upon which I now begin to distinguish a half-mistakeable thickening

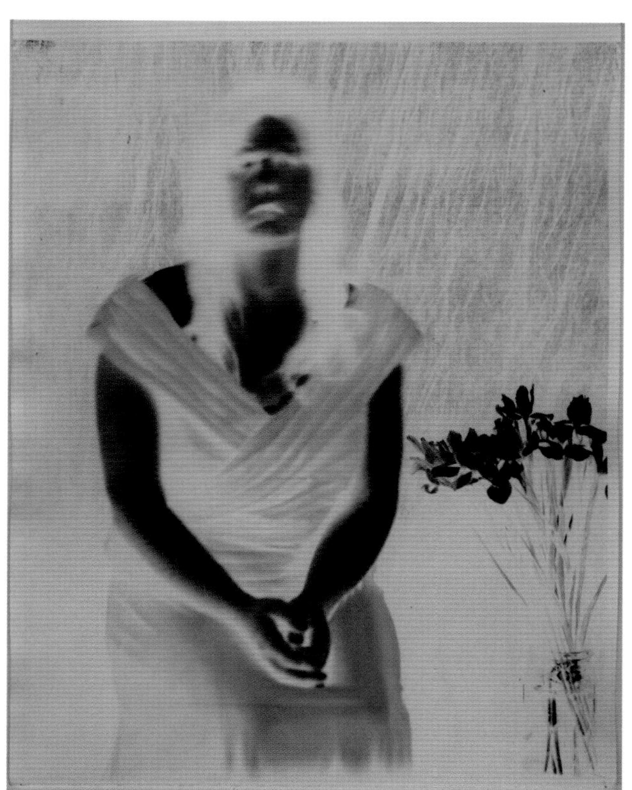

of something along the borders where the dark slide gripped it; and I might as well be in some New England forest of my boyhood, looking out through the trees at some creek-horizon or faraway wolf-hill, wondering which cloud will fly toward me — it's a grey ghost; it's blackskinned, white-lipped, whitehaired Dolores! — then when the negative appears slightly too dark (which is how photos should look beneath a mostly banked safe-light), I lift it out by the front right corner, drain it, deposit in the stop bath, not releasing the grip of my tongs until the far edge supports itself upon the bottom of that tray, which I now swish happily for twenty-odd seconds, fix the image in two successive baths for thirty seconds each, turn on the light, discovering the negative's true tones and details (shadow-light curving along the underside of her dark arm, pearlescent and often blurry greynesses in the whitish hollows of her eyes), and then decide whether I wish to do all this again. I generally do.

I have been known to compromise by employing one of my 8 x 10" wooden field cameras, but that I'll confess in my merest darkroom whisper.

My successful silver gelatin prints, both negative and positive, are later selenium toned to extend the tonal range. That only adds two and a half hours, mostly from washing. — Does this seem too long to you? My friend Tom Robinson sometimes washed his silver gelatin prints for a couple of days, remarking to me: "Those optical brighteners in the paper only last thirty to fifty years, so I try to get them out as soon as I can and find out what I'm working with." The cheerful determination of his words — Tom was going neck to neck against time itself — continue to gratify my aspirations of independence. I will grub my way toward death in my own fashion, thank you, in or out of a dress, striving to please myself as honestly as I can. Now that paper, film and chemicals are getting rarer, I have even less excuse to cut corners.

I have always thought that a paper negative is like a sonnet or some other rule-structured poem: limited in what it is allowed to do, and therefore potentially quite expressive. But it is well to consider the making of one as less equivalent to composing verse than digging in the dirt, not knowing whether some rock will suddenly grate against the shovel's edge — for the holders sometimes leak light, and Dolores does not always succeed in holding as still as she thinks. Digging a hole certainly possesses as much value as any other task, and if I do it for Dolores, why shouldn't someone do it for me once it comes my time to feed the grass?

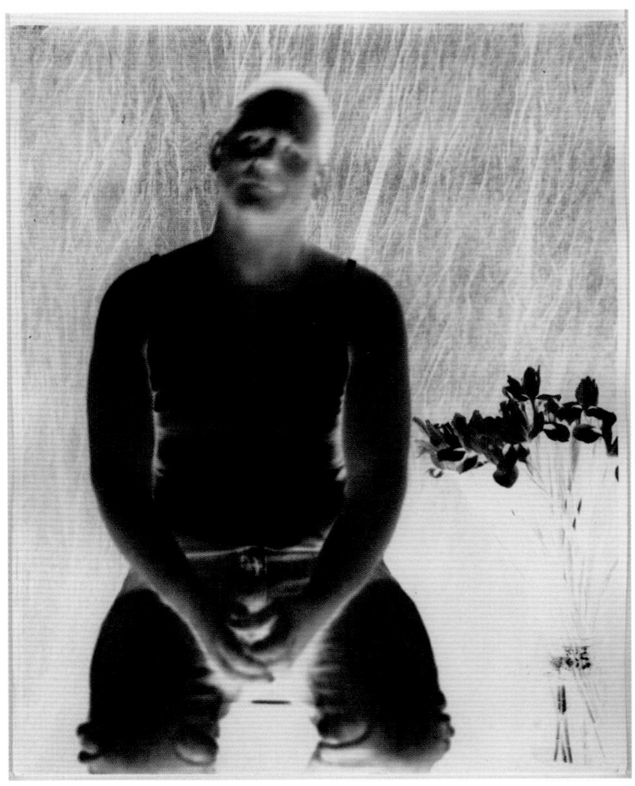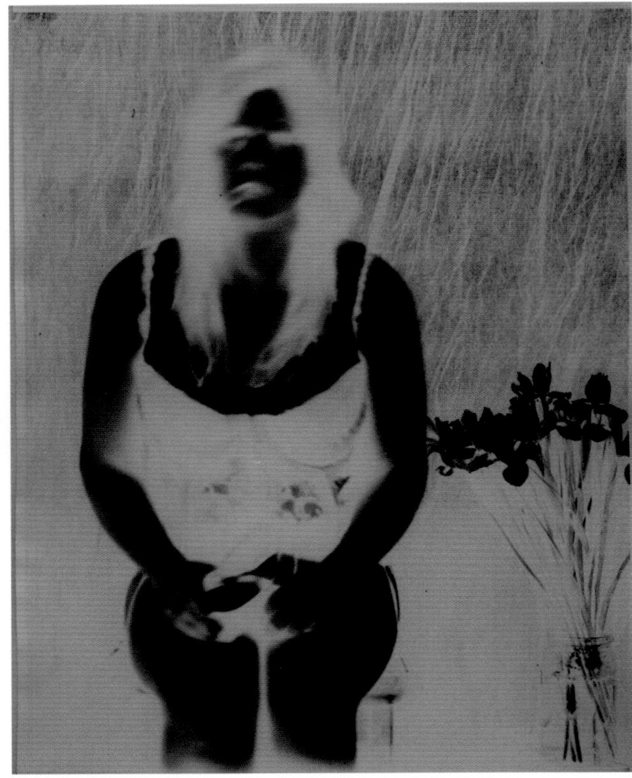

The long exposures bestow on Dolores a stiff, melancholy quality, in keeping with her name. The reversal of tones which darkens her skin renders her face rather masklike. That light in the sockets of her eyes might derive from her soul, her tears or something else. In these negatives she appears both vulnerable and distant, when in fact she was merely posing patiently at the time. I try to remember this when I peer at the stiff dead souls on old daguerrotypes: These may be our only visual traces of them now, but once they were released from their slavery to the lens, I'll wager they could laugh and caper as well as the rest of us.

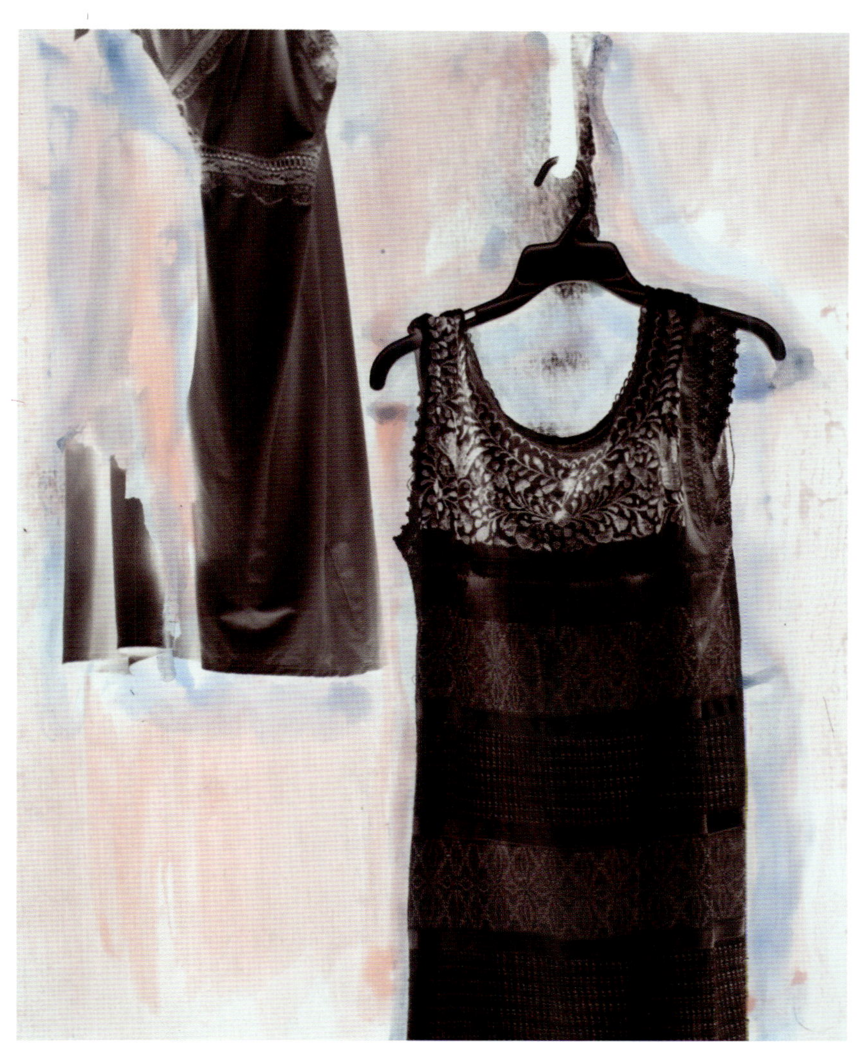

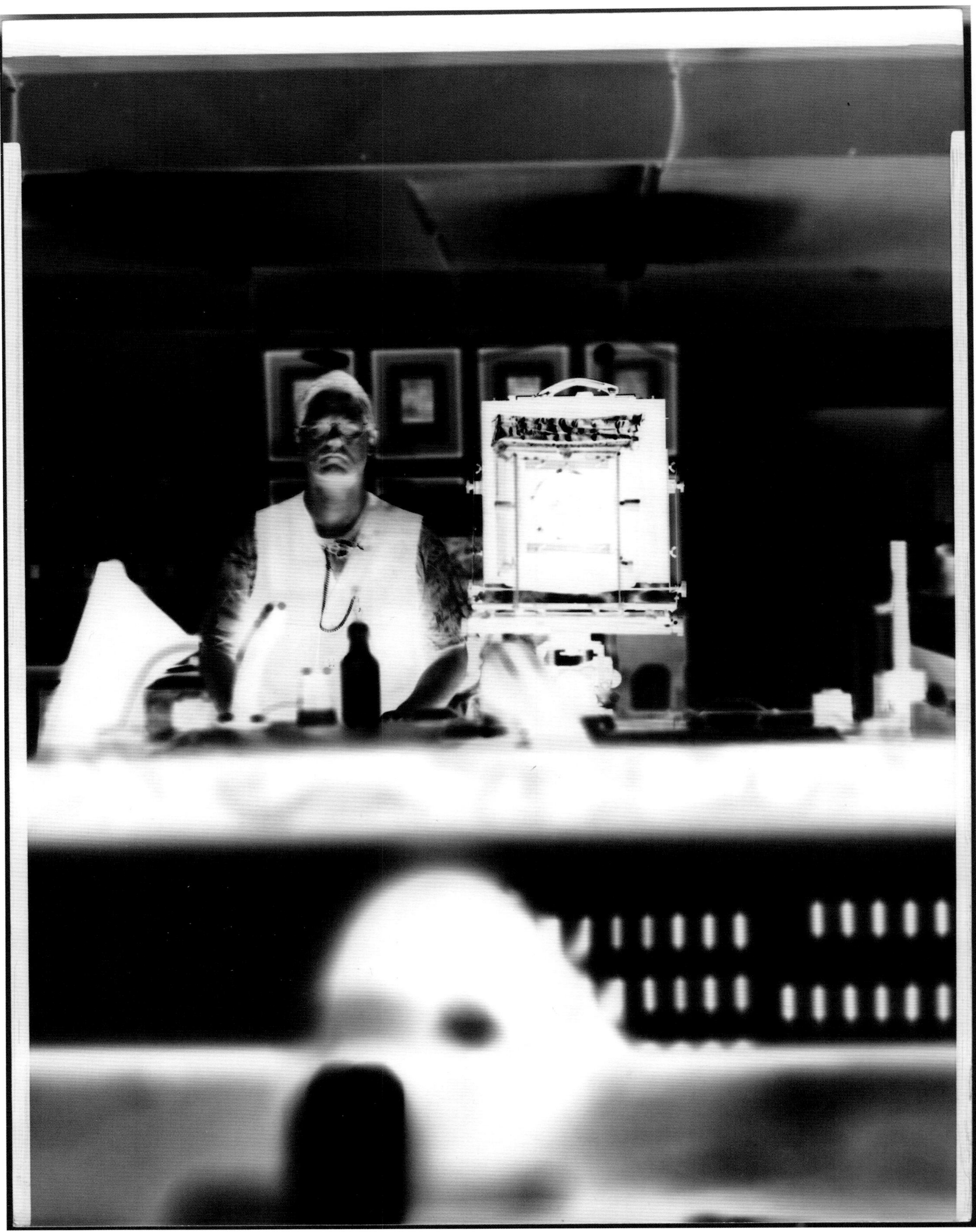

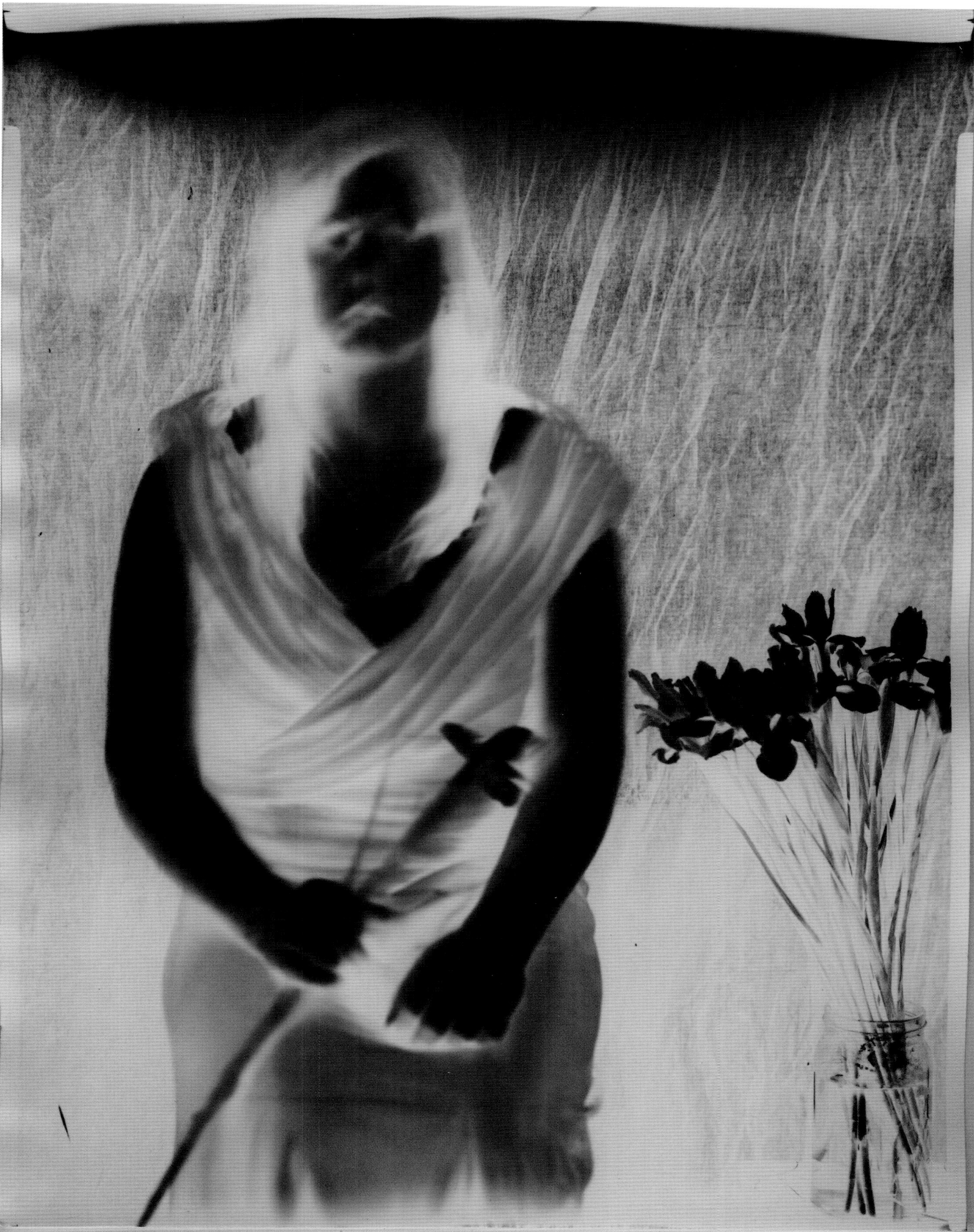

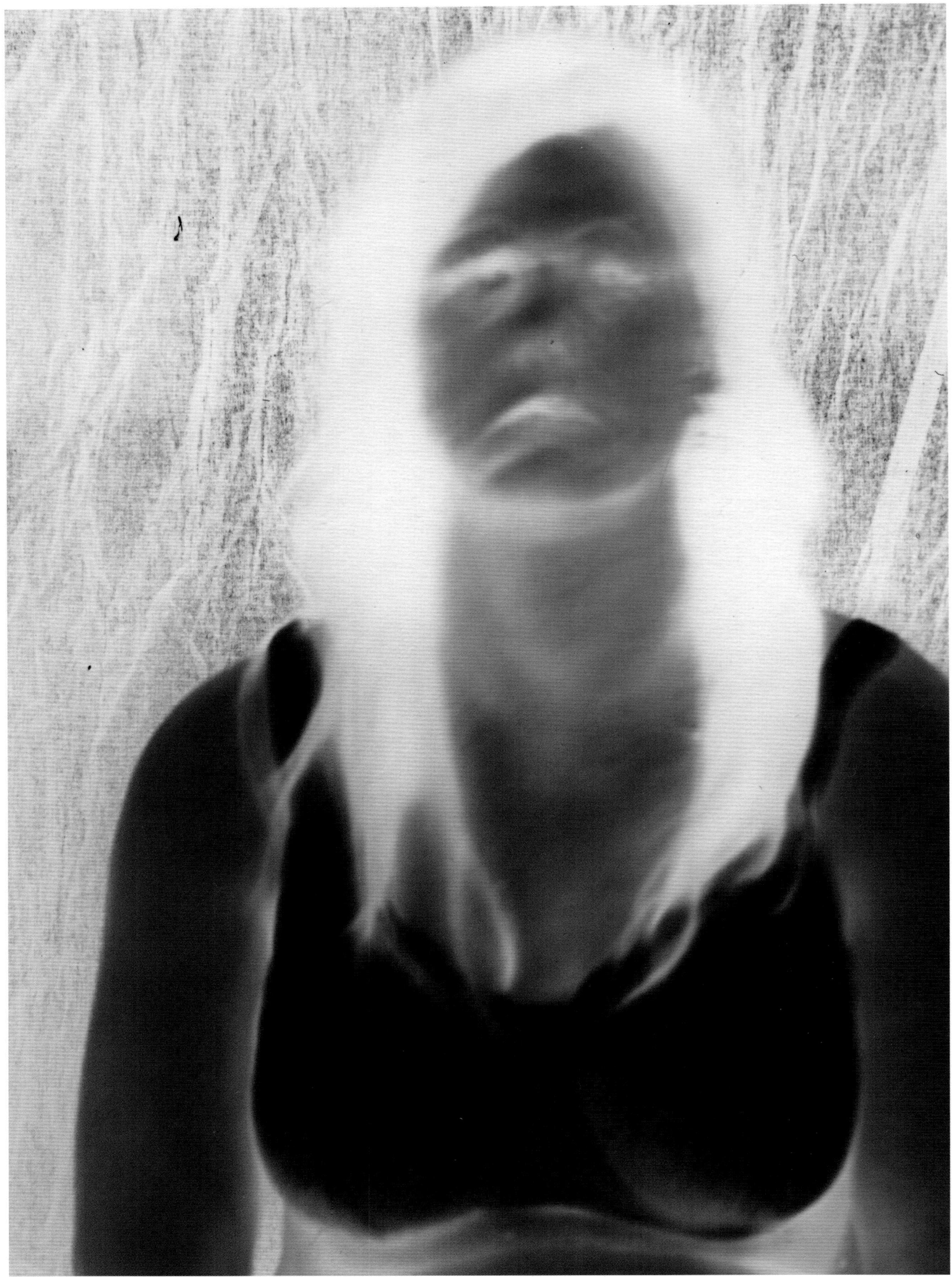

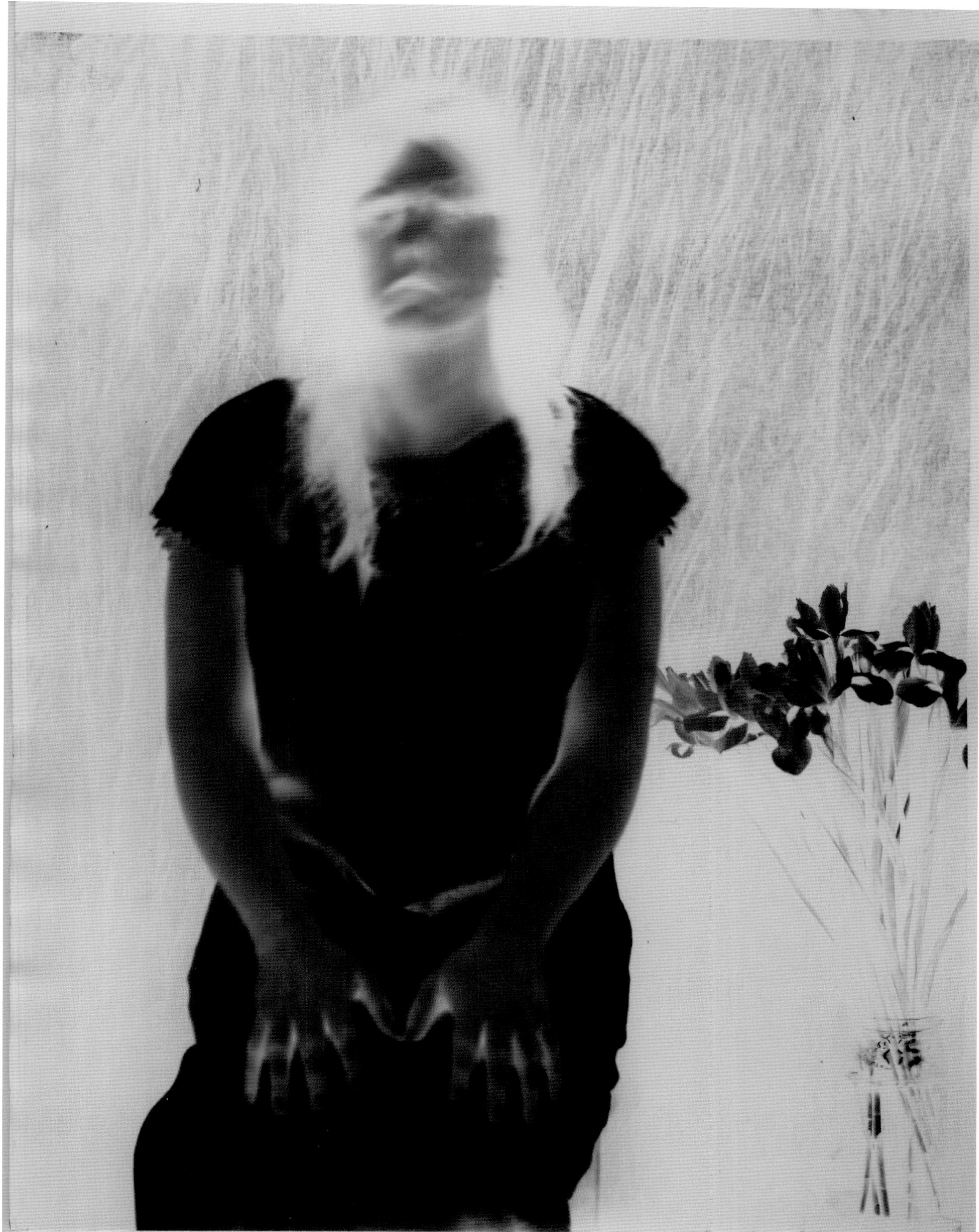

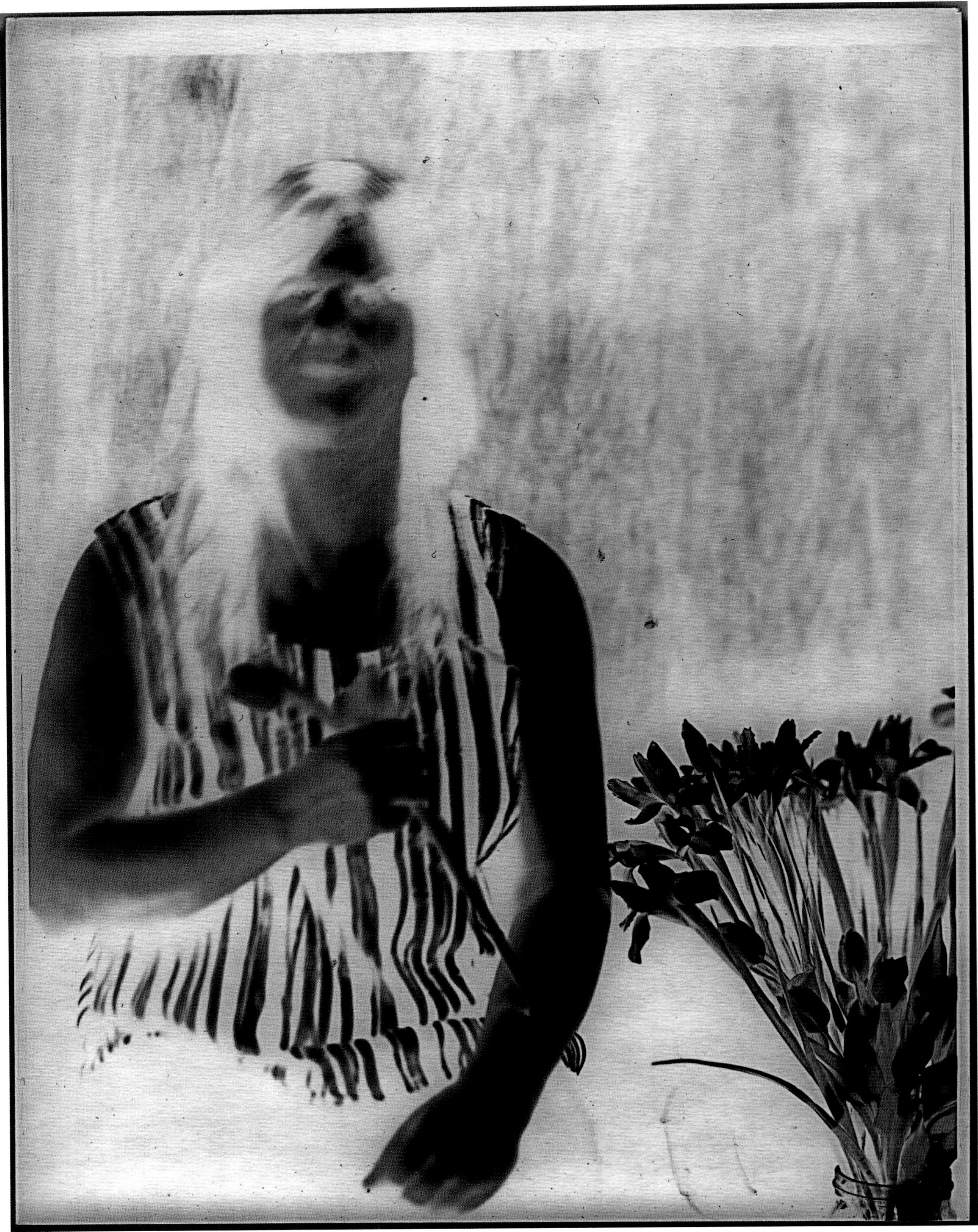

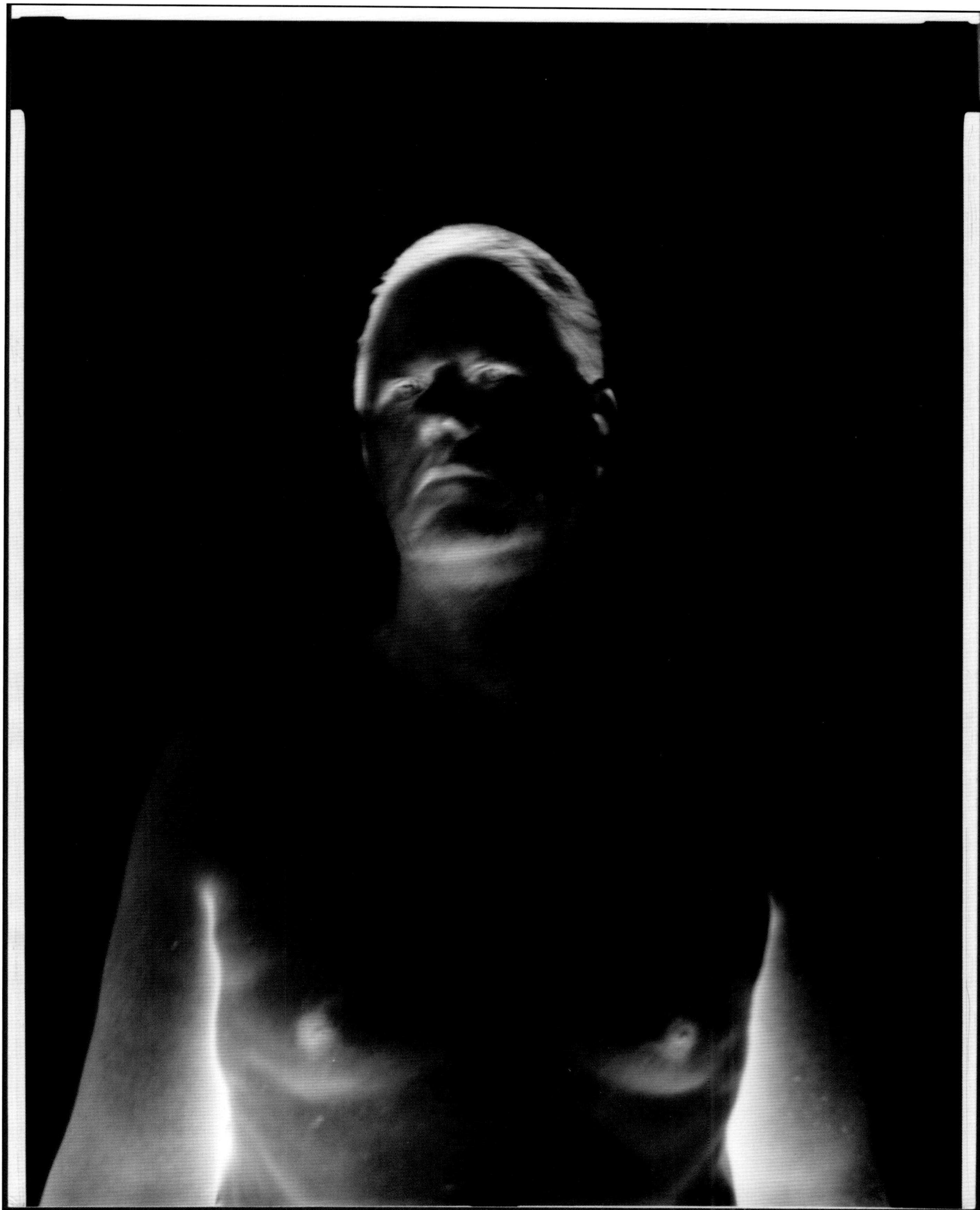

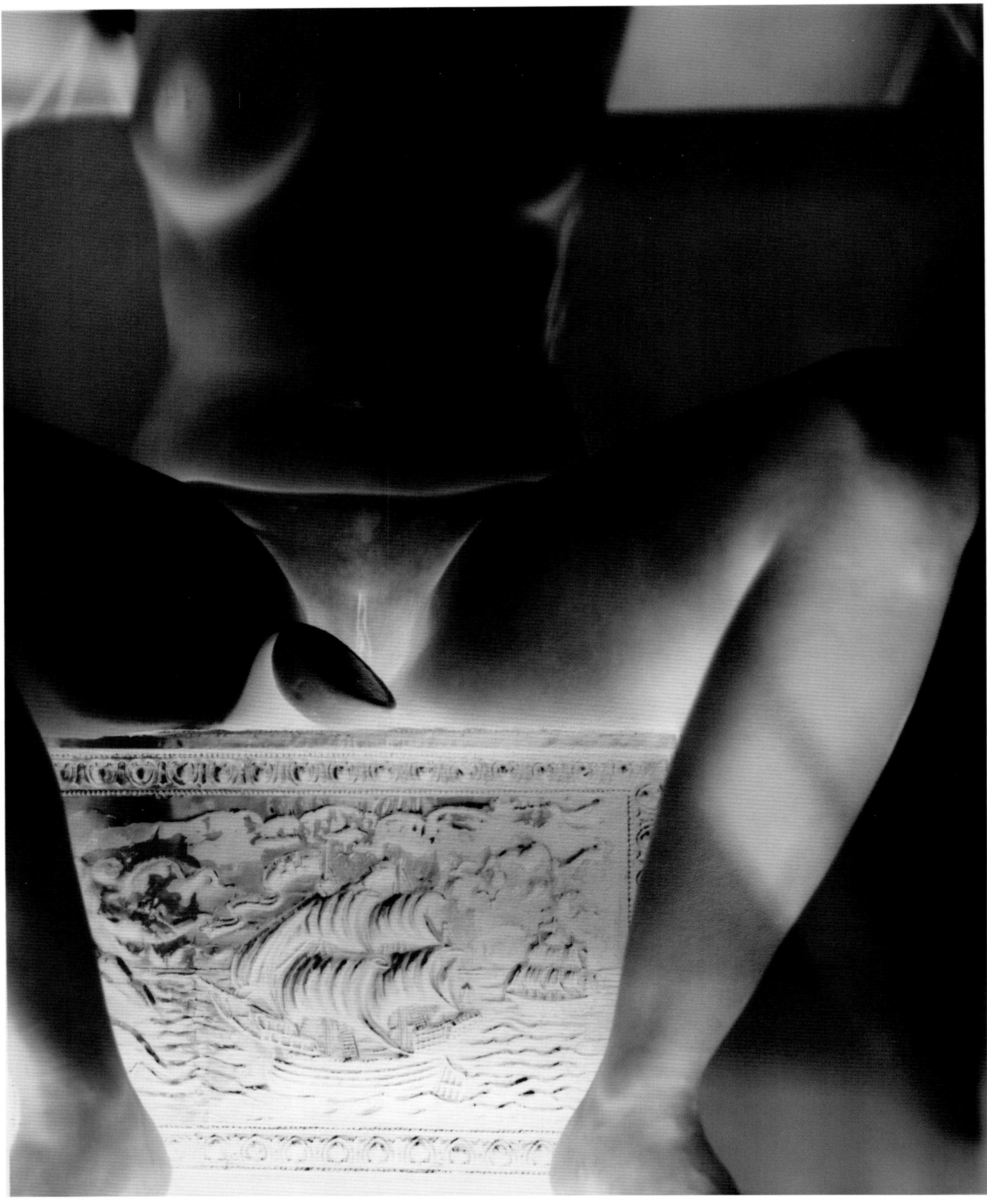

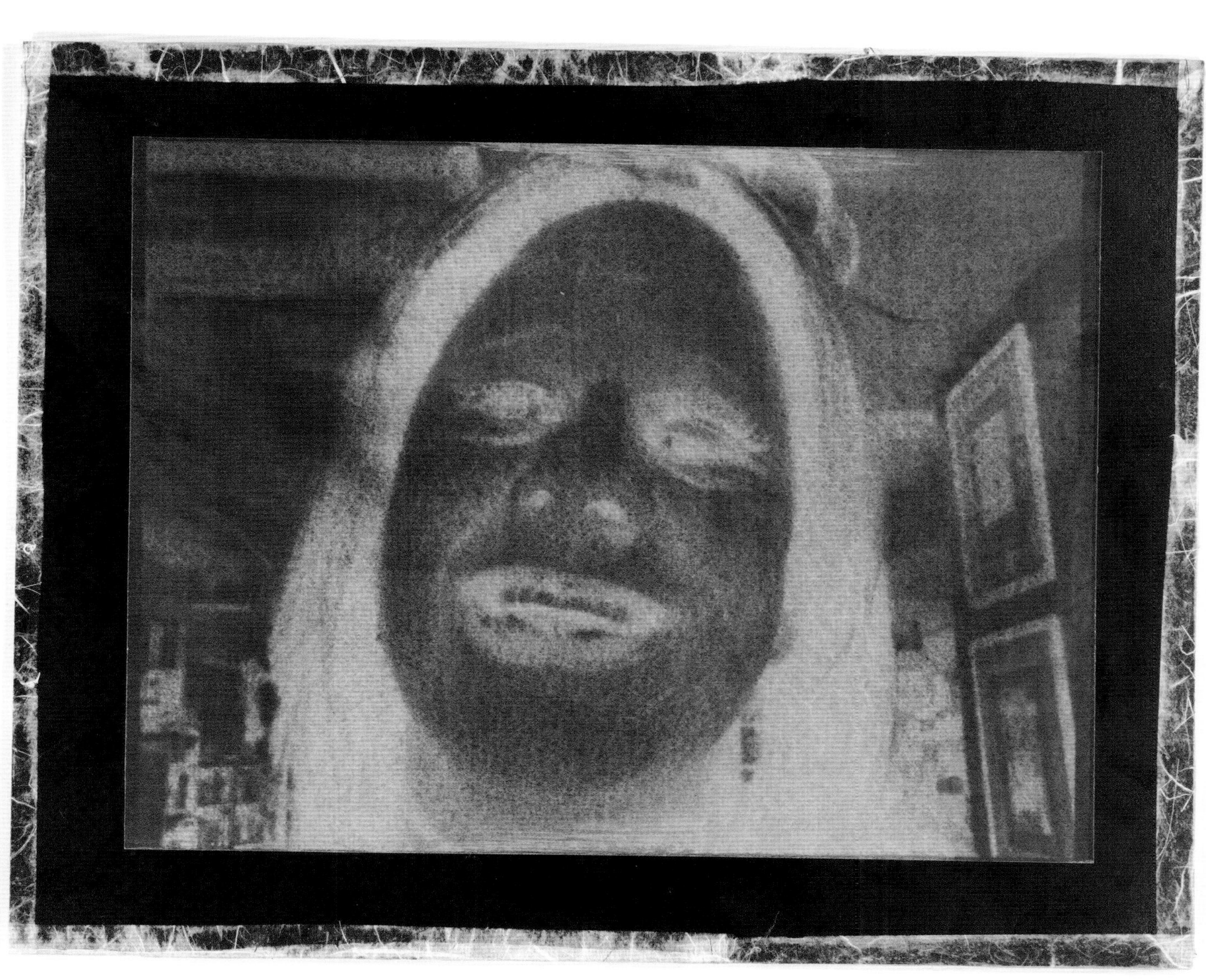

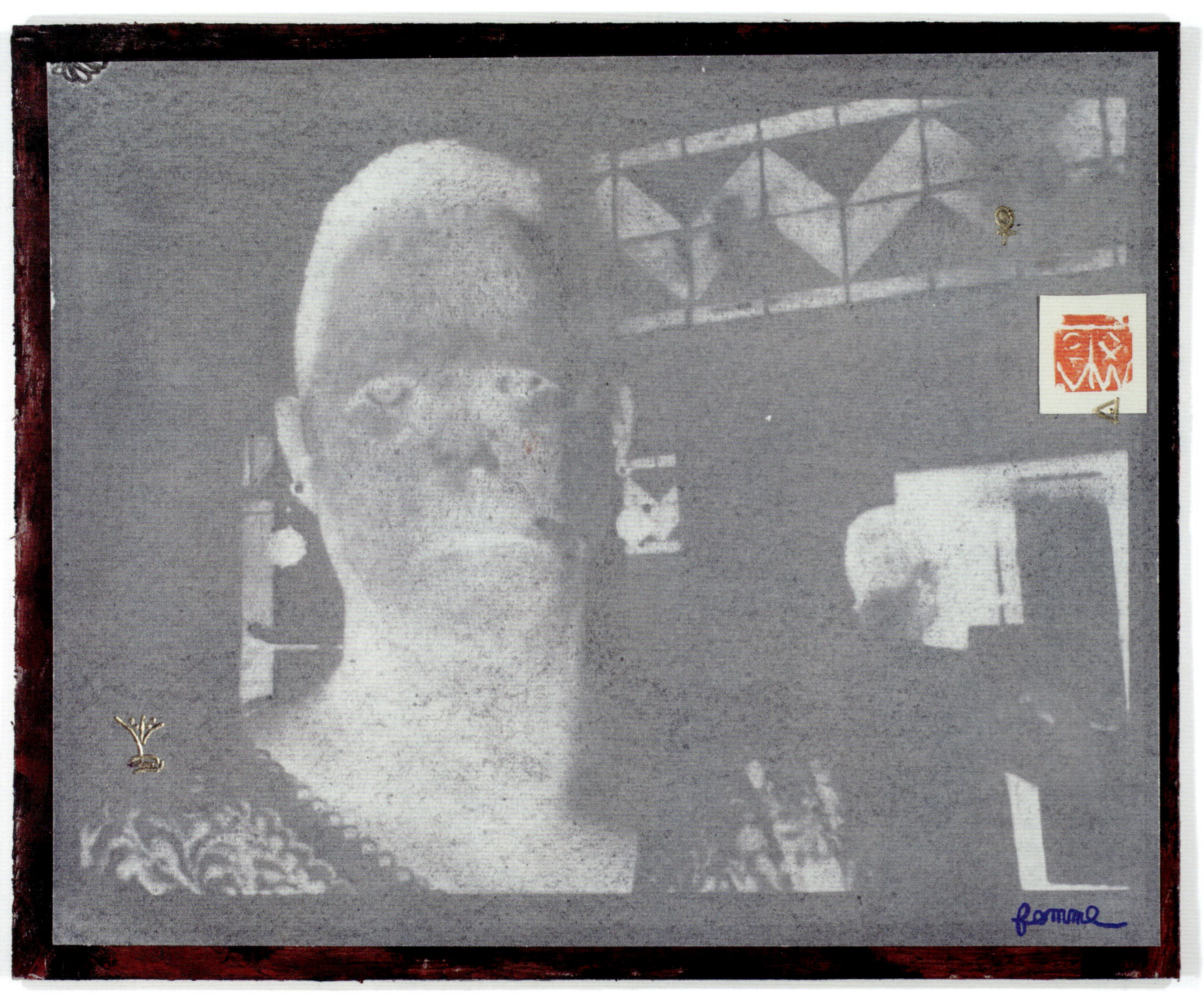

femme

2.5: Silver Gelatin Positives

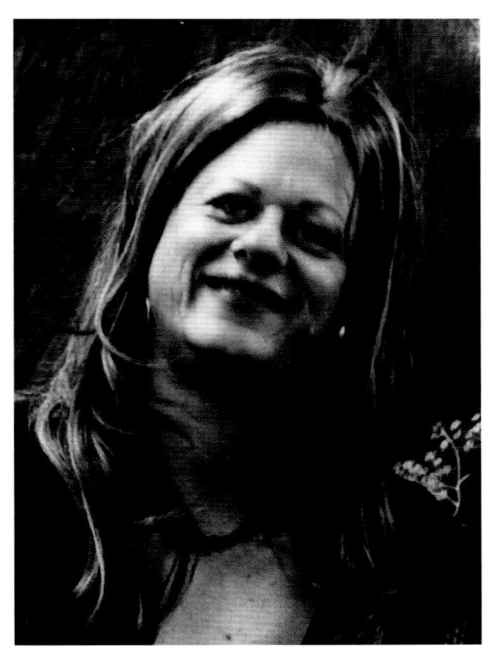

Shooting film is almost as instant as making paper negatives, but not quite, since I hire my friend Jeff to develop the rolls for me. He runs the last black and white lab hereabouts. Recently his wife told me: "Jeff's been fixing machines all week. The tank developer's broken, and so is the horizontal 8 x 10" enlarger. All these companies are long out of business. When I see him struggling in there, I want to cry." Hearing this, I was all the more pleased with Jeff's business acumen in wangling such a lucrative client as I. Sometimes I give him two or three rolls in one go. He drives in to my side of town to pick them up, and then we take a long lunch and chat about someday making daguerrotypes. The most interesting part of that activity will be learning how long we can hold our breaths while bringing mercury to a boil.

When I get my film back from Jeff, I inspect the negatives on a loupe. If I see half a dozen that interest me, I go into the darkroom and print them. I tone them on the same day. Silver gelatin is not yet arcane enough for me to detail the process here. However, the diptych of Dolores beside her jar of weeds deserves an anecdote. Its pair of negatives were 8 x 10" Kodak Tri-X sheets, which as I write have just gone out of production. I shot them in my ancient Kodak 2D field camera and Jeff developed them. Then I printed each one by laying it over a sheet of 8 x 10" Bergger warm tone paper on my enlarger easel, flashing the room light on, counting four seconds aloud, switching off the light, and developing the image in Dektol. That was some of the easiest printing I ever did.

More often I invoke my elderly Leitz Focomat enlarger, which I bought from my friend Tom up in Portland. Recently it shorted out, so I picked out a nearby electrician from the Yellow Pages and got a very Christian ex-engineer from the Ukraine; he expressed displeasure at the test portraits of Dolores thumbtacked to the walls of the darkroom, but forgave me once a genetic woman dropped by. Taking the enlarger apart (he had never seen one before), we discovered that it had been insulated with tiny hand-lacquered rings of brown paper. So it seemed that the wires had lasted since the 1950s. Now, thanks to this electrician and his painstaking crimpings and wrappings of vintage cable, it is in pretty good shape. Since the incandescent light bulbs it employs are disappearing, I bought a handful of those.

My friend Kent Lacin runs a commercial photography business here in town. It's mostly digital videos now. He gave me his sturdy rectangular LED timers when he shut down his darkroom. Both of them are getting spastic now. Kent pities me for doing what he used to do, and also, naturally, for being a host organism to that humiliating parasite called Dolores. Twenty-odd years ago he told me that he was considering making a series of photographs of himself, and I wondered why he couldn't escape from his head. Now here I am.

In the dark I grin and dance to the music of up and coming or at least almost new musicians from that recent decade when I was in college and had never heard of prostatitis; while the Focomat projects a spider-monster shadow on the ceiling and a sheet of 11 x 14" Bergger warmtone paper, whose like is unavailable now, lies pallid within the metal frame-bars of the easel, receiving upon its dully shining glossy surface that negative image of Dolores for, let's say, a minute and thirty seconds, for forty-five seconds of which I will dodge her face with my ovoid-headed wand, hoping that Kent's timer won't short out again. The lens must be stopped all the way open now that the paper, after seven years of curation on the refrigerator along with leftover meals, has gotten weak, and with it the various developers (official shelf lives of unopened concentrate: two years). Don't we all store up treasures for moths and rust? So far, more light for a longer period of time, followed by longer development in a more concentrated solution, still rescues my prints, but the end approaches, not least because my eyes cannot so easily judge the progression of development nowadays as I stand under the safelight, peering down into the dark, dark liquid, whose fumes begin to make me nauseous. Thus one of my exaltations. Robert Demachy, 1904: "For initiated, or perhaps for the insane (this is a question of words), there is a most exquisite pleasure in the contemplation of fine shades of deep and translucent black independently of form."* I hope he finds nice black vistas in his tomb.

I begin each enlarging day with joy and hope. Staring down at the image on the easel is a lovely meditation. After eight or nine hours of standing on concrete, my back hurts. An hour's wash, and then six minutes of shuffling a batch of prints through concentrated selenium toner heated up in my tea kettle, and then another batch or two, followed by a another hour's wash, and I eat chili cold out of the can before squeegeeing my photographs with a windshield wiper blade. Even nowadays I can turn out a pretty decent set of matched prints, but as the paper and chemicals I love continue to age, silver gelatin becomes for me slightly more akin to such alternative processes as platinum and gum: more finicky, less consistent. I do not like this, of course. But Dolores never liked getting old, either. She and I had better accept our losses.

Jeff, by the way, is mildly disgusted by some of the Dolores images, particularly when harsh light accentuates the condition of her skin. To me she sometimes appears not unlike an Indian brave, longhaired yet masculine.

---

* Bill Jay, *Robert Demachy 1859-1936: Photographs and Essays* (New York: St. Martin's Press /Academy Editions, London, 1974) p. 27 ("On the gum-print").

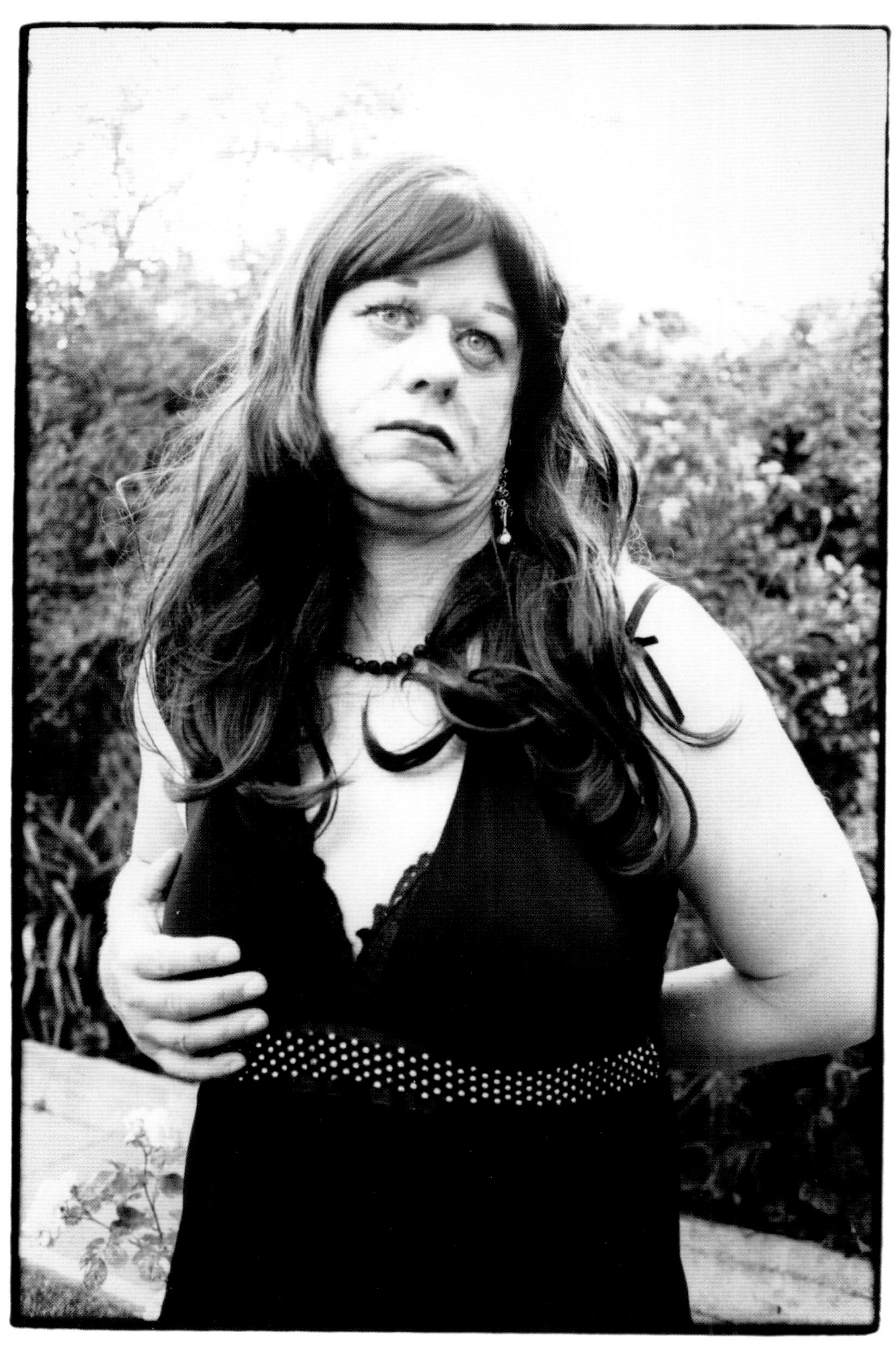

Hoping to pass

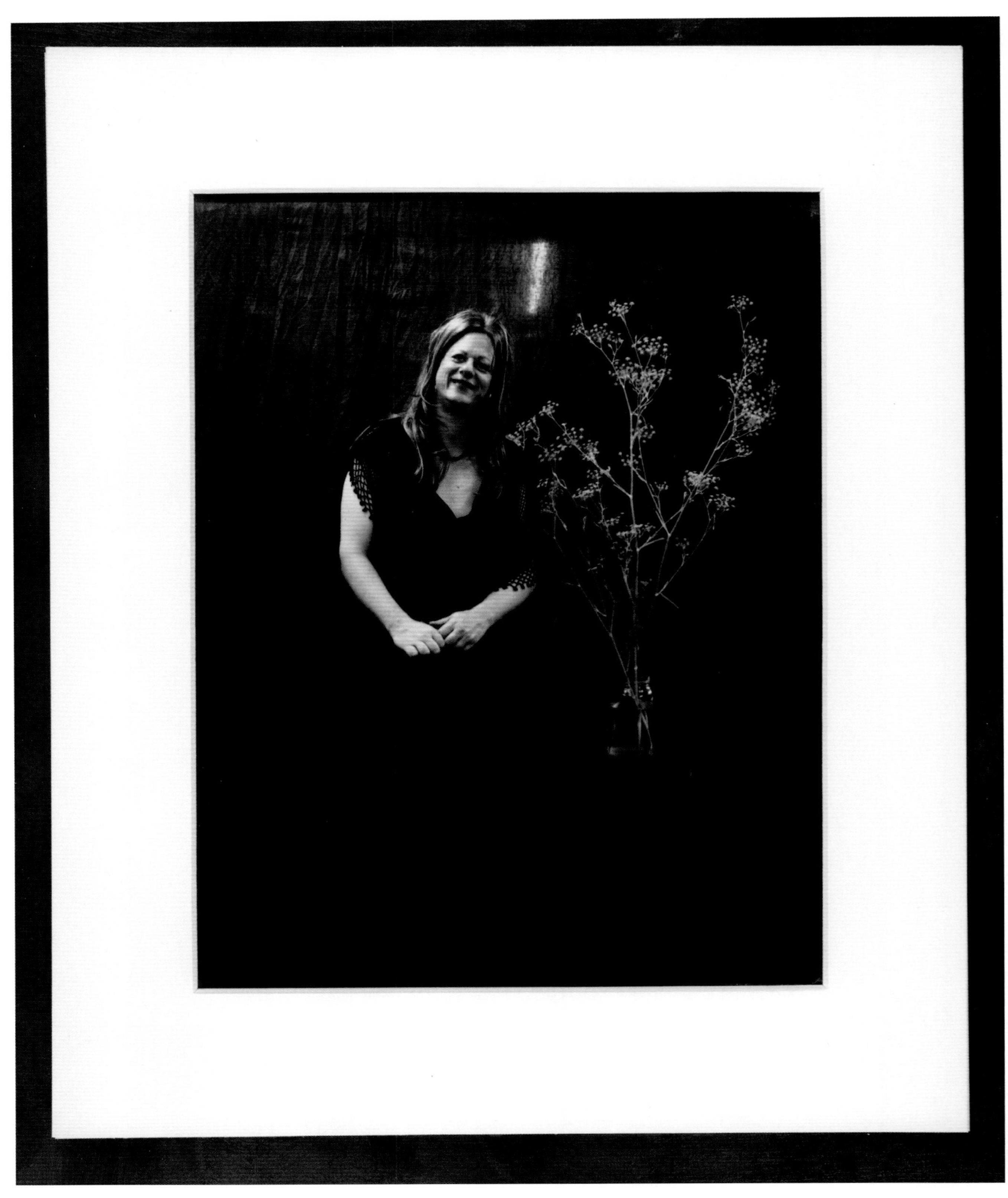

8 x 10" contact printed diptych

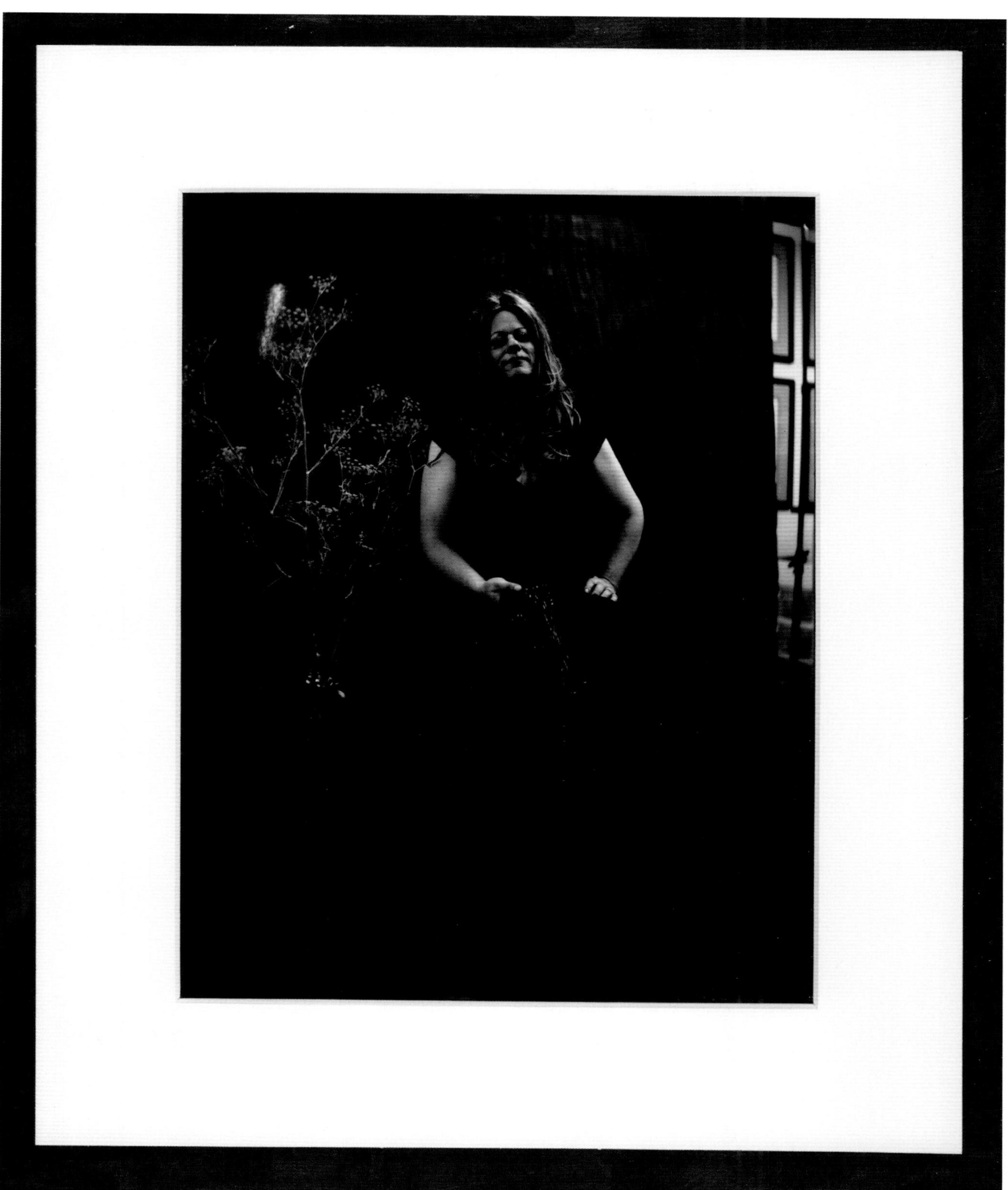

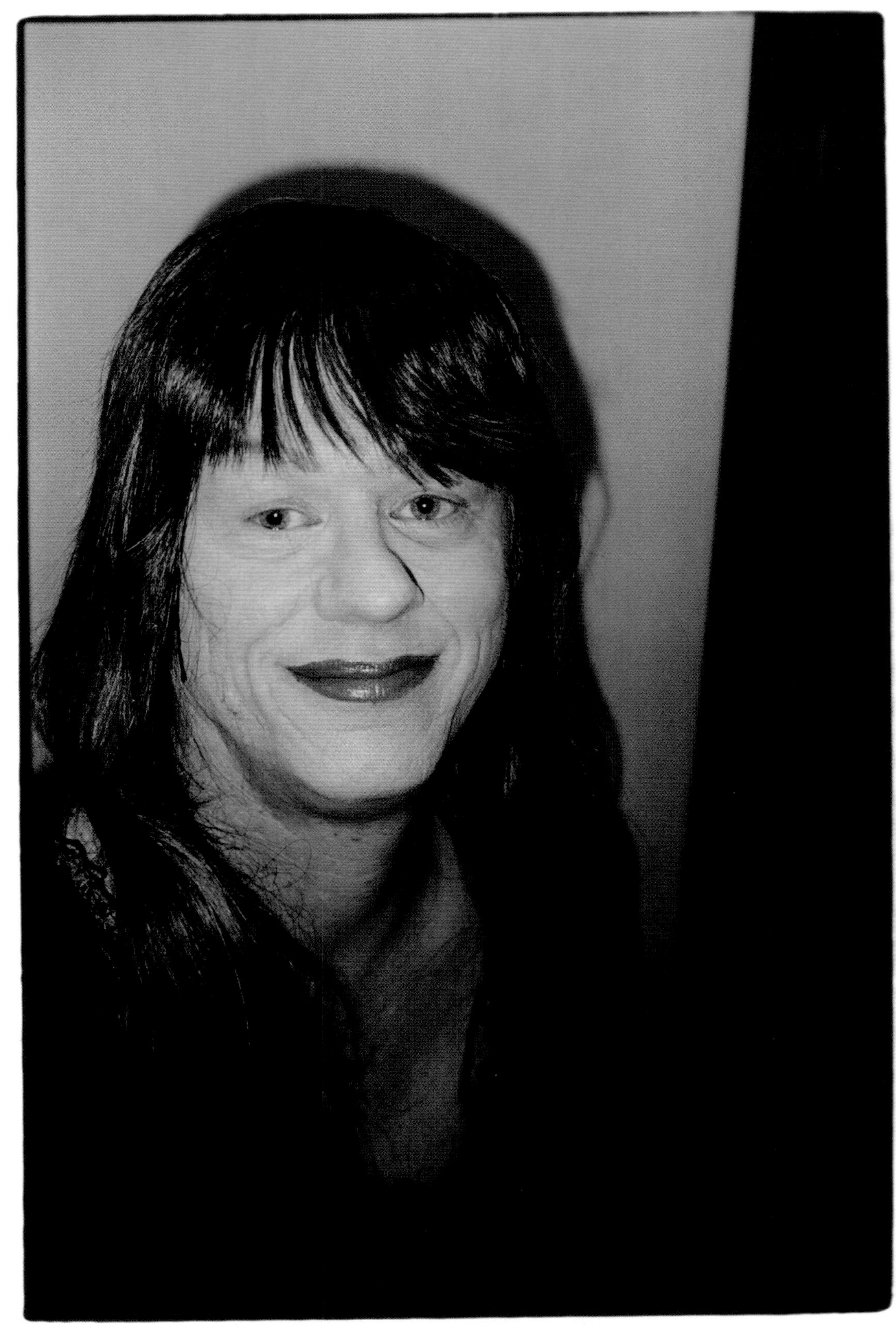

Alone

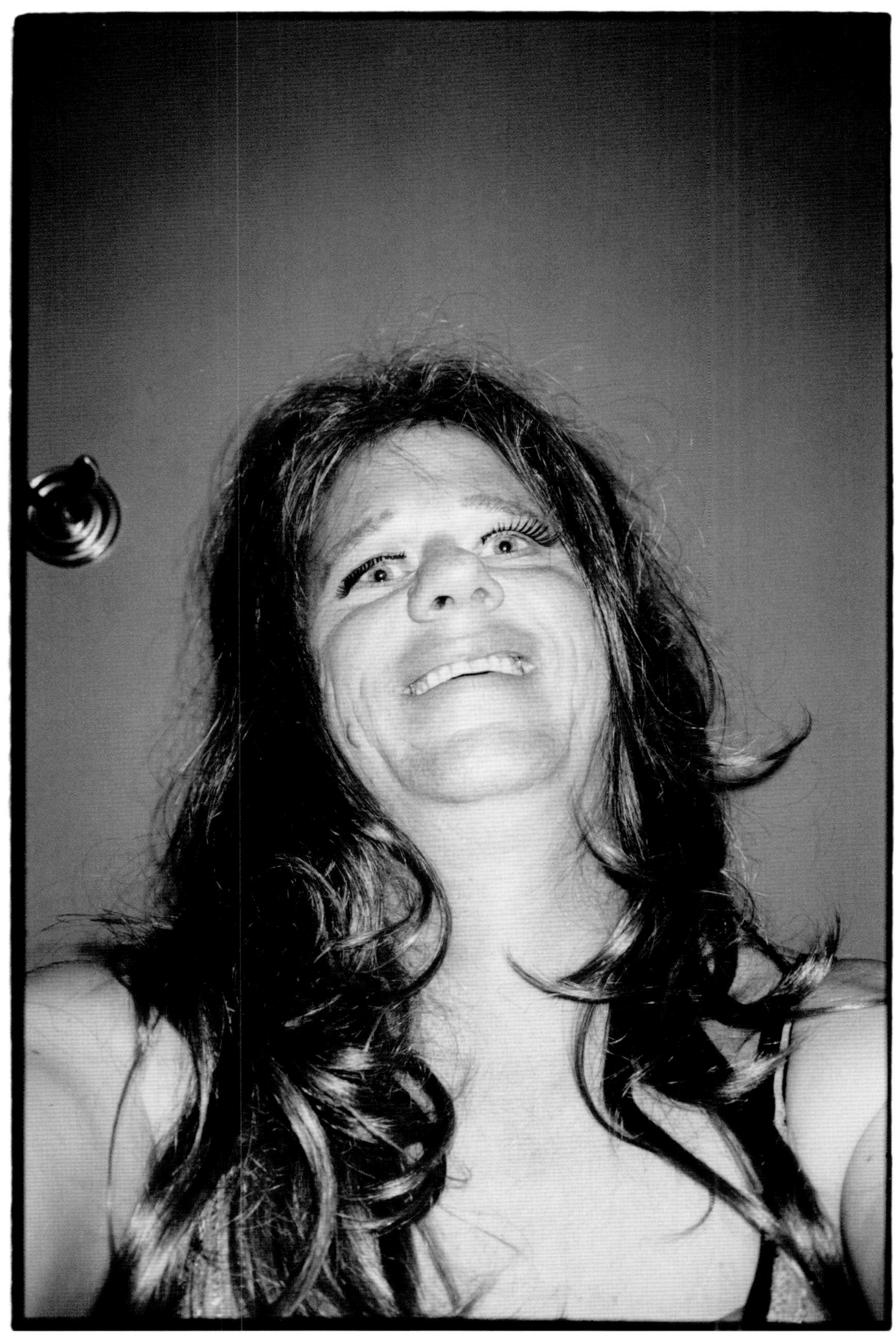

Blood level

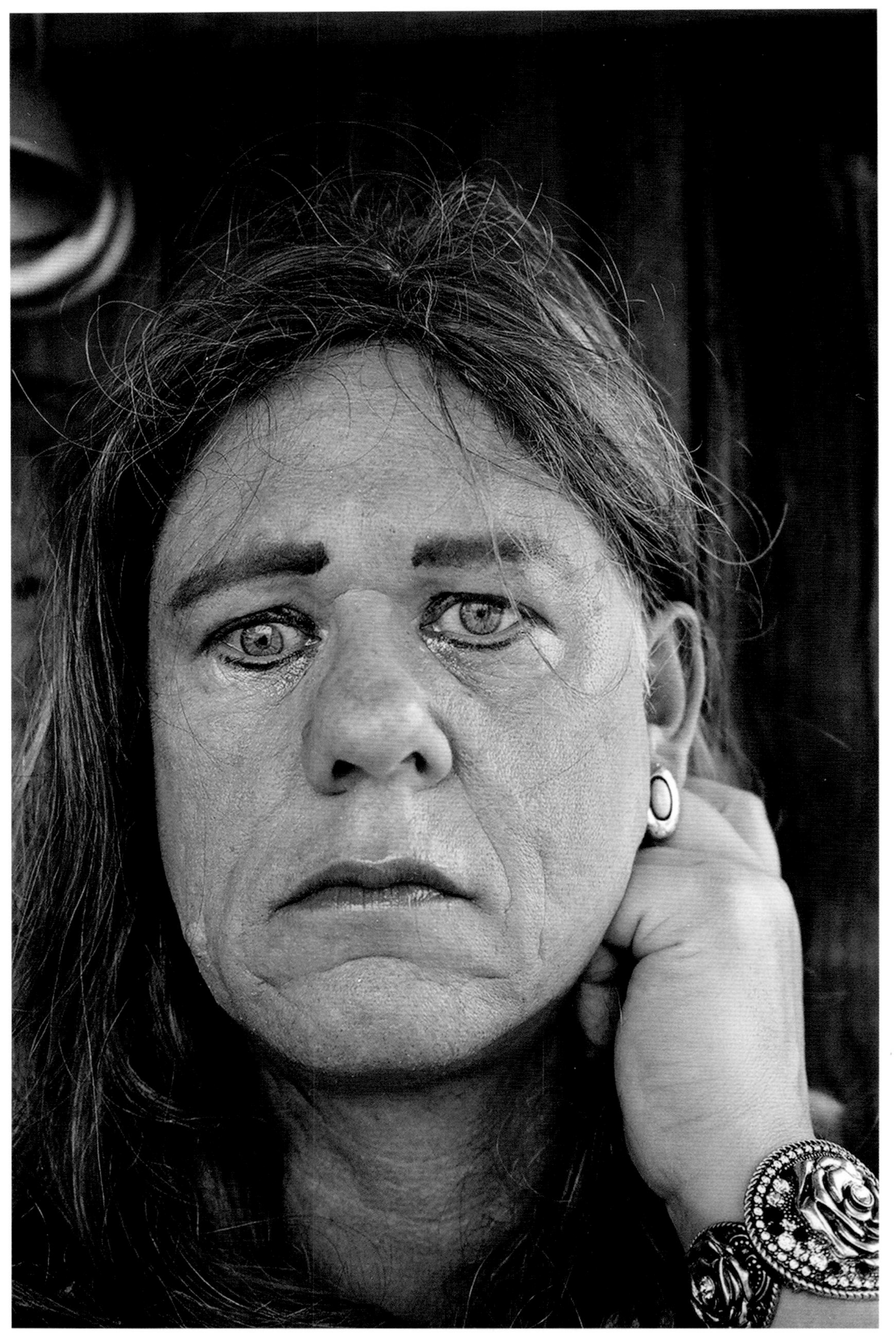

In Montana

2.6: Color Film Positives

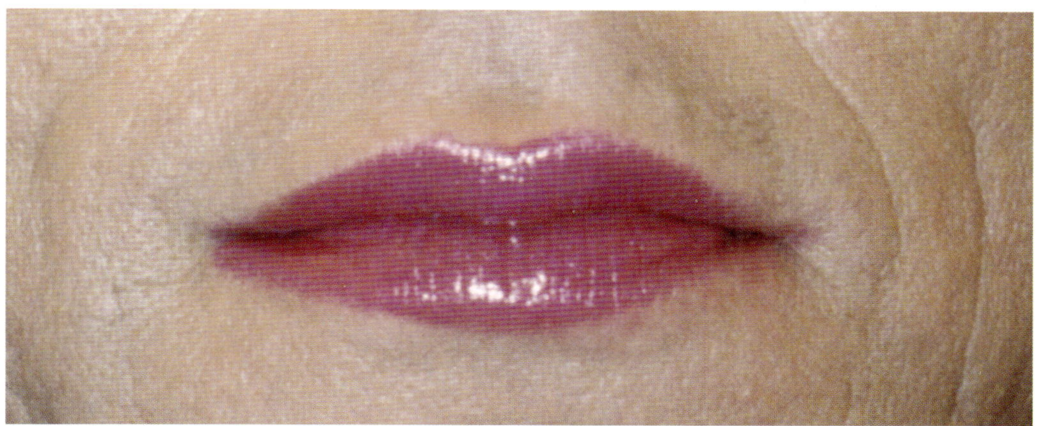

Detail from outtake snapshot

Of all the the portrait methods in this book, color film is most unforgiving , as the above enlargement of Dolores's mouth area proves. Laptop photos obscure some pores and wrinkles behind pixellation, the high contrast of tonal reversal of paper negatives creates a convenient obscurity, and silver gelatin positives can always be under-exposed or -developed a trifle. I hardly ever shoot color film, but not for that reason. Why go to trouble and hazard for the sake of impermanence? When black-and-white labs began to wink out of business, I sometimes used to send magazine editors quickie color prints of my black and white rolls. The price was low and the time really no more than an hour. The tones would be either bluish or sepia; sometimes the one-hour people would even let me choose. These snapshots, taped to my wall in bright sunlight, have already lost contrast after a mere decade. I say screw all that. But since this book will doubtless be printed in fugitive inks, I shot a few rolls of Fujicolor, just for you.

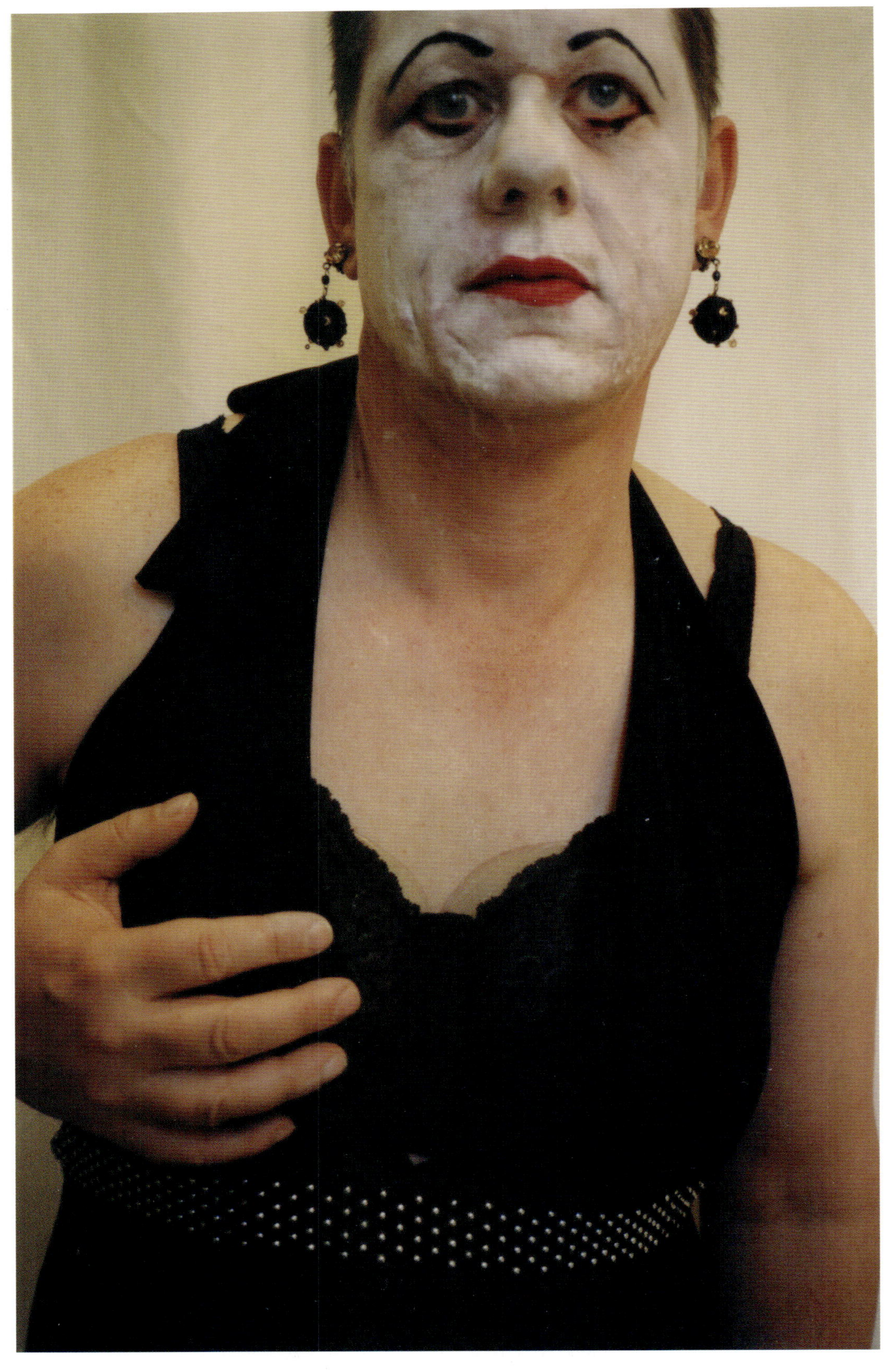

Beauty queen

144

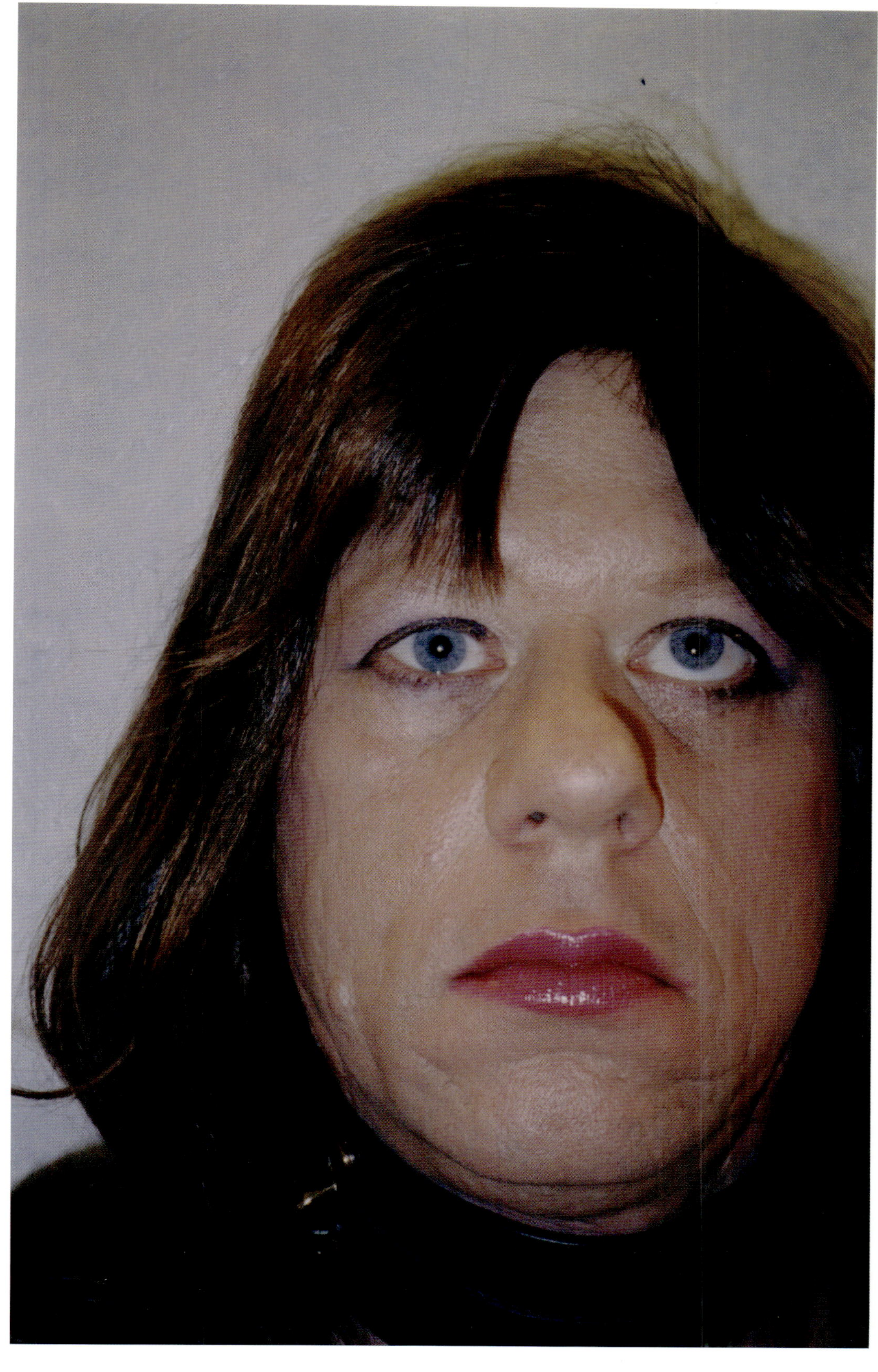

Collar and lipstick

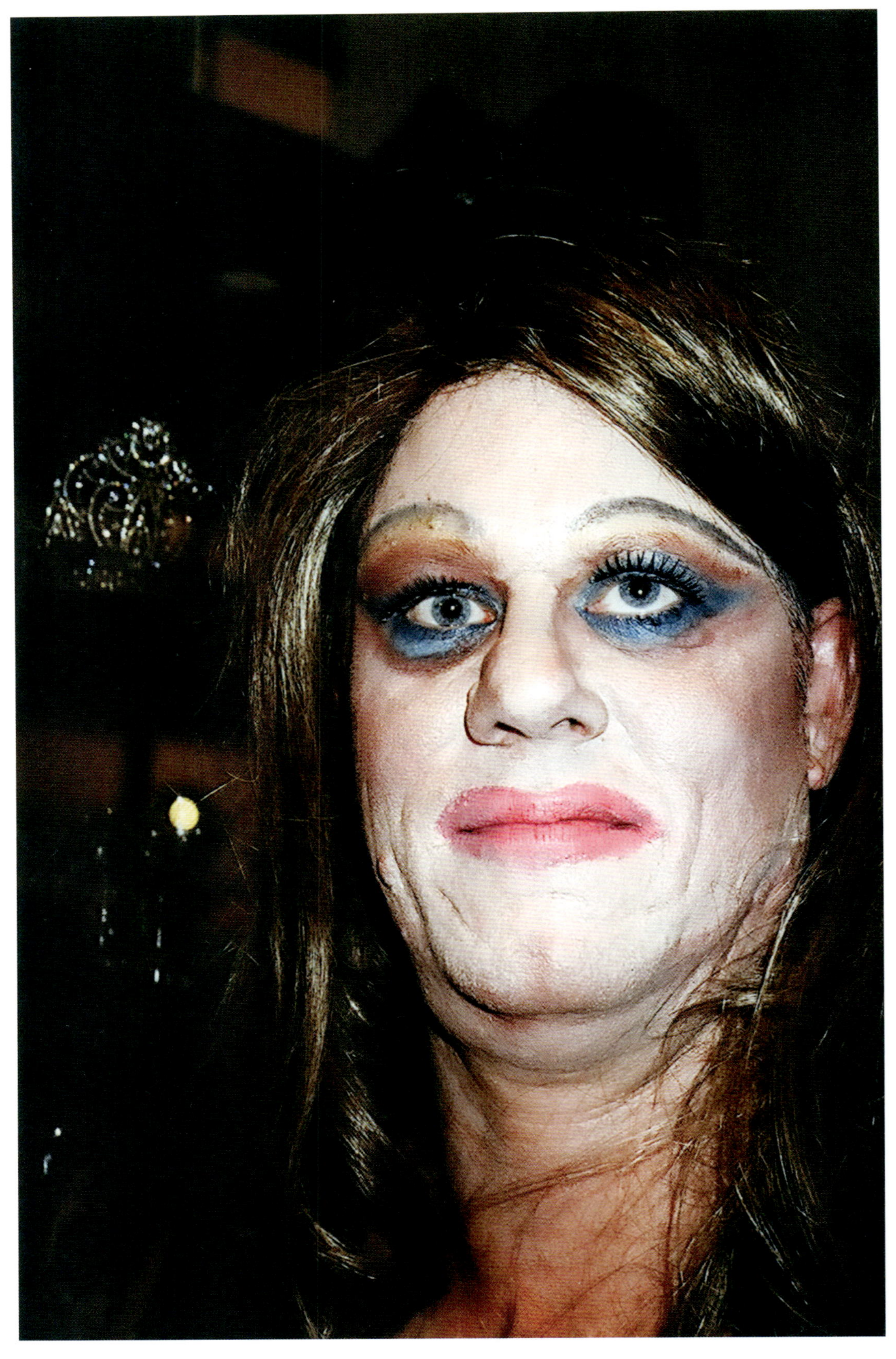

Katy's makeup

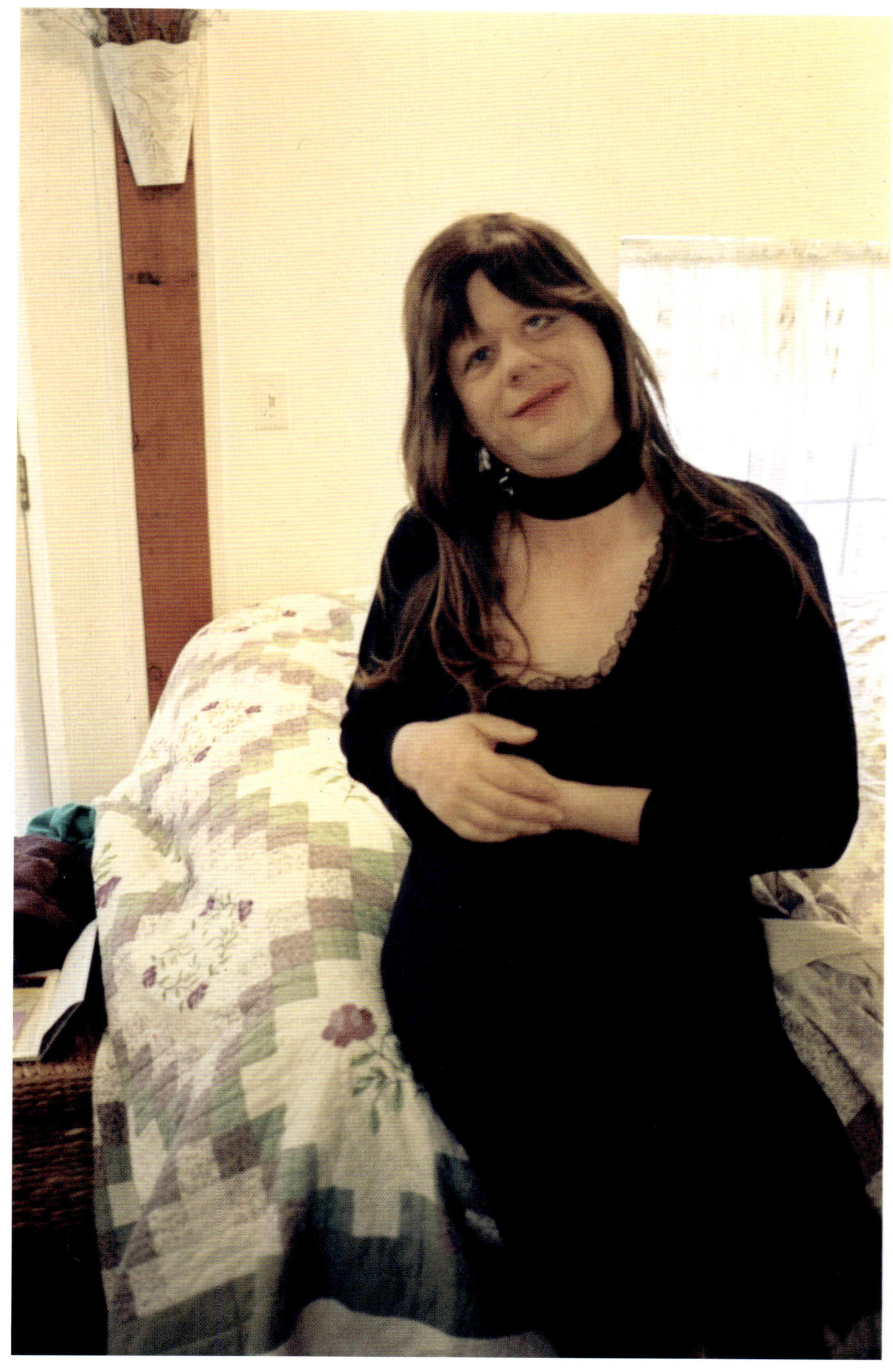

Available girl

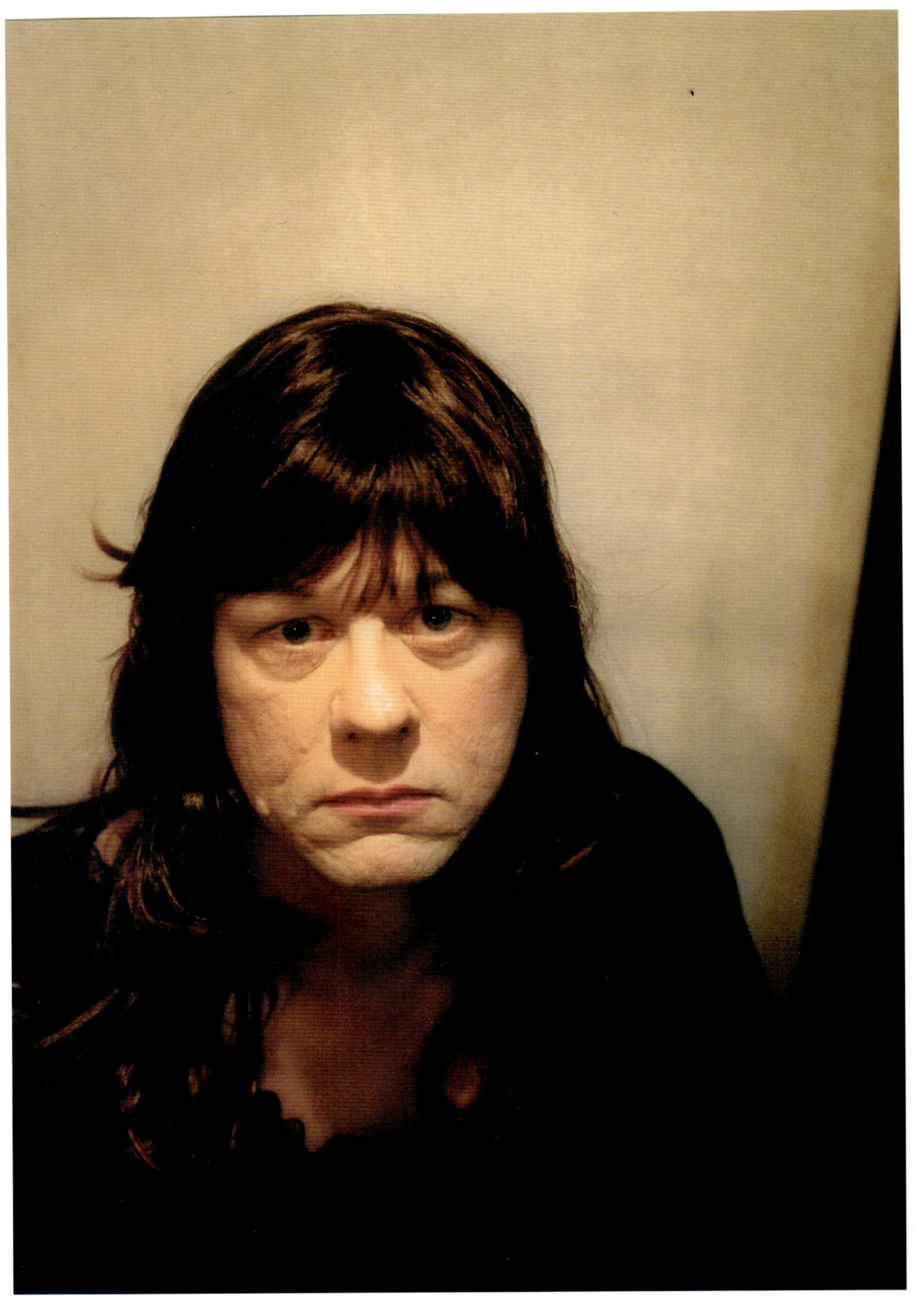

In the stairwell

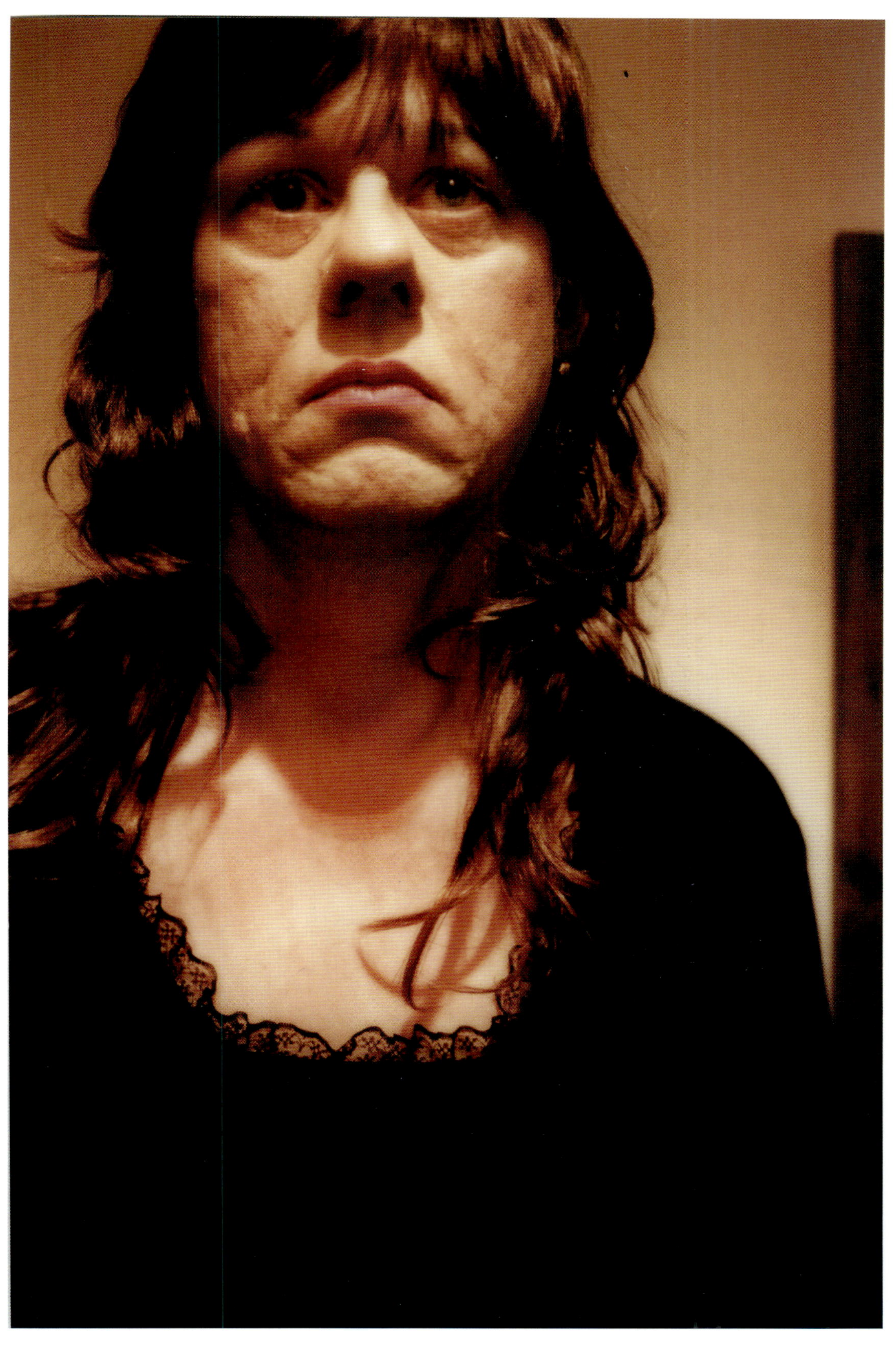

Black nightgown (with slight digital blur)

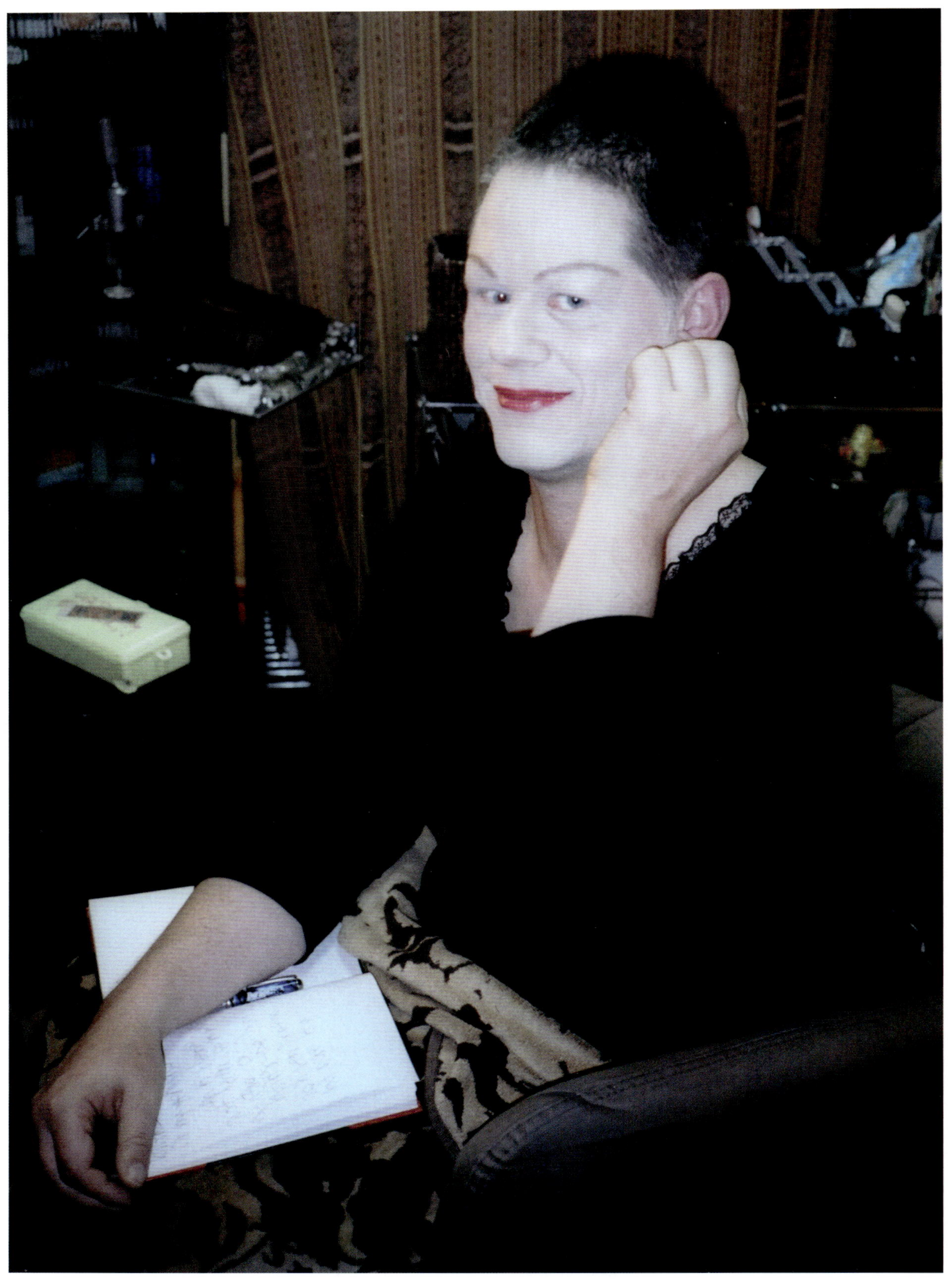

Japanese makeover

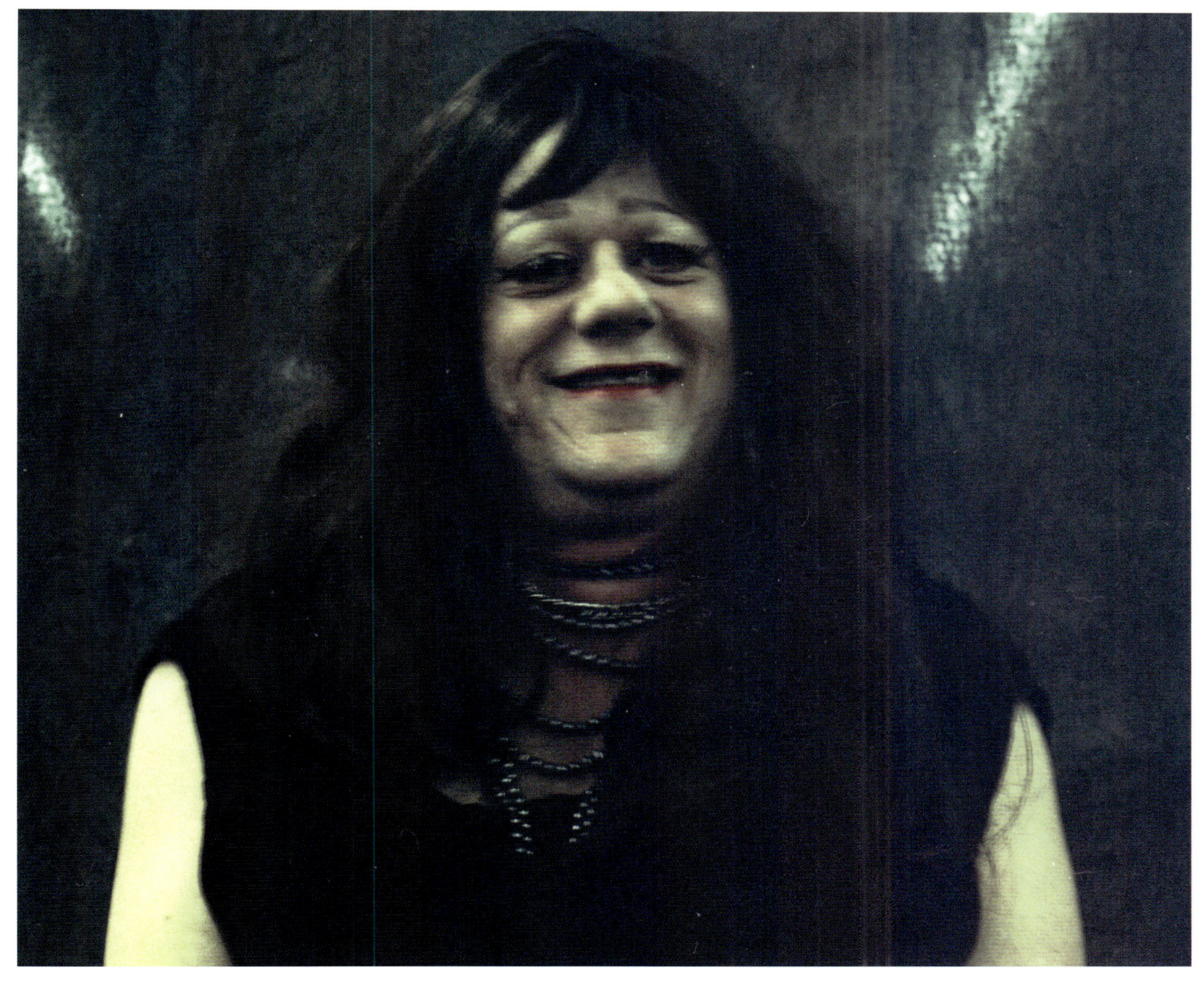

Happy woman

2.7: Gum Bichromate Prints, *or,*
It Will All Come Off in the Clearing Bath

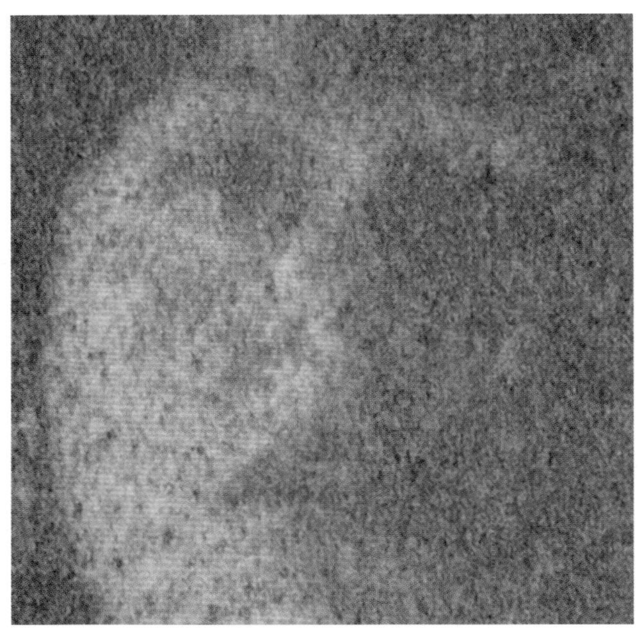

Detail from "White dress"

The nineteenth-century gum bichromate process entails the contact printing of a negative or photogenic drawing onto a sheet of custom-sized watercolor paper which has been brush-coated with a mixture of watercolor paint (diluted in gum arabic) and any one of three chromium salts, which will render the watercolor photosensitive. Exposure to light makes the coating insoluble in water, in proportion to the transparency of the negative. After the proper amount of time (determined by trial and error) in the sun or under a bank of ultraviolet lights, one removes the paper from the negative and places it face down in a tray of water in a darkened room. A weak image forms by subtraction. The print is held vertically to drain for a moment, then left to dry overnight. The process can be repeated almost indefinitely, with the same or a different color. Thus tone, saturation and color complexity build up — theoretically.

Many gum printers employ a single black-and-white negative for each print. The procedure then is simple. The great French gummist Robert Demachy did this, often printing in single or multiple layers of black or red. His photographs can resemble chalk drawings. I myself have learned to print portraits and landscapes from silver gelatin negatives (11 x 14", commercially enlarged from 35 millimeter) with, if I may say so, considerable success. No matter how many color layers I employ, the topmost invariably dominates; and an image whose tonal scale possesses a single apparent hue — for instance, the greys of an untoned silver gelatin print, or the Prussian blues of a cyanotype — receives far more indulgence from our eyes than attempts at true color. Man Ray's solarized portraits are eerily lovely. It is difficult, although certainly not impossible, to imagine an equivalently pleasing effect in color. Back in the days when there were still travel agencies, I used to be depressed by the window-posters of, say, the Adriatic coast, whose reds had bleached out, leaving pallid bluish-white memorials to that vanished magenta information. Old snapshots afflicted by a yellow or brown cast, or by the disease appropriately named "red eye," demonstrate their own enviable achievements of color inbalance. A gum print made from a single negative is potentially no less beautiful than one from color separations, but the effort required is far less. One simply prints the negative over and over, until a sufficient tonal scale has been established.

The incomparable Stephen Livick gets true color by employing separation negatives, and I once thought to do the same. Since Dolores appears to love colors, it seemed an act of kindness to her to render her in color. The softness of gum printing, which I foolishly imagined to be forgiving, seemed to promise great things for her skin. All in all, I imagined an equivalent to the soft focus portrait lens which represented 1930s Hollywood movie stars to advantage. I can still see in my mind's eye what I supposed these gum prints of her to be, and who can call what I visualize impossible?* In the

---

*   My decision to use the poor-quality laptop camera, which I thought would improve Dolores's skin, was a further miscalculation

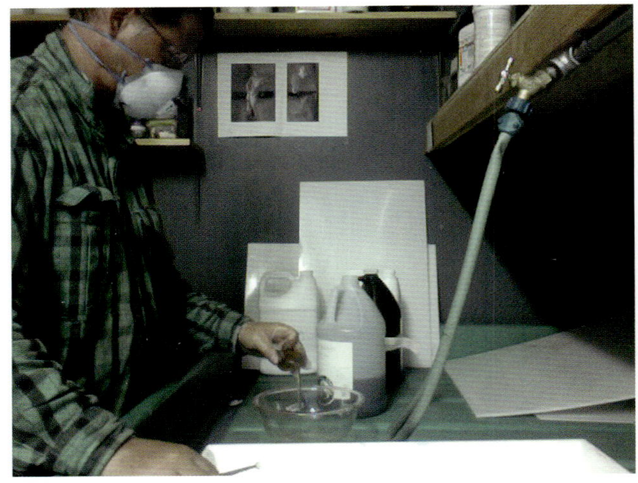
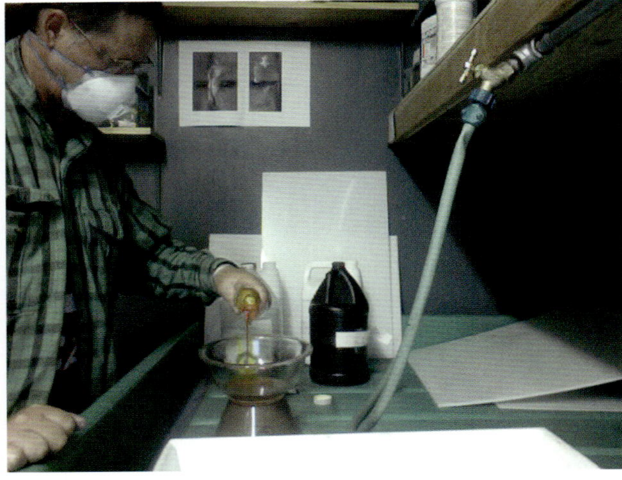
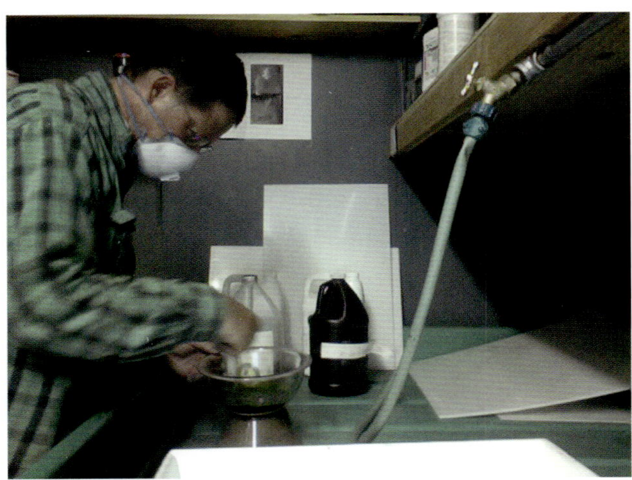
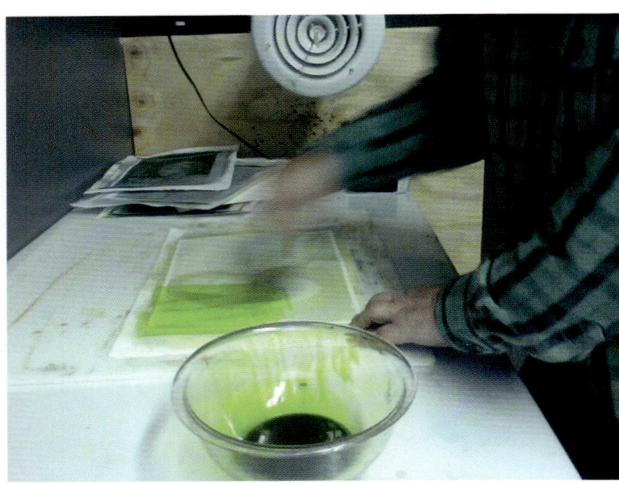
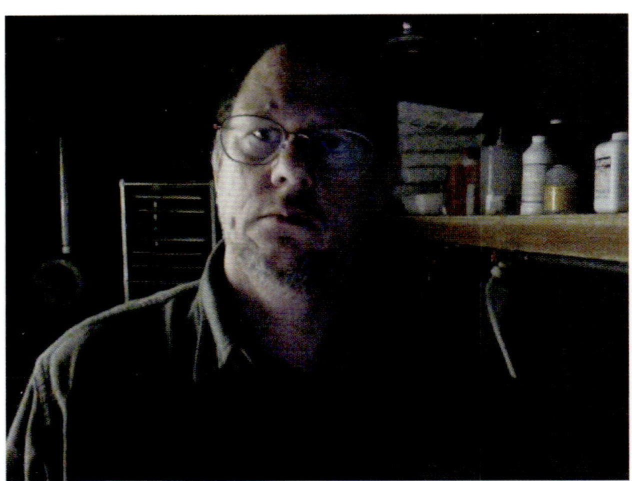
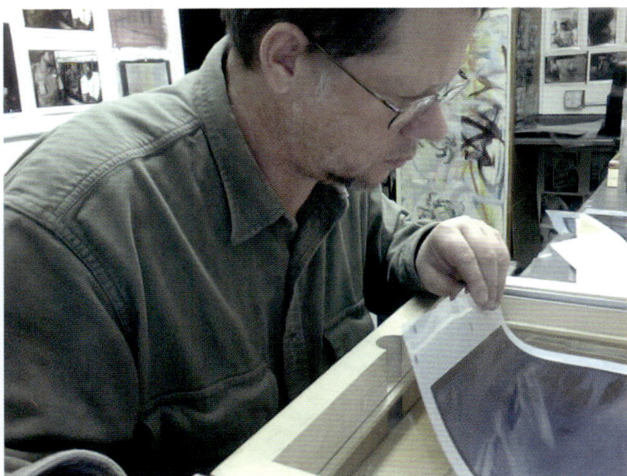

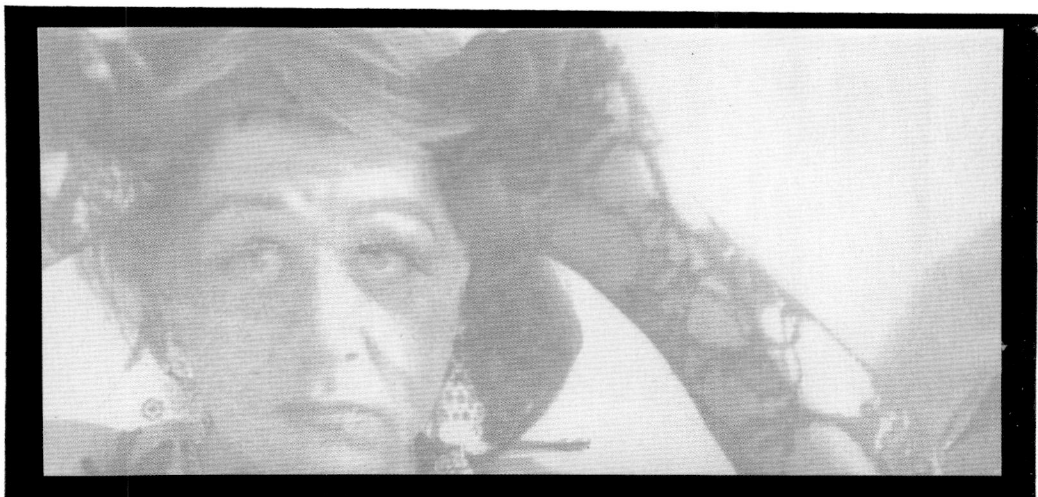

four-color separations which I mostly employ for the gum portraits of Dolores, true color was aimed at, missed, and finally abandoned. When after several years of struggle I gave up this aspiration, I felt sadness, disappointment in myself, and, mostly, freedom and joy.

The shorthand for four-color separations is CYMK (or some other scrambling of these letters, depending on one's order of printing). The C, or cyan negative will obviously be especially transparent to blue — for instance, in the pupils of Dolores's eyes. Y is yellow, M magenta (perfect for lipstick) and K contains the darks: shadows and outlines. It is possible to print with the K layer alone (as you just saw in the "Black gloves" version above), which produces a nicely contrasty, "graphic" result but of course omits midtone subtleties.

The four negatives can be printed in any order, but I have had my best luck in printing the K layer last. Although the Y layer distinguishes itself poorly from the whiteness of the paper, there is much to recommend about printing it first, because a yellow-orange dichromate stain builds up with each successive printing, rendering yellow tones ever more obscure. Hence that chimera, an experienced worker, reminds himself that when the colors of a four-separation print appear to be balanced before the final clearing bath, the print will not actually be yellow enough.

One of the many difficulties contingent on four-color printing is this: When printing a single negative over and over, one reinforces one's previous effort. But when overprinting different negatives one upon the other, only the transparent areas common to the entire set (in other words, the shadows which will be finally nailed down by the K layer) get solidified. Let's say one begins with the C layer. The result resembles an underexposed cyanotype, except, let's say, in Dolores's eyes, which now seem nearly blue enough. On the following day, our hopeful photographer essays the M layer.

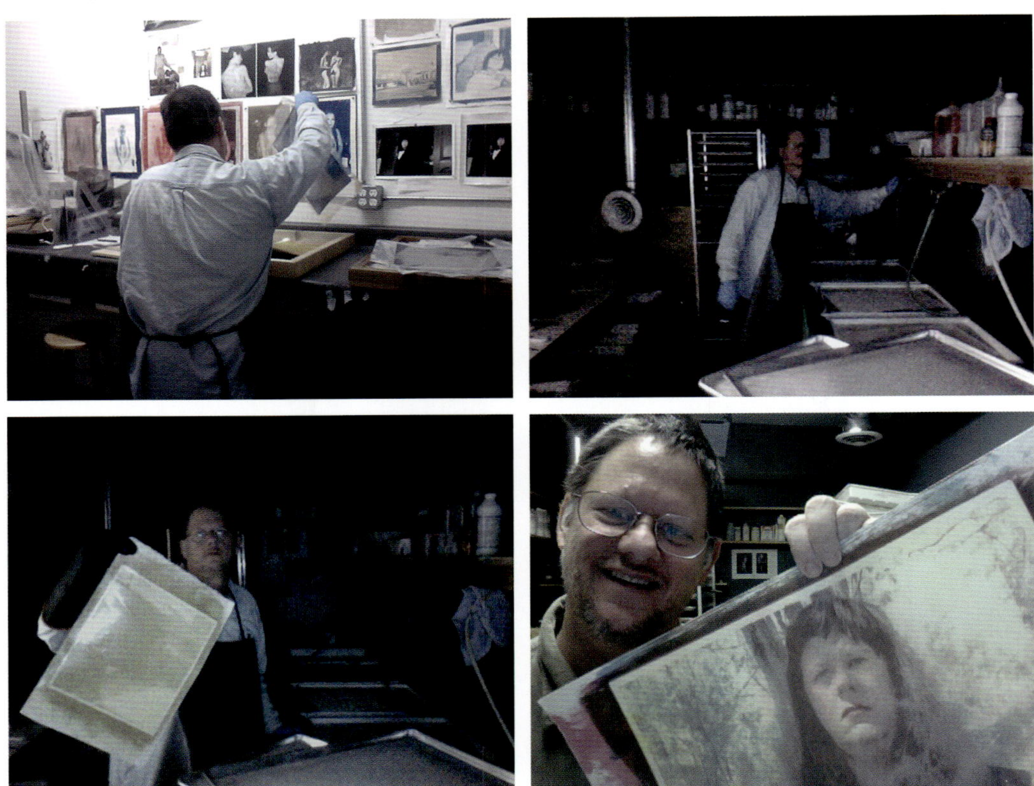

Dolores's lips begin to look good, but her eyes seem less blue than he remembers. By the time the Y layer meets its two predecessors, creating some approximation of flesh tones, it may be necessary to print another C layer. By then, unfortunately, Dolores's pink lips are losing their color.

My first defense against this retrogression was to print each layer twice in immediate succession. Thus each finished photograph required a minimum of eight days before it could enter the final clearing bath. So far, so good; effort improves the soul, they say; but that was how I learned that four to six printings was the most that the watercolor paper I had chosen could safely withstand. Sometimes, to be sure, I did put in my eight days and get lucky; more often the seventh or eighth day marked the matriculation of that set of prints into the wastebasket, after which I got to start again.

The difficulties of the process do not stop there.

Too great a pigment concentration will result in flaking off of the dark areas. Too dilute a concentration will require many, many printings in order to reach a reasonable density, any one of which might fall out of register. Extra printings are additionally dangerous because after an unpredictable amount of soaking and drying, the paper, having been tortured more than it can bear, will abrade without warning. Indeed, as I have implied above, it is my frequent experience for the print to improve layer by layer, day by day, until its color and depth are nearly breathtaking — up to the streaking, spotting,

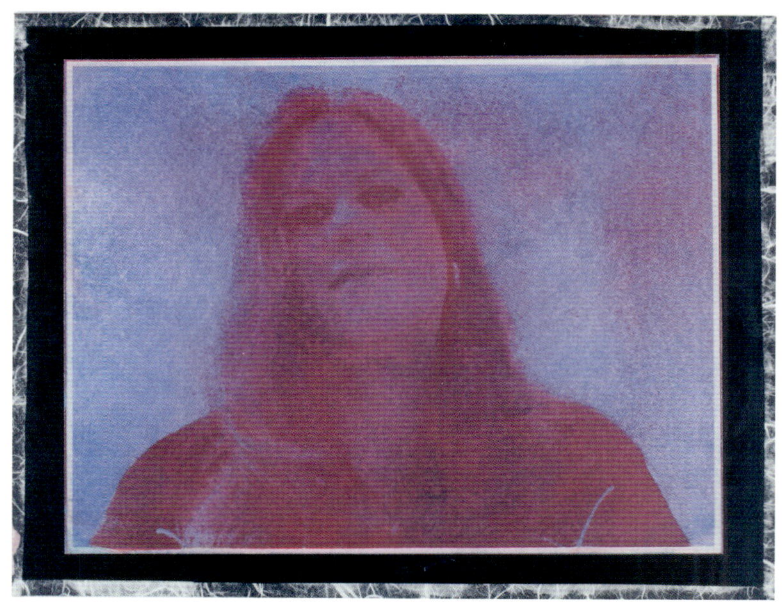

Top: First printing in quinacridone coral (M layer) and second printing in cerulean blue (C layer) for portrait "Melissa's work," from tricolor experiment

Bottom: Cropped version of "Melissa's work," printed in cadmium yellow and quinacridone coral only

speckling, poxing, hideously coarsening decay, disease and dissolution.

May I continue? Too heavy a sizing will make the pigment flake off. Too light a sizing will cause the picture to sink in. Too short an exposure will cause the picture to dissolve away during development, or, worse yet, in the final clearing bath, after many layers of apparently successful effort have raised the photographer's hopes. Too long an exposure causes staining, because the light-baked gum loses solubility. One pigment's optical properties will surely not match another, so blue prints more slowly than red, and may be thinner or thicker in the final print. A set of prints can dry down beautifully for the first two hours, and then bleed gruesomely overnight; but waiting until tomorrow to complete the set would likewise show imprudence. Humidity and temperature affect exposure so drastically that a given negative and pigment may require four minutes one day and six or seven the next. Pre-mixing volumes of consistent pigment concen-

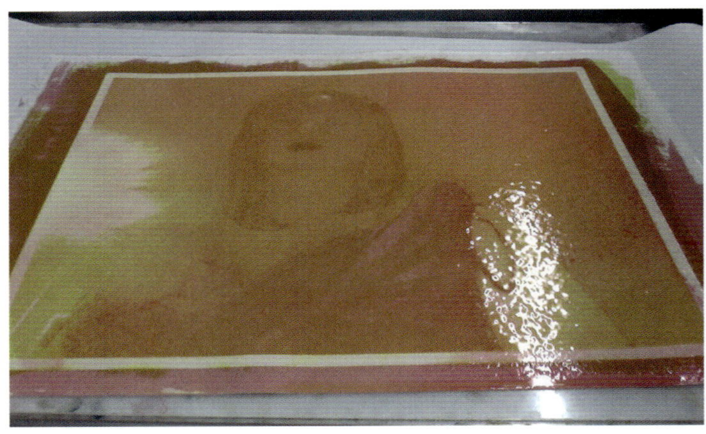

trations would seem to be a good idea, but in practice the colors tend to settle to the bottom and the gum arabic has a cunning way of evaporating from tightly screwed jars, so I have learned to mix my hues as I go, by eye, drawing a brushful up along the side of a glass bowl to observe its "legs," as if it were fine Scotch. (Demachy was good at this.) It has come to my attention that cadmium yellow possesses a nearly overpowering tinting strength, so that I had better squeeze out only a trifle (I can't tell you how much, but as the man said about obscenity, I know it when I see it) in comparison to an azurite or turquoise. Cerulean blue, by the way, differs markedly from those two aforesaid mineral cousins, being most prone to staining, so that one printing of that stuff is either insufficient or else ruinous. Quinacridone gold and amethyst both achieve a remarkable tonal range in one printing; however, in four-color printing the former render yellows as brown and the latter will degrade the separation between red and blue — which doesn't mean they can't be used; one simply needs to be wise. When coating a print with any colored gum preparation, each layer had better be a little more dilute than the previous one, in order to avoid abrading and damaging it. The gum should spread on the paper easily; its consistency ought to be in between that of water and that of syrup. Older manuals advise the use of a blending brush, a feathered brush, and this and that; I for my part recommend a foam brush. All of the above items of knowledge pertain only to the one watercolor paper I know, Rives de lin. So there you have it, and good luck to you.

Gum printing has been one of the great joys of my life. I have always loved to watch a silver gelatin print develop out of blankness in a tray of developer. While making the first layer of a gum print is mostly an exercise in deferred gratification, each additional layer resembles a drink of absinthe, the aesthetic pleasure building on the tongue and in the brain until conviviality ascends into heavenly drunkenness. Who would have thought that rhodonite over golden ocher could be so beautiful? Sometimes I lie awake at night marshalling my army of phantom watercolors around me, wondering which color I will print tomorrow. I rush to the darkroom, so excited that I put off friends and taxes for later. Often the day is half over before I know it, and I stagger into the shower, sweaty, worn out and impregnated with sinister chemicals, but already determined to rectify my errors and secure my victories as utter triumphs by printing a moderate bloodstone K layer tomorrow for four and a half minutes, unless of course I decide on bone black for three minutes and forty-five seconds. Once upon a time I was dying to print in pure silver. I got a few grams of that from a numismatics company, and began straight away with the K layer. Only one print survived the clearing bath. I later rejected it. But now I wonder whether I ought to try again, coating the silver more dilutely and printing longer, or heavier and longer, or something; then I would surely get it right. Because I never know for sure how a print will turn out (although often I think I do), every good result is a gift for which I am humbly grateful. I am free to hope as much as I like, but I cannot expect, as I can with silver gelatin, to achieve what I envision, and therefore I cannot deserve it.

What an education in life gum printing is! When I open the statement of my mutual fund account and learn that it lost a third of its value in the last month, at first I feel fright and discouragement, of course, but then I remember that all these numbers are imaginary until I cash out. So it is in the world of gum bichromate. What perfection a new quartet of negatives promises! These will surely produce my best photograph ever. And after two layers, or seven, when I have to start all over, I have it all figured out — a printing of amazonite just for the eyes, and then I will be a gum god! Already everything is looking more and more splendid. Who could ever have imagined how accomplished I would have become? Next, of course, comes disaster — frequently

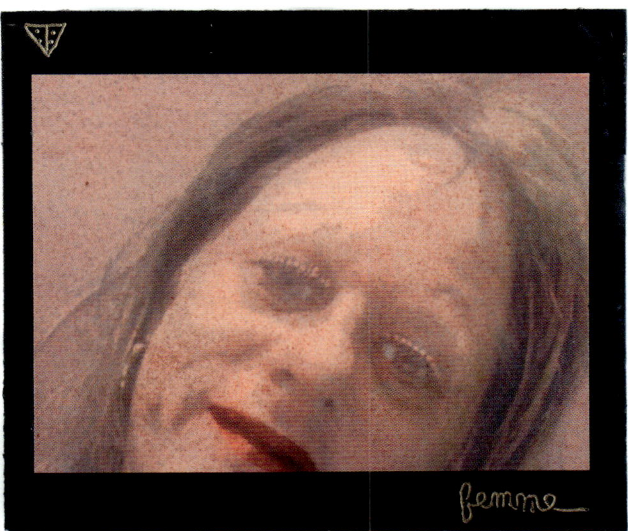

at the very last possible moment, when I am ever so carefully withdrawing the glistening print from the rinsing tray after the metabisulphite clearing bath, and then coarse particles of bloodstone come tumbling out of Dolores's hair and stick all over her face. I used to feel terrible then. Now I laugh, although sometimes I still feel terrible; by the next day I have figured it all out again. In Demachy's words (1905): "Fancy what a saving of time — two or three little squirts of coloured paste in a small saucer, a liqueur glass of gum, and a little bichromate, a vigorous churning with a hard brush and all is ready for coating."* Once again I gaze at a reproduction of his "Behind the Scenes," 1897: Two young ballerinas stand chatting, the one in the foreground with her ankles crossed and light gleaming on her heel; their tutus could be pencil-strokes or pastel-work or anything; as for this precious light in hair and on a face and on a door, I suppose Demachy made it with a brush, or by swirling around in sawdust-water.**

The photograph of Dolores in her red corset, standing by the vanity (the original laptop version is on p. 000), cost more than fifty prints before I got a single good one. In

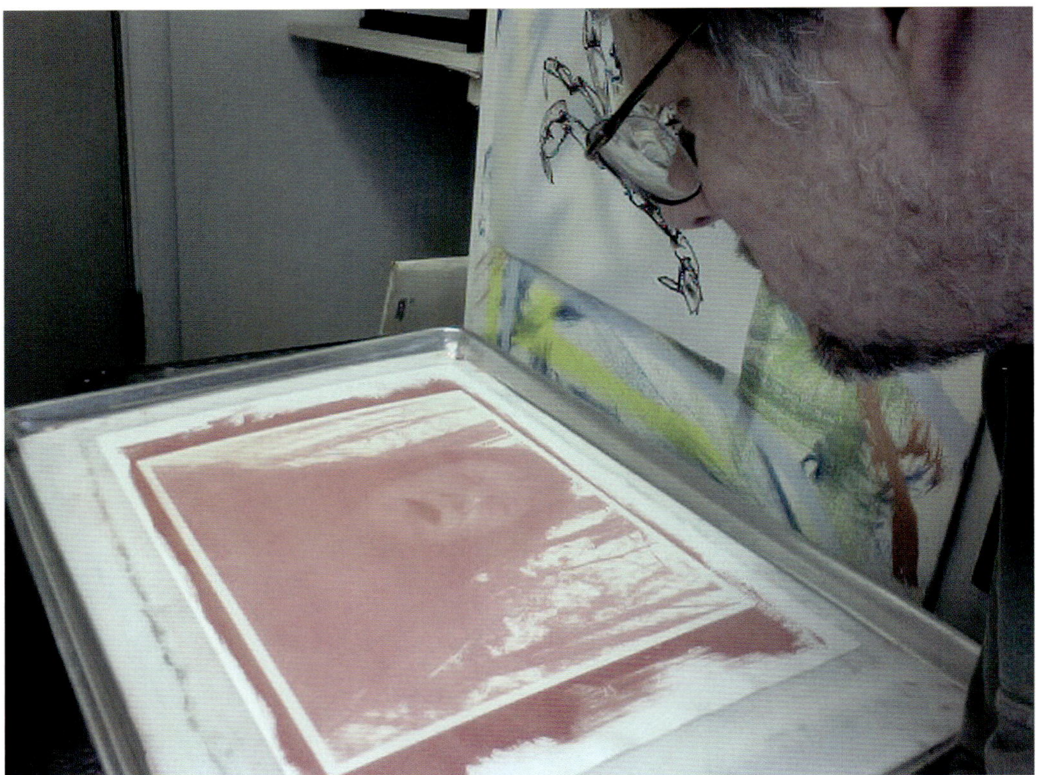

fact, as I study it now, it appears that I'll need to make about five more in order to close out my edition of five. What if I deleted that image from the portfolio? Nobody would know or care. My friends recommended cutting it out; I was getting sick; I was falling behind in paid work; the planet was warming without me. But I now established that my mistake in "Red Corset" had lain in the yellow layer, which insisted on staining at any plausible concentration. If I settled for a lesser vibrancy, I knew I could pull it off. Or I could go for broke and print it eight times — finishing it off in the paper shredder, no doubt, in order to start over and print it another six, or even another nine, grasping

---

* Quoted in Newhall, p. 147.
** Ibid., p. 148.

the impossible. The more I printed, the less my failures and successes mattered, and the more accomplished I got, at least to my own mind.

As of this year (2012) the four-color Dolores portfolios are about one-fourth completed. By the time I finish, Dolores's face might have dissolved away for real. I hope to give her something by which to remember herself.

I feel grateful for the beauties I have seen in my years of darkroom work, the reds and yellows blending on the glistening print so that Dolores's skin shines like peaches and sunsets, the yellows and blues subtly outlining her eyelids and nostrils while adding

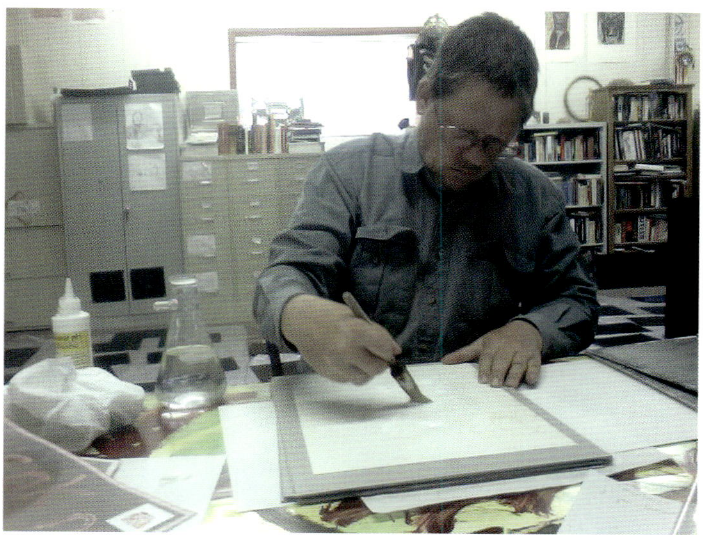

mass to the stuff of her evening dress which will at the end be black; and because I imagine myself a photographer I imagine that what I (or rather the watercolors) might make will remain forever; but even Ansel Adams met disappointment when his lustrous white-planked barns and whatnots dried down; for just as the glowing pebble plucked from the creek is to the dry dead thing which the child soon abandons, so is the wet print fresh out of the bath to the coarse dull changeling all warped and curled in my baker's rack; moreover, as the wet print is to the dry, so, miserably often, is the dry print to the one which has passed through its final ordeal in the metabisulphite bath. How many glorious colors and ethereal outlines have sloughed off by the end of the final rinse, how many radiant Dolores-faces have treacherously pitted themselves with slag-stuff of bloodstone or sodalite which, tumbling out of Dolores's hair, left it so pockmarked with whiteness that only the wastebasket will serve! (Come to think of it, how many times has Dolores imagined herself to be pretty, only to inspect her portrait with her spectacles on?) Print too heavily, and this will happen for sure. Print too lightly, and in the clearing bath your tones will bleach away. Expose so that your prints will take long development in the clearing bath (remember that this must be done at least four to six times for a four-color print), and sooner or later the paper will abrade in the water; the image will be ruined. Expose for short development, and it will all come off in the clearing bath.

Perhaps I ought now to advise you what to look for in a gum print. Most of the time (Mr. Livick's prints sometimes excepted*) you will not see the detail which might be taken for granted in one of the conventional color photographs of our day. When a gum print dries for the final time after its swim in potassium metabisulphite, the

---

*   This is really a very kind enchromium of mine.

color reticulates into something not entirely unlike the dots of various hues in which the ophthalmologist invites his patient to seek out hidden numbers. Moreover, most watercolors, especially including the mineral pigments which I delight in, are famous for granulating. Watercolorists prize this; gum printers often do not. In short, when a gum print is at all bold, it tends to be coarse — particularly with my low-resolution negatives. (When it is not bold, it can be flat.) In comparison to results achieved by other processes, these qualities may be fairly considered defects, except to members of the secret society of grain-loving perverts. But remember: A gum printer can make his photograph any combination of colors he likes. Only a painter possesses so much liberty. Gum is mood; gum is art. Gum is appropriate to Dolores, because, like her, it looks better from farther away. Unlike Dolores, who will fall into her grave without delay, gum is permanent; it will last as long as the paper; the only other color photographic process which does so well in this respect is carbon printing, whose difficulties I decline to embrace. Cibachromes, they say, last for two or three hundred years; I don't know where to order those anymore, and anyhow I would rather make my prints myself. If you like the ones you see in this book, I thank you; if you dislike them, I forgive you as cheerfully as I do myself.

Right: Untitled portrait, contact printed twice in azurite,
from 8 x 10" silver gelatin in-camera negative

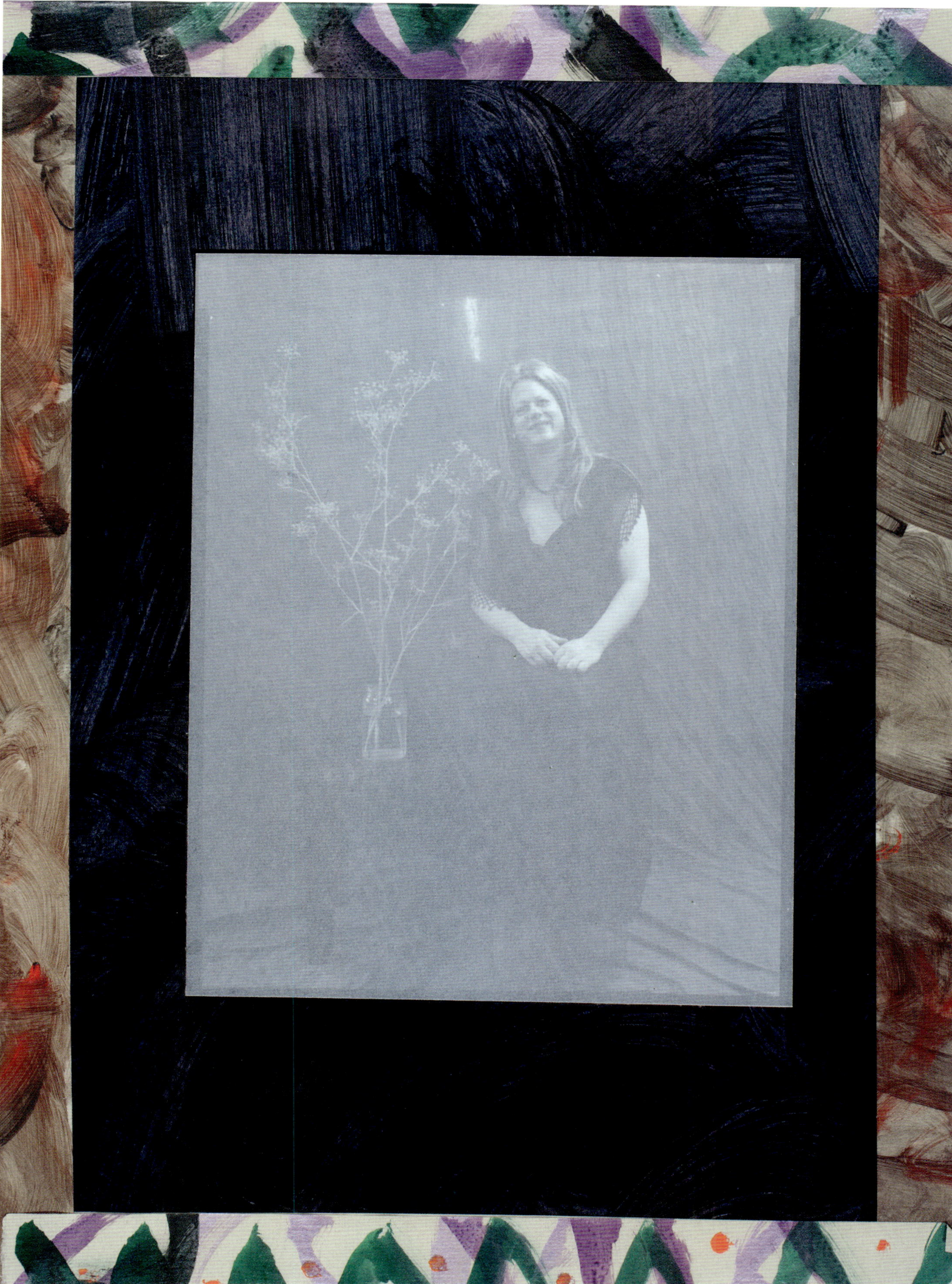

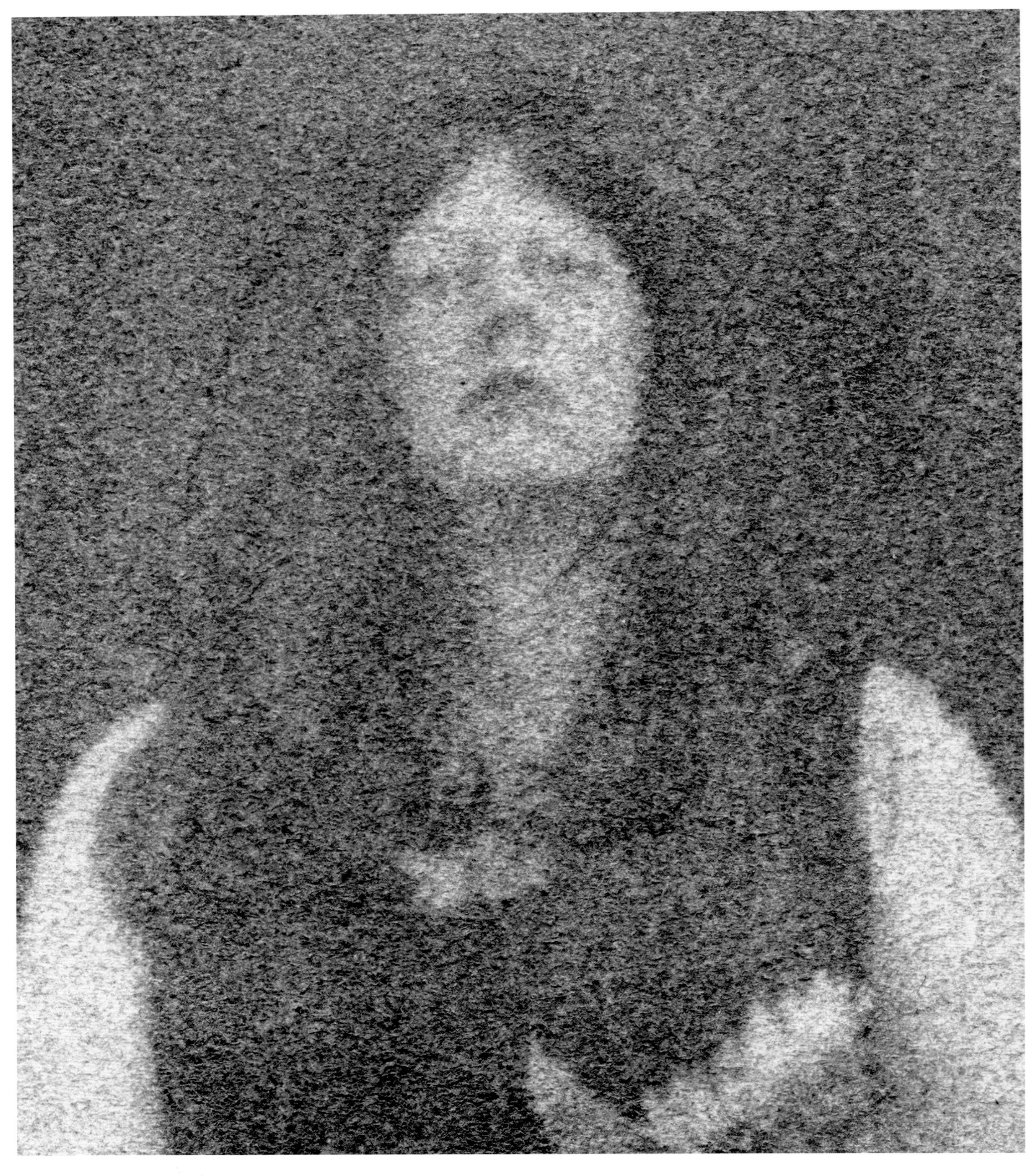

Detail of another untitled portrait, contact printed three times (cadmium yellow, ivory black and cerulean blue) from 11 x 14" silver gelatin in-camera negative

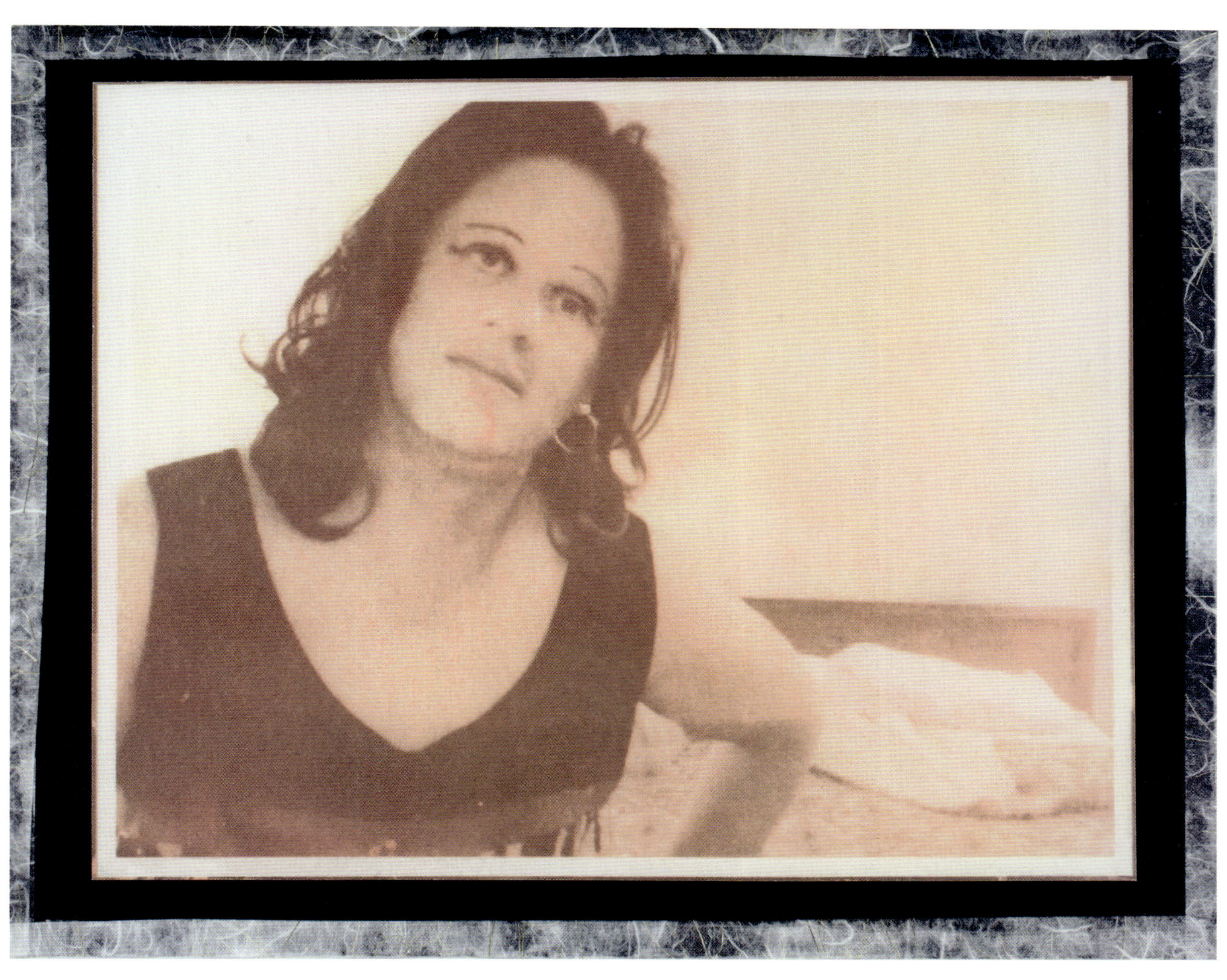

"Desert light," which is a single-negative image derived from a laptop capture. This version was printed with quinacridone coral, quinacridone gold and Van Dyke brown

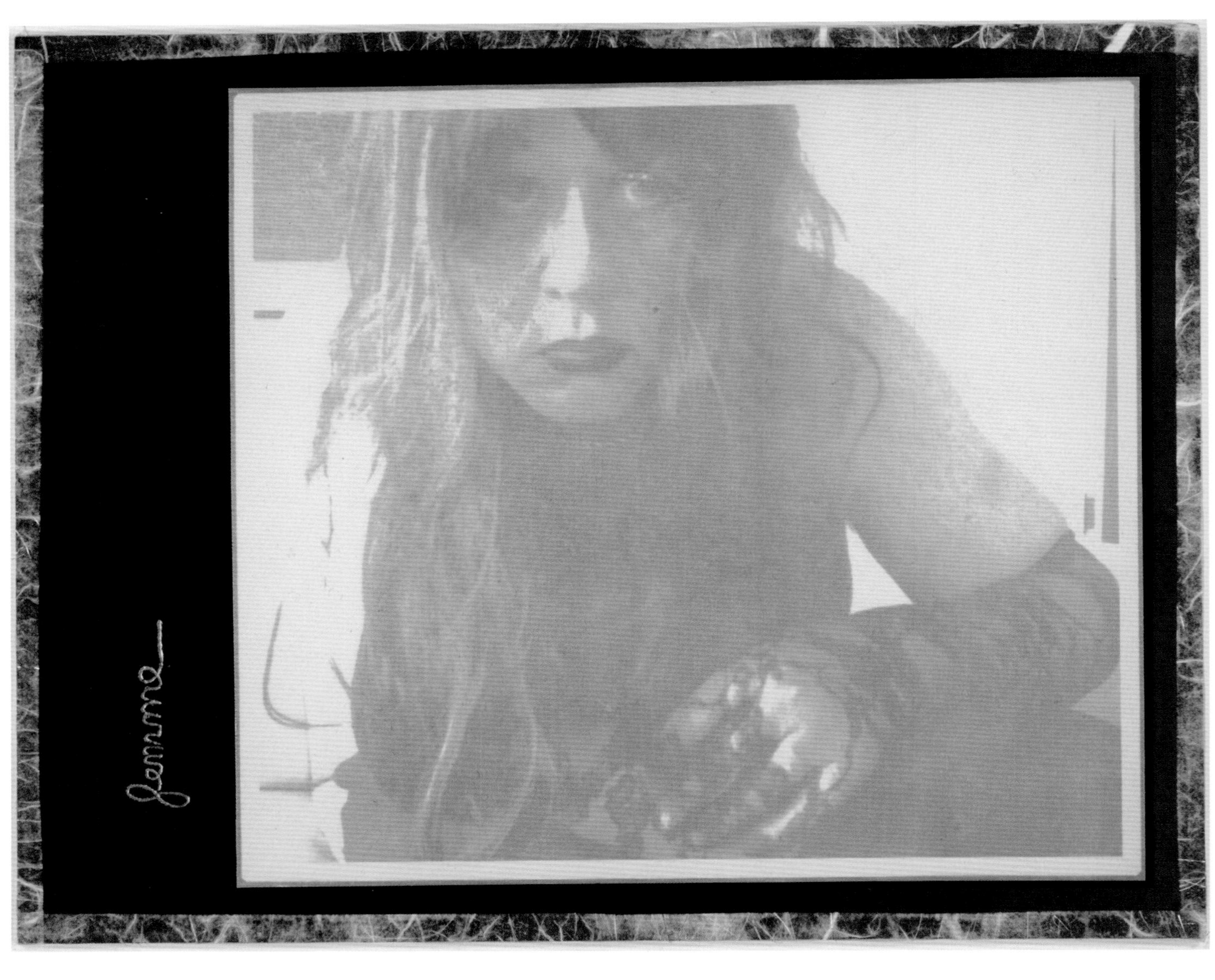

Single sodalite K printing of "Black gloves"

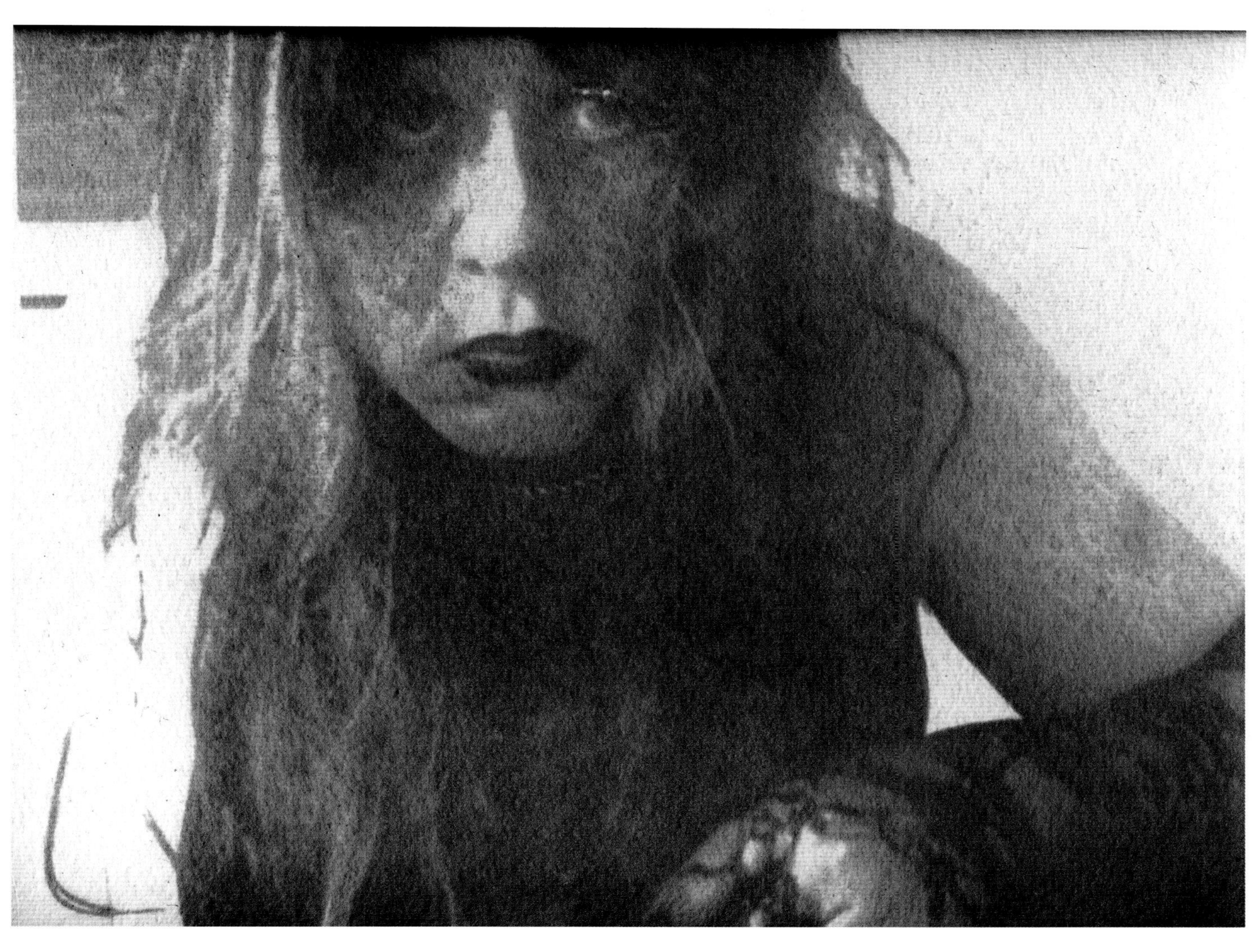

Detail from single ivory black K printing of "Black gloves"

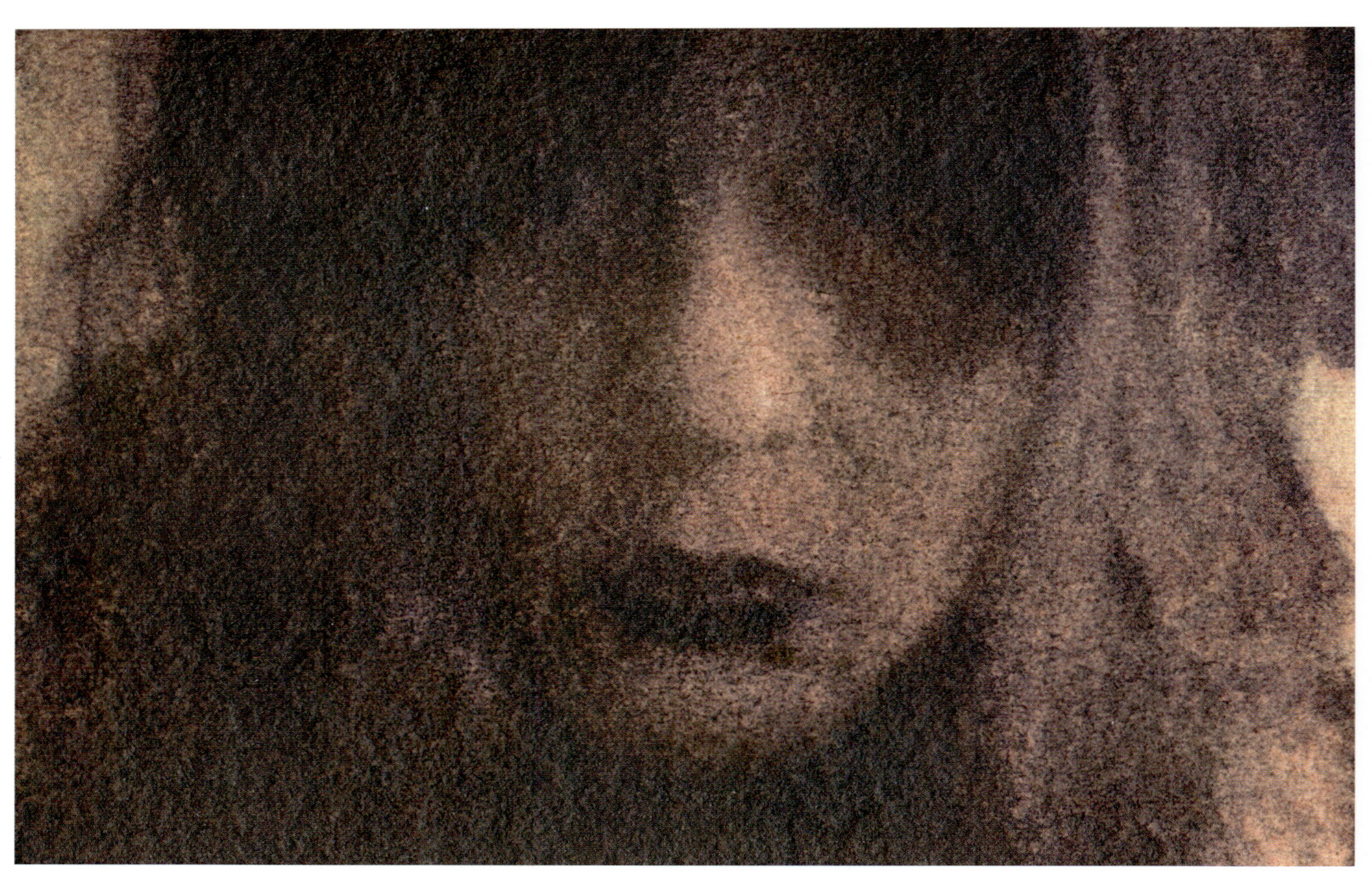

Detail from a different 4-color print of "Black gloves"

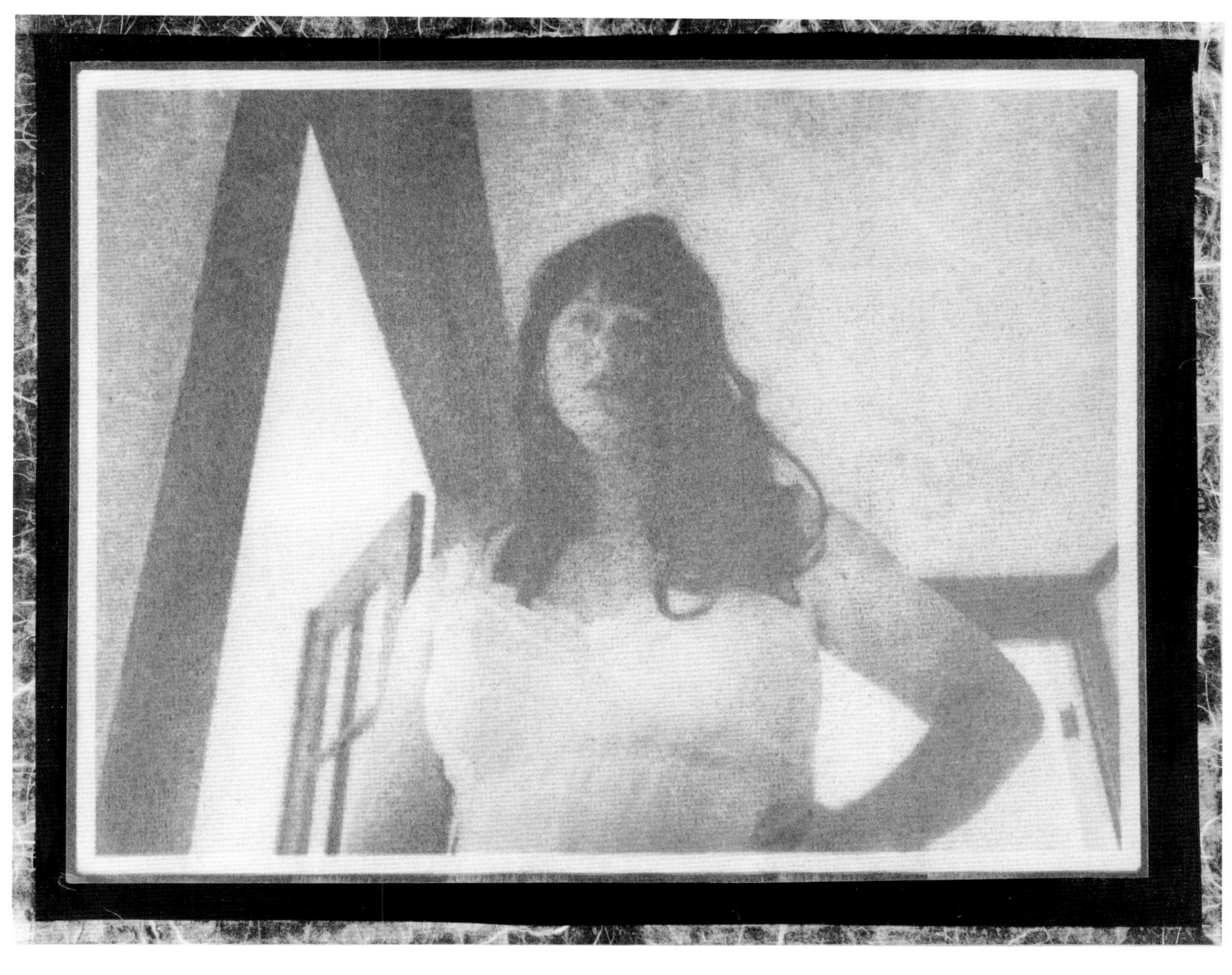

White dress

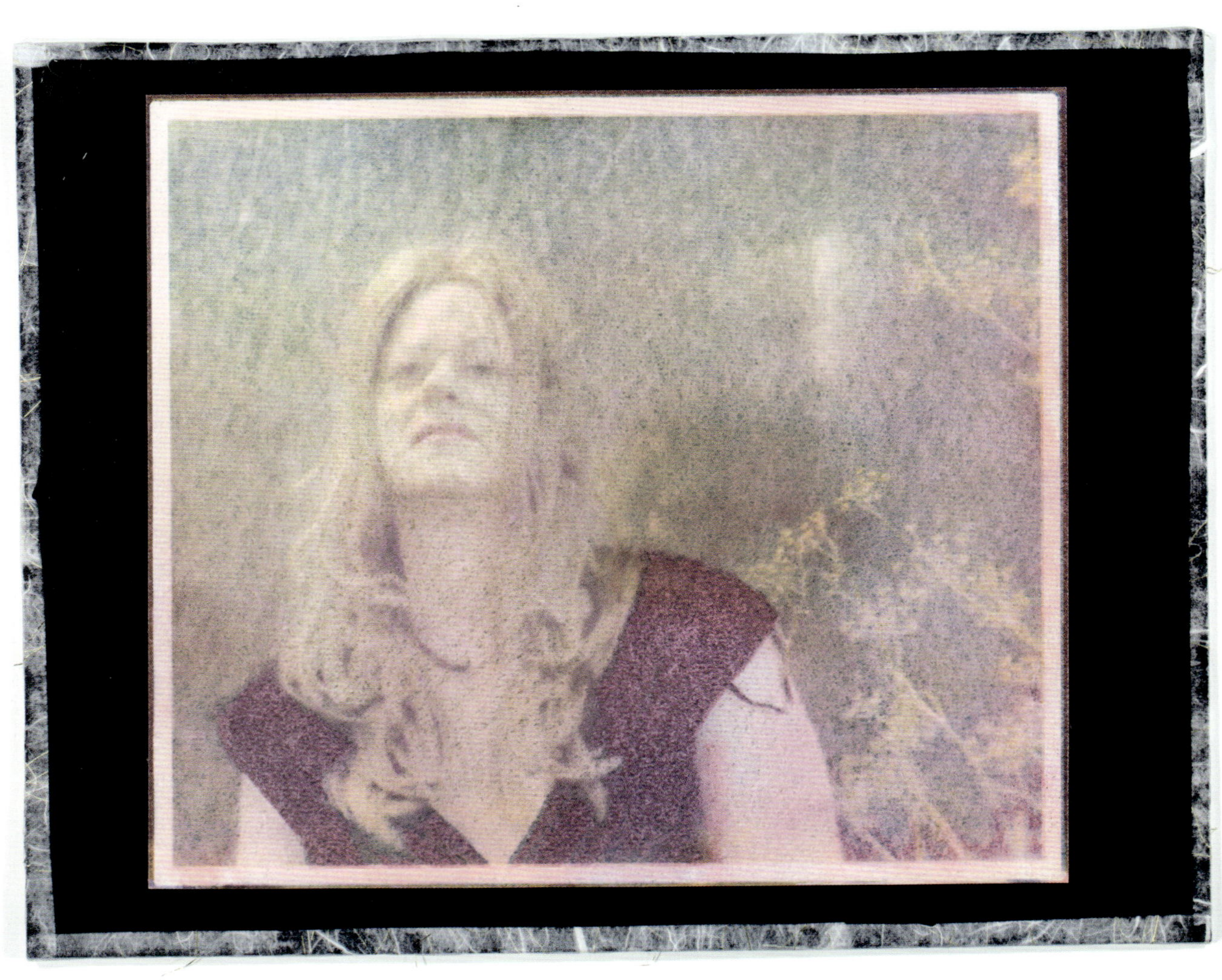

Above: Blonde

Right: Corset strut

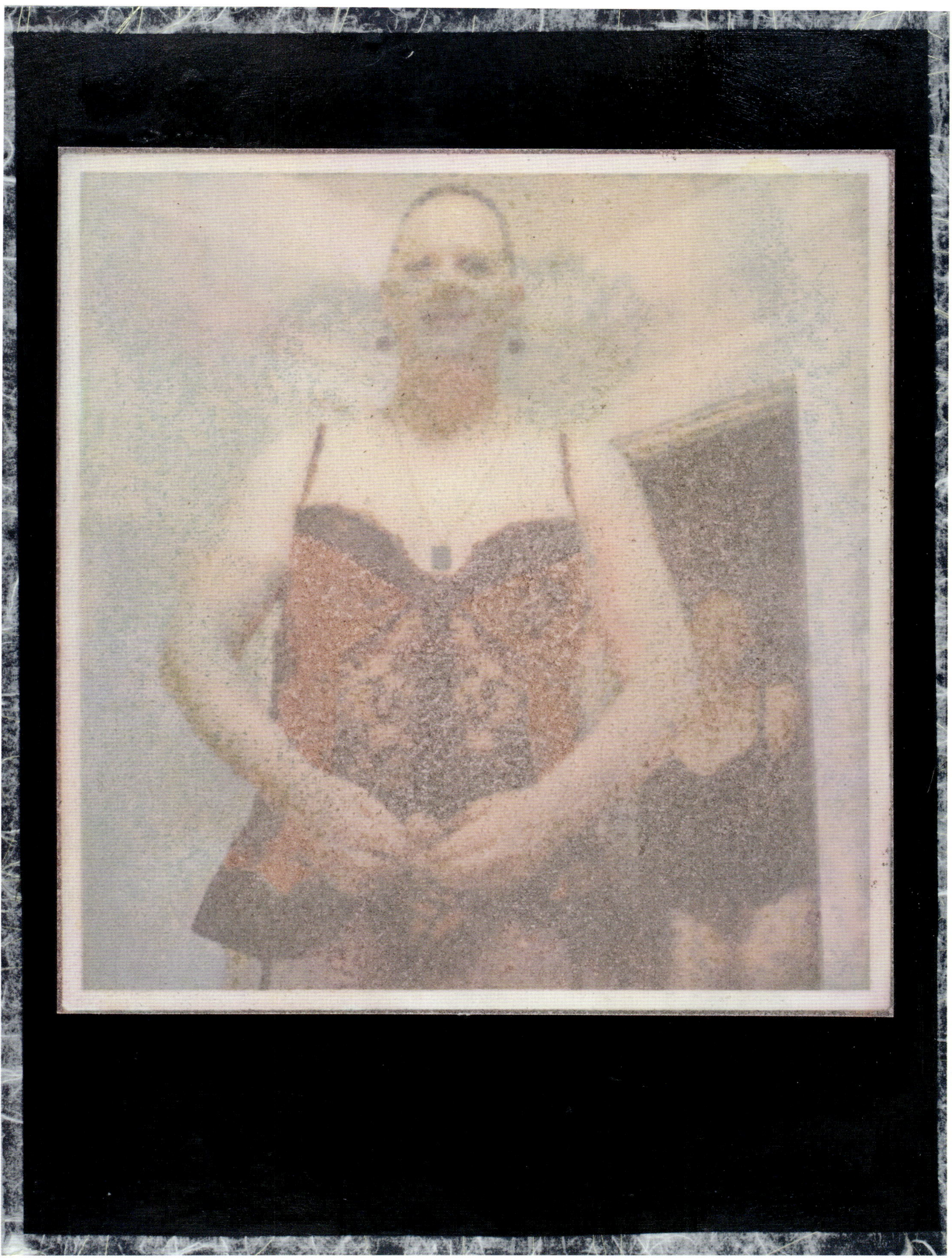

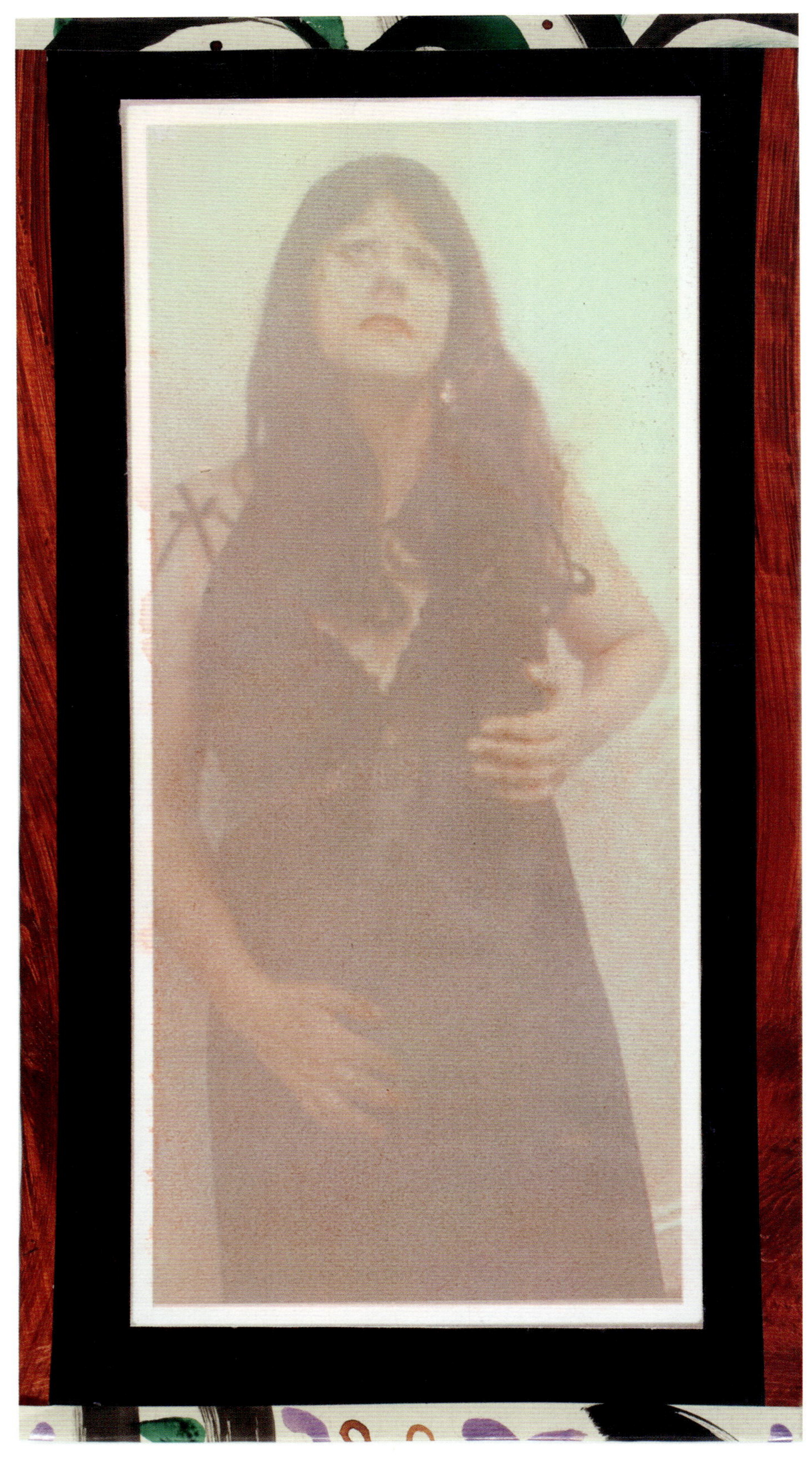

Evening dress

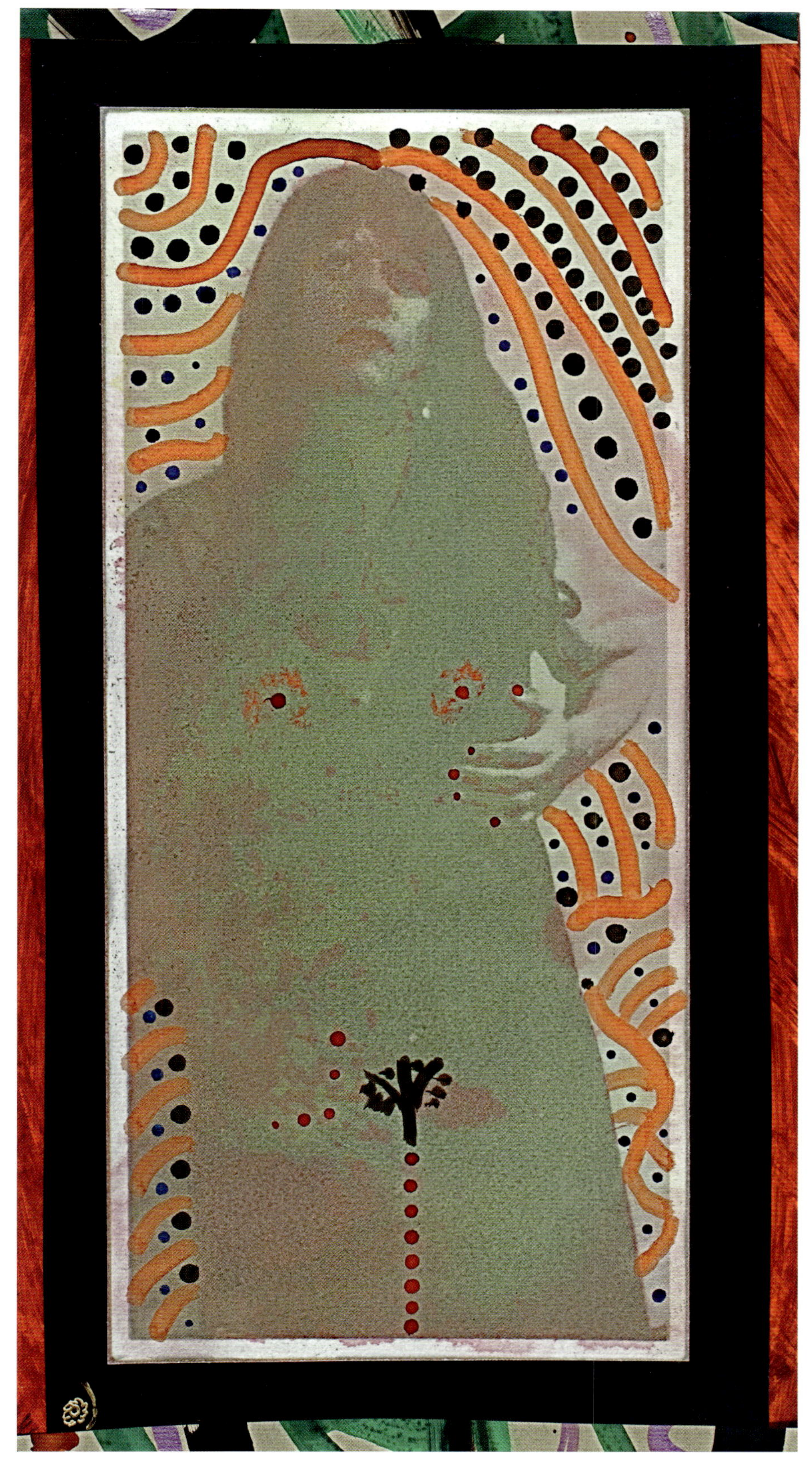

Evening dress (variant)

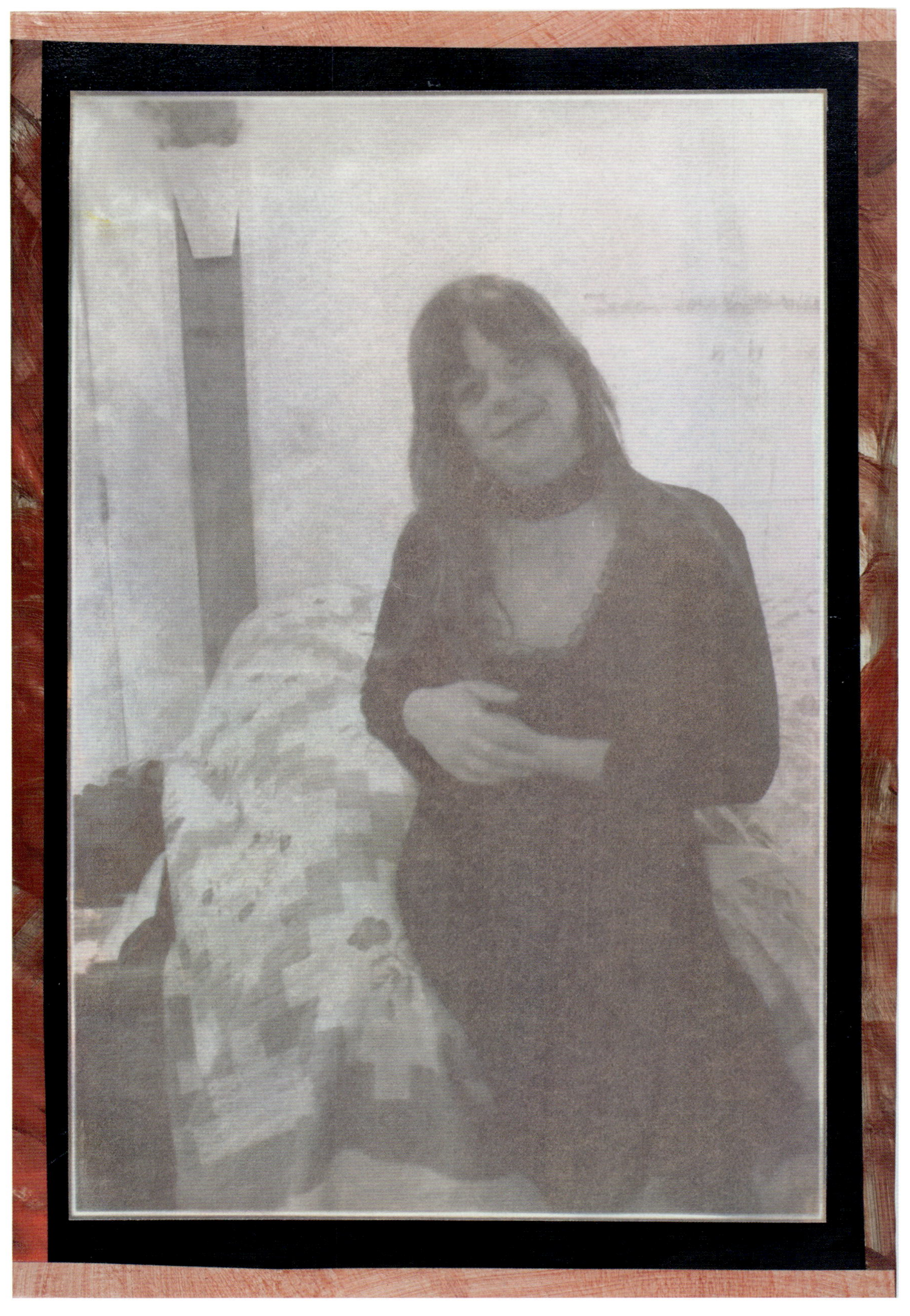

Available girl

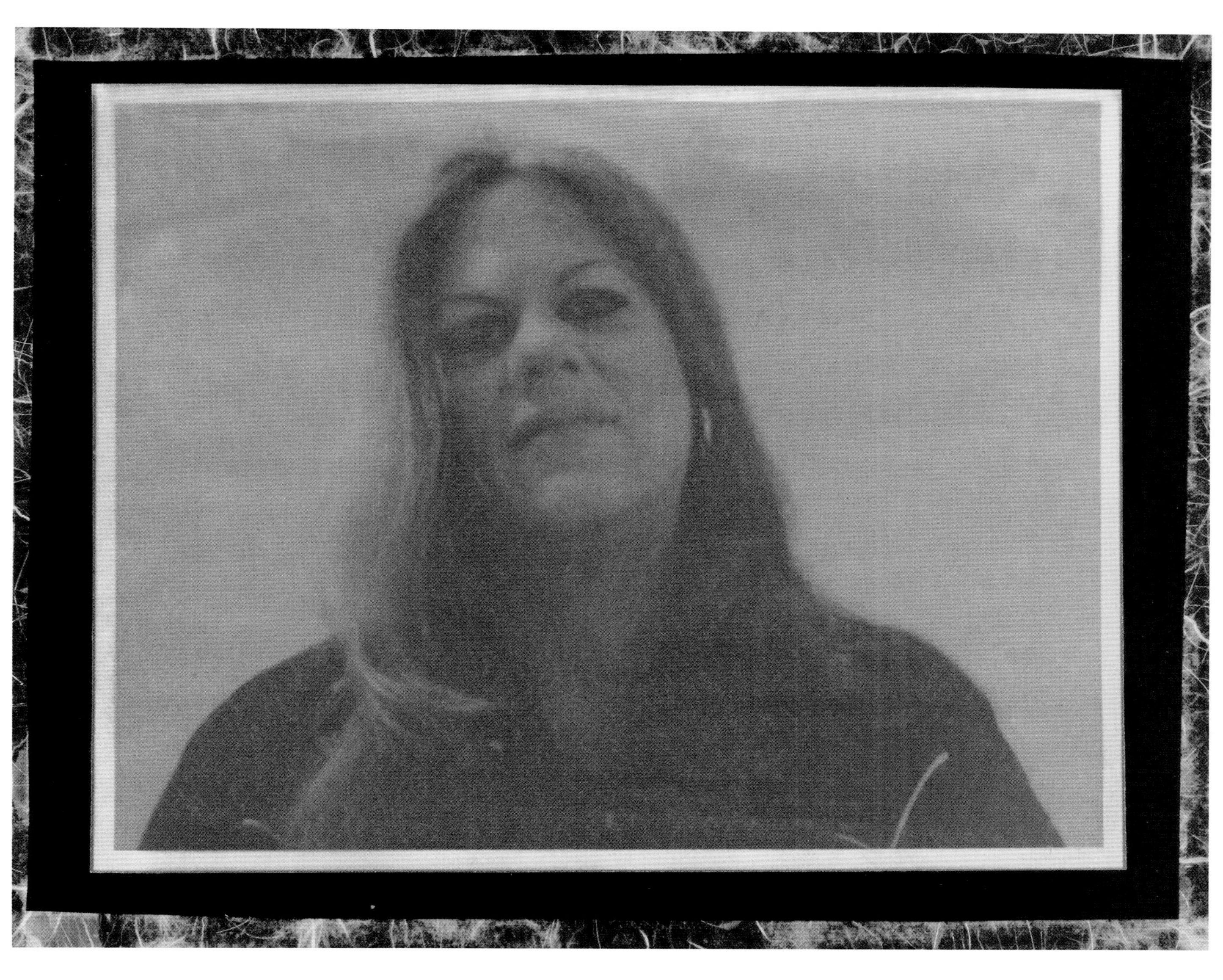

Melissa's work

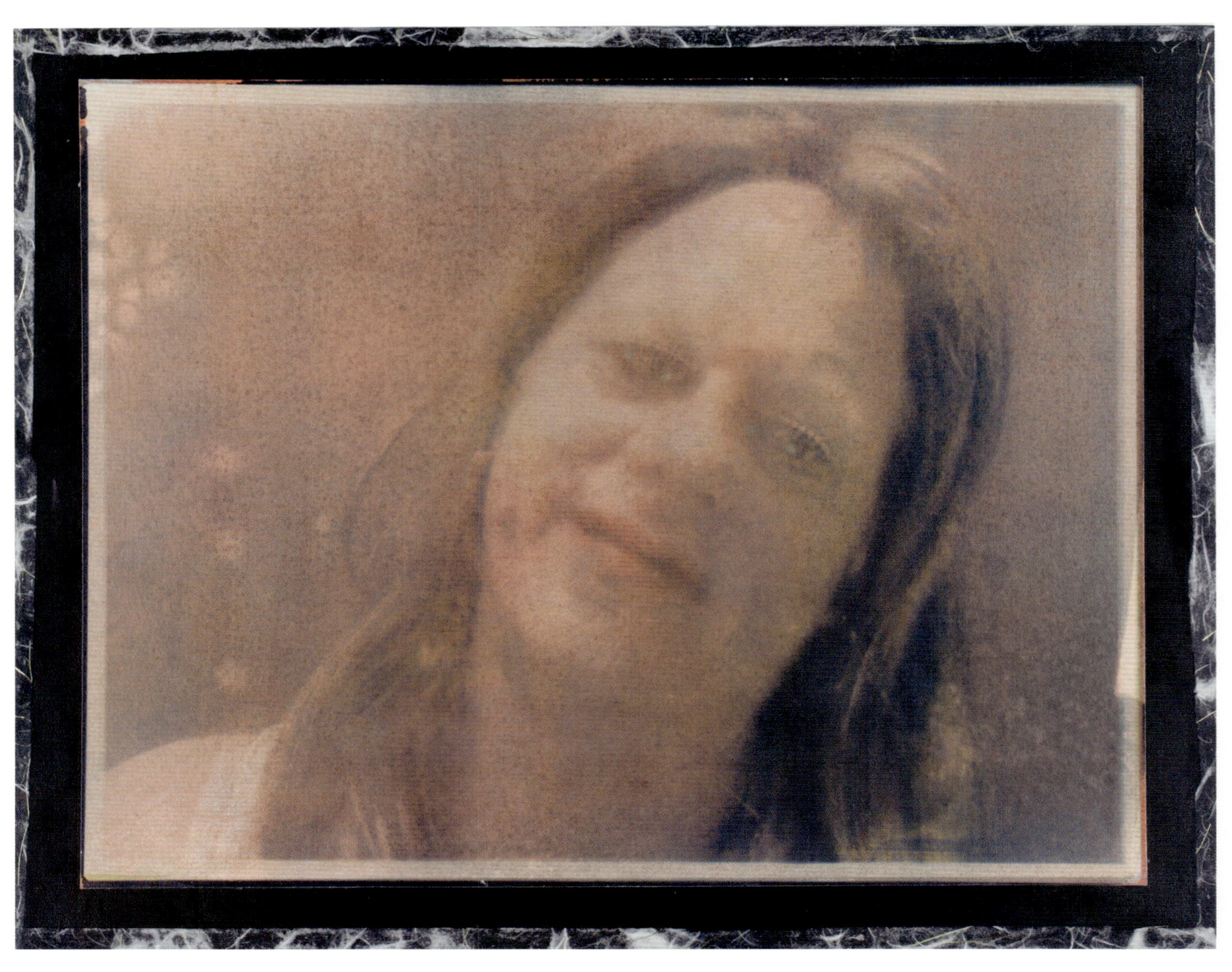

Tilted smile

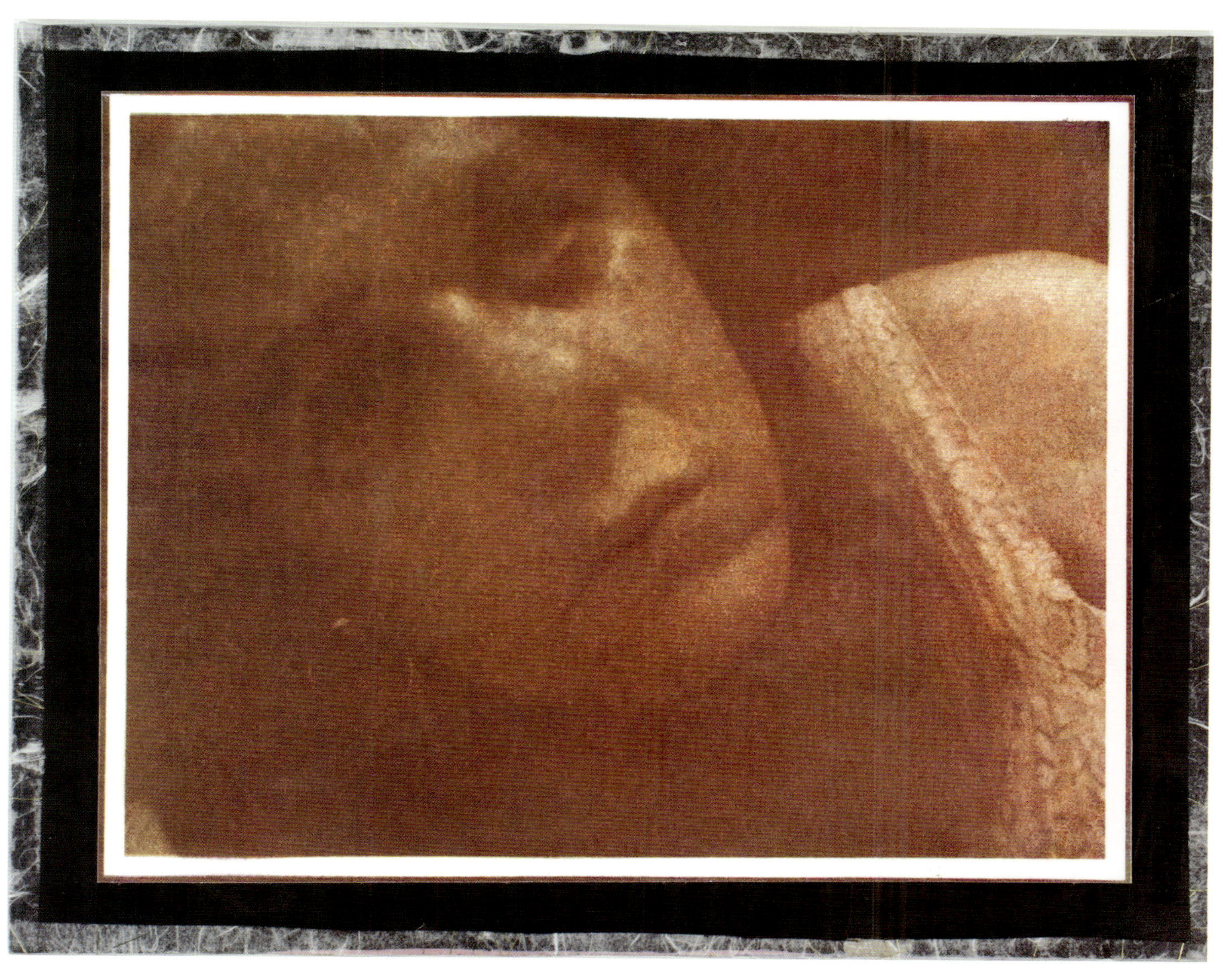

Hoop earrings

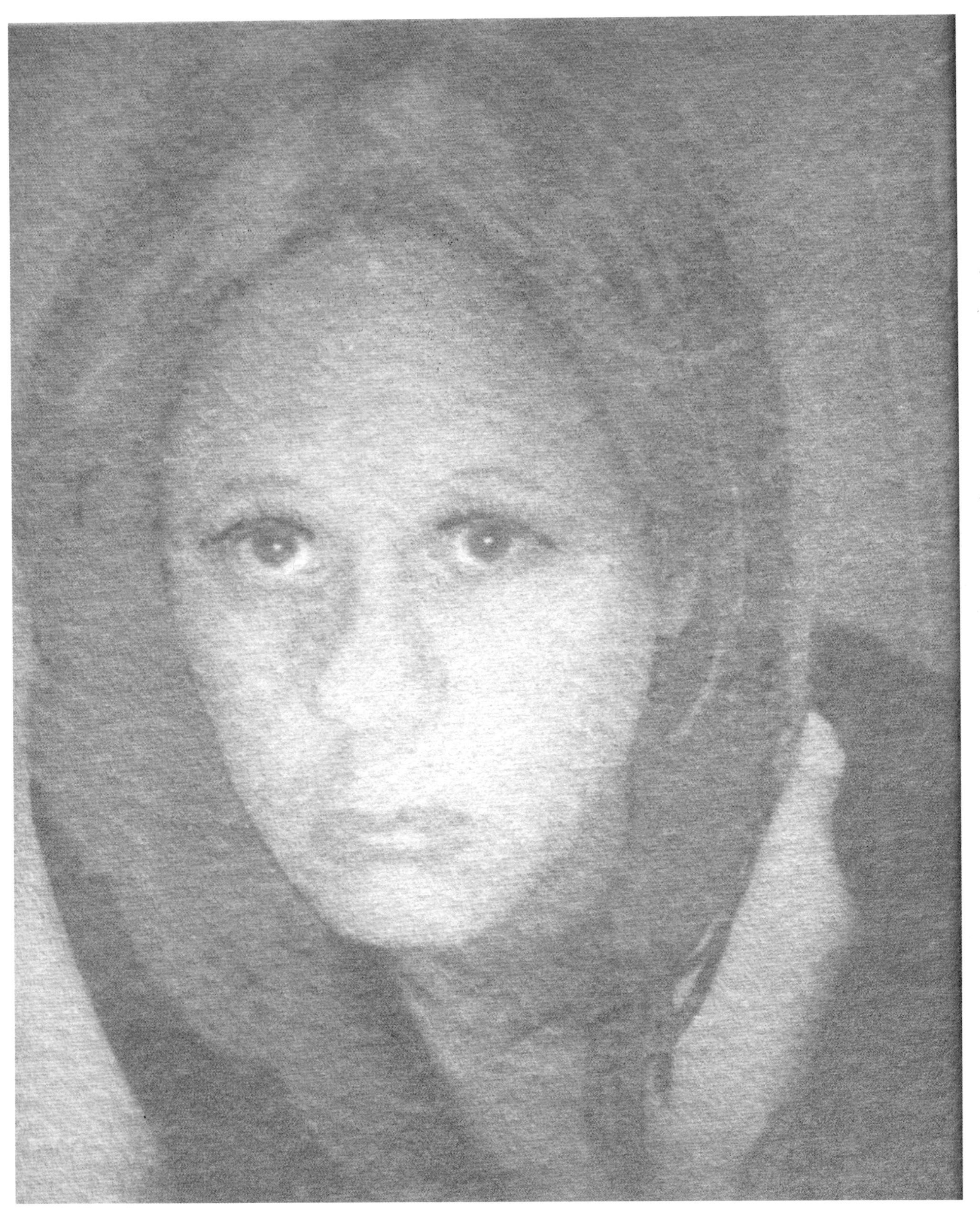

Detail of variant "Meat locker woman" (C layer printed in sodalite instead of cerulean blue)

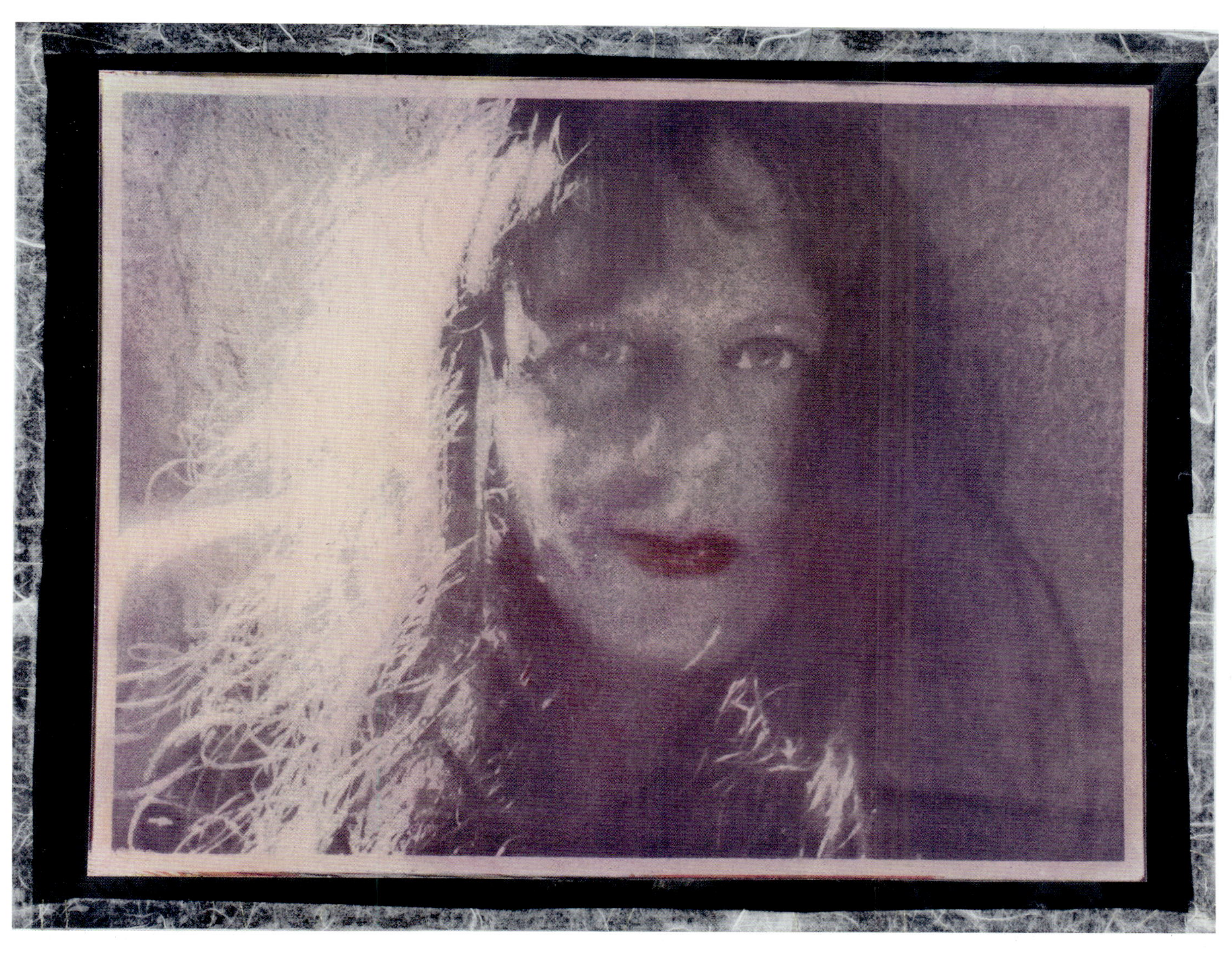

Cave witch

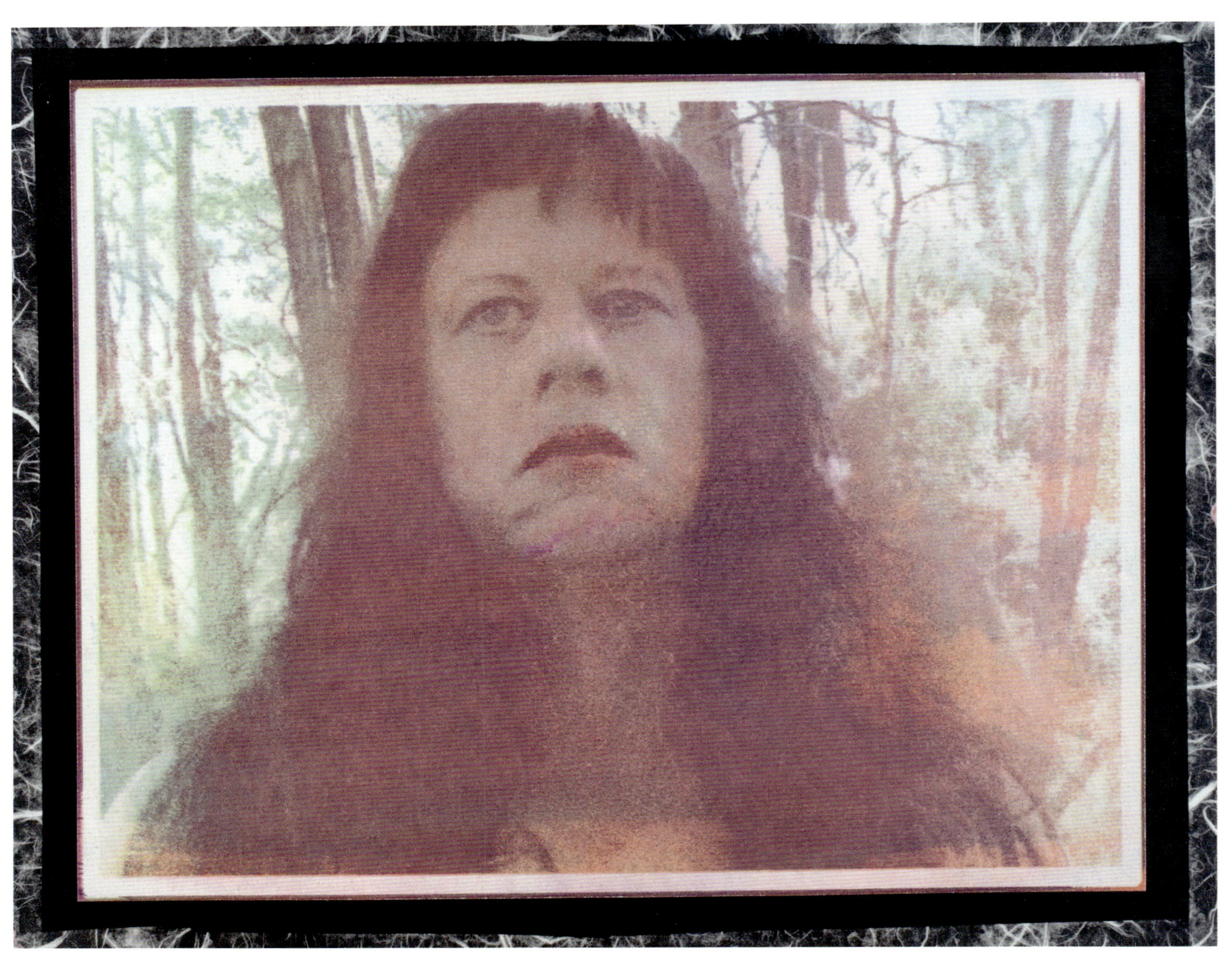

Forest

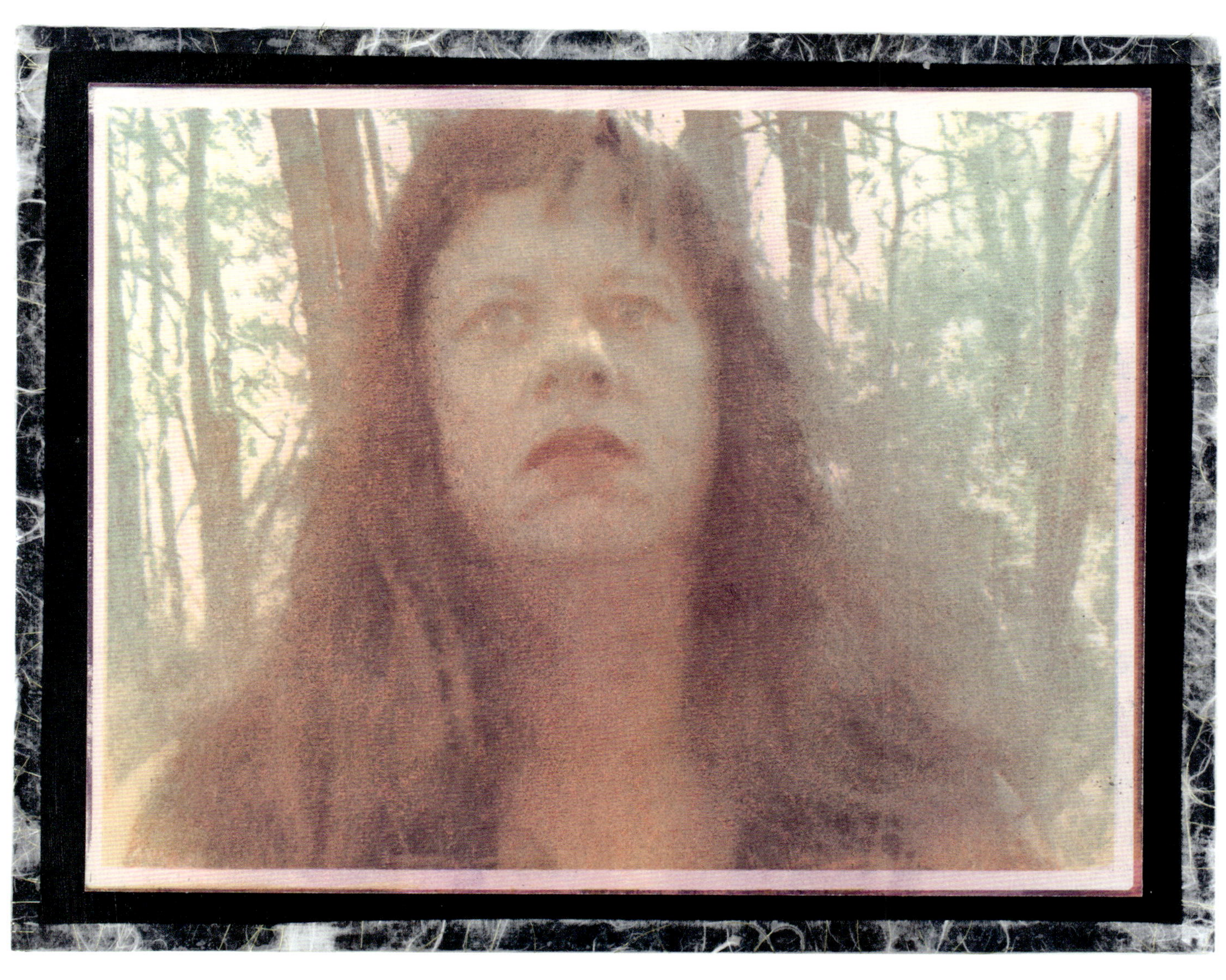

Forest (variant)

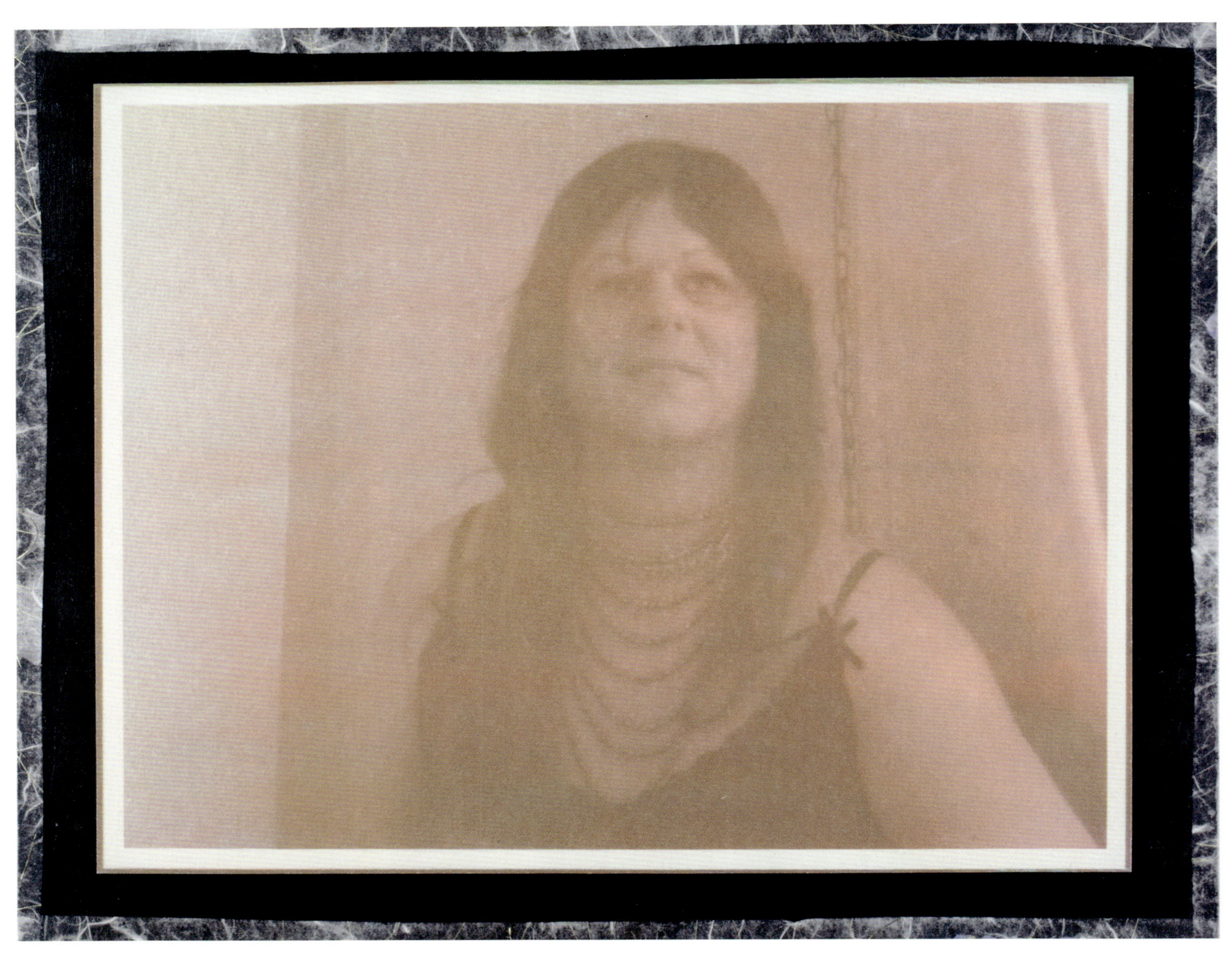

Necklaces

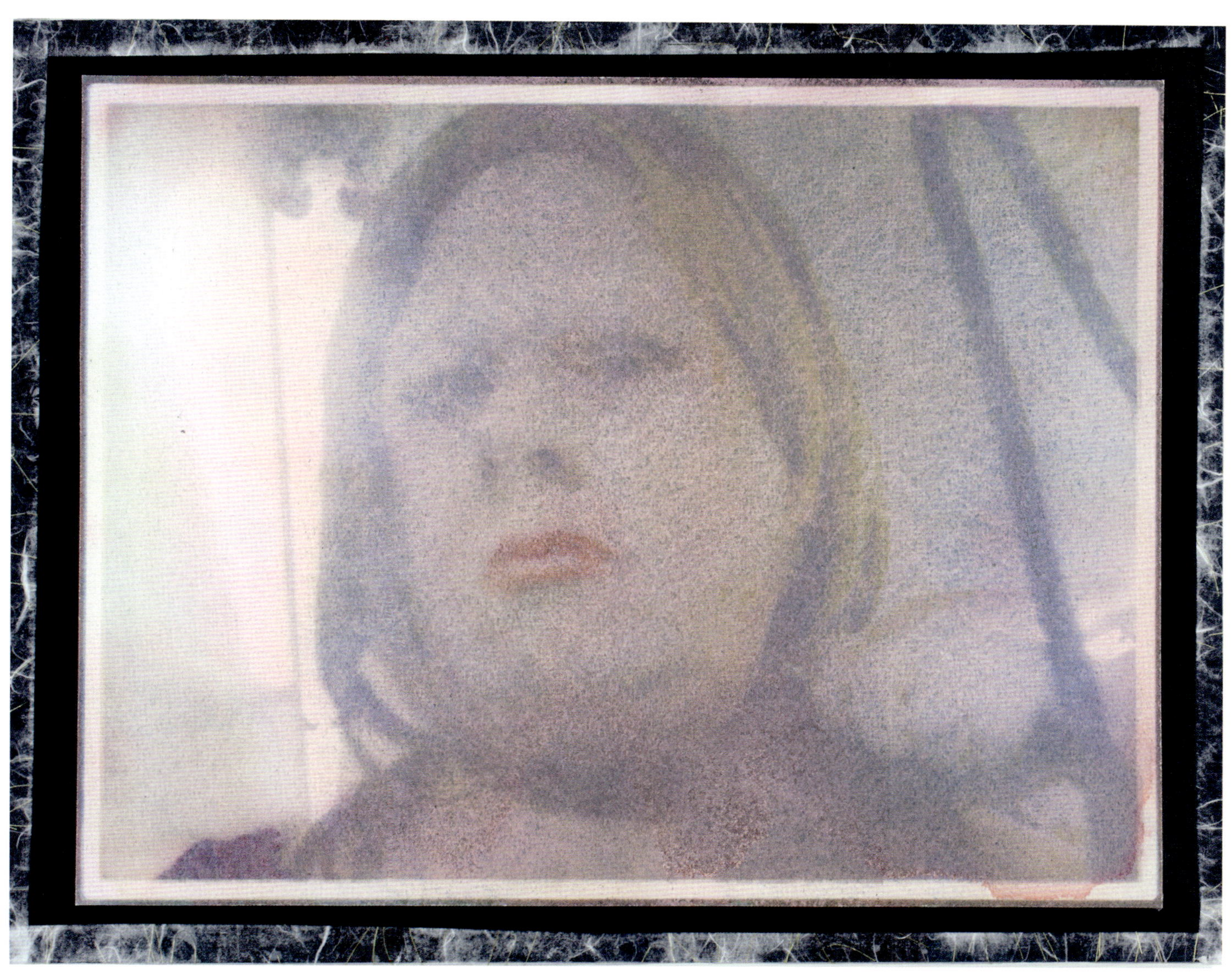

Noose

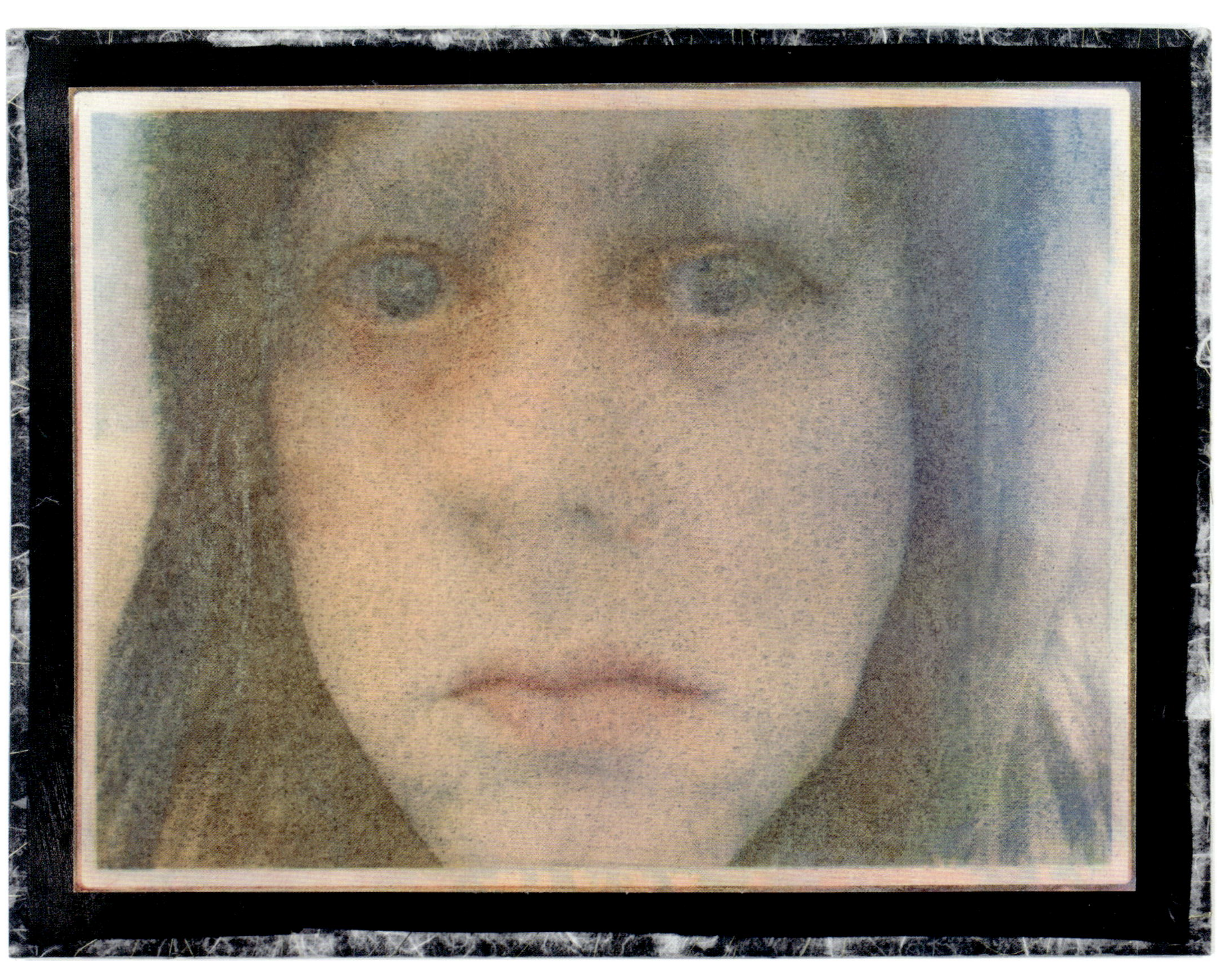

Blue eyes

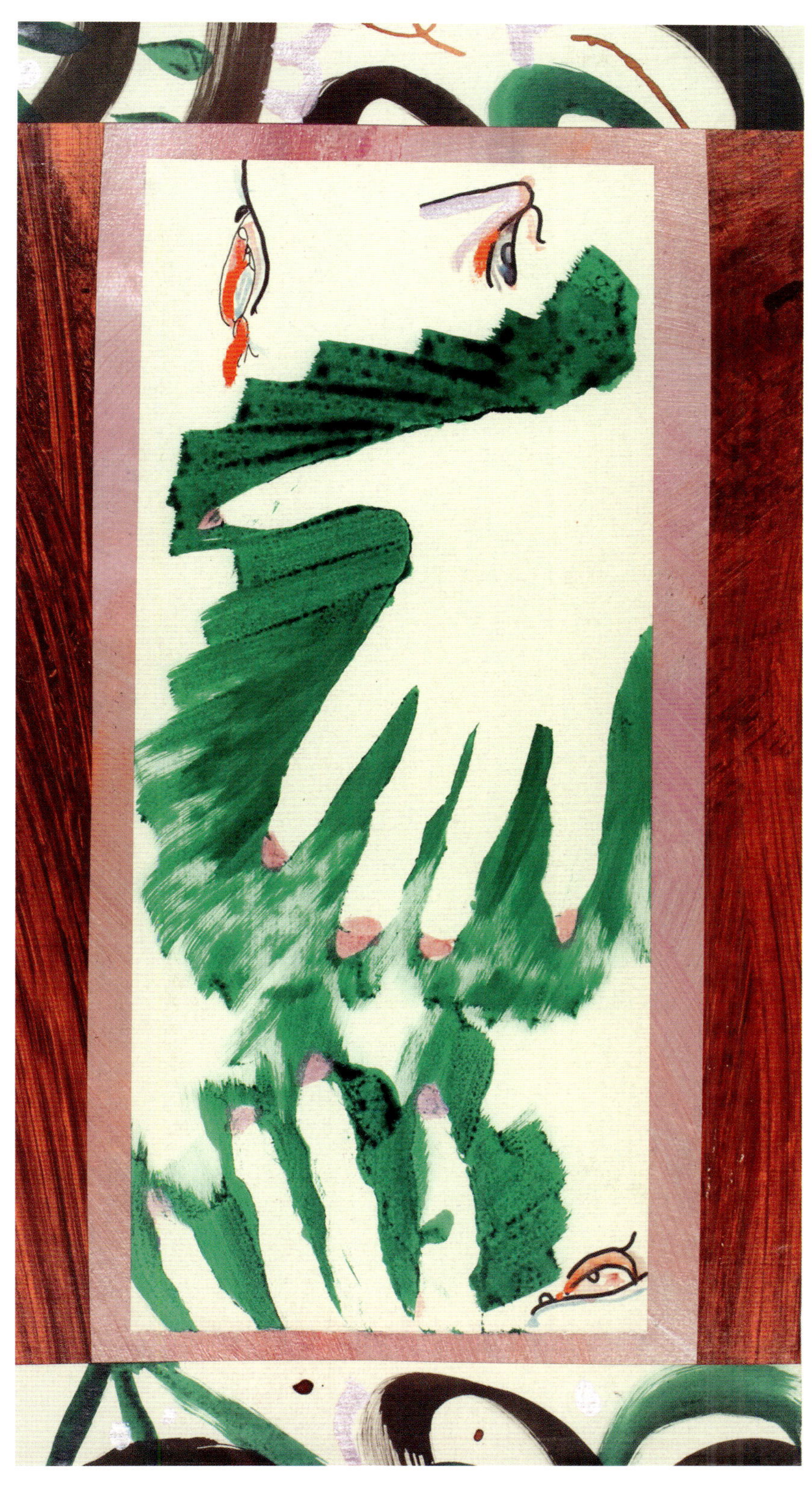

Reverse side of a Dolores gum print

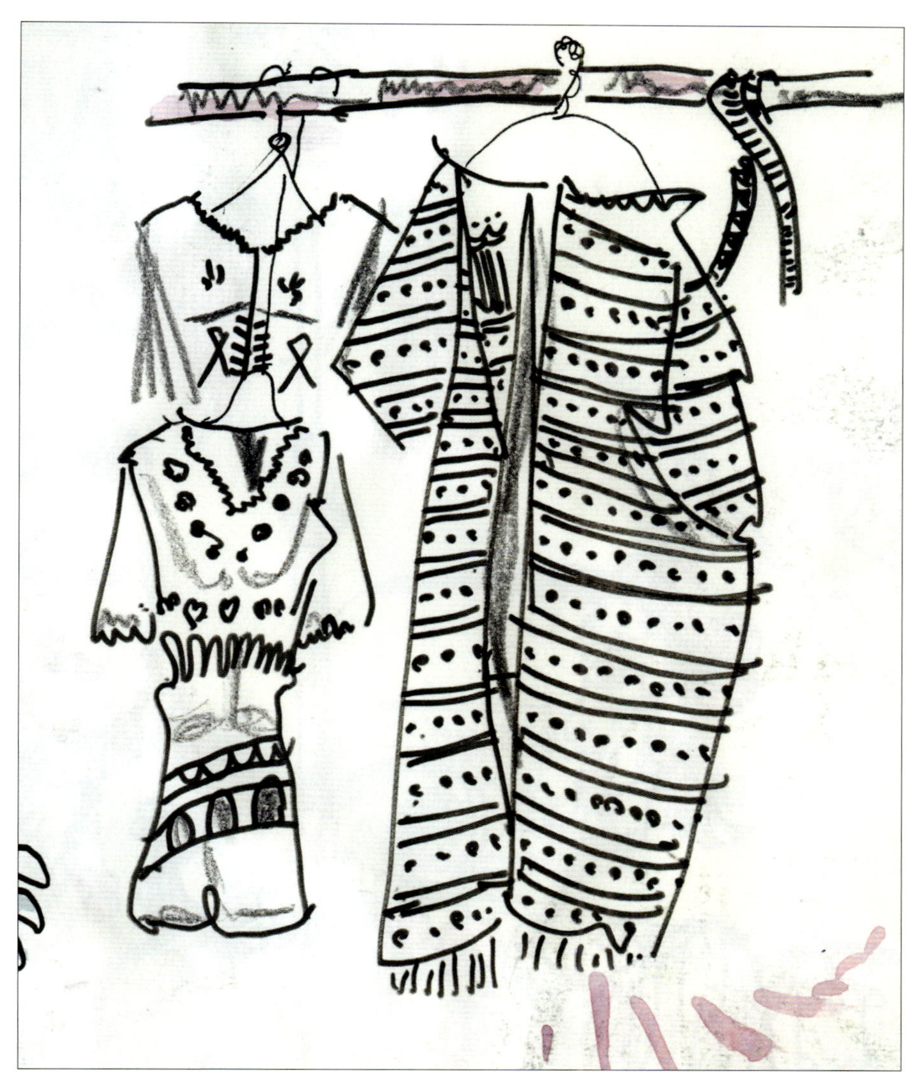

3.1: My Gum Bichromate Procedure

This is offered in hopes that it may be of use to other devotees.

SIZE PAPER (minimum 3 days)

1. Cut 19" x 26" Rives de lin watercolor paper to 13 x 19".
2. Mark back side.
3. Soak in warm water for at least 1 hour, shuffling sheets periodically.
4. Hang to dry, at least overnight.
5. Soak in hot gelatin solution, prepared by dissolving 40 grams of reagent-grade gelatin in a liter of water, allowing it to "bloom" for an interval, and then heating to a specified temperature.
6. Squeegee and hang to dry, at least overnight.
7. Wearing mask and gloves, soak in formaldehyde solution for at least ten minutes, shuffling all the sheets continually (about a dozen in 3 liters of solution), handling each sheet in the stack at least twice.
8. Hang to dry, at least overnight.

PREPARE SENSITIZER

9. Wearing mask and gloves, dissolve potassium dichromate crystals in hot distilled water.

PRINT (usually 10 days)

10. Wearing mask and gloves, pour dichromate sensitizer into large glass bowl.
11. Add equal quantity gum arabic solution.
12. Squeeze in the selected watercolor, carefully mash with a brush, and mix into the solution. The amount is determined by intuition and experience with each watercolor.
13. Wet foam brush and shake it out thoroughly.
14. Coat the sized paper smoothly, rapidly and evenly.
15. Place each sheet on the baker's rack to dry.
16. Wash bowl and brushes.
17. The gloves and mask can come off now. Leave paper to dry at least 1 hour in darkness.
18. Place negative and sized paper in a contact printing frame or in sunlight and

expose for between 3 minutes and 2 hours, depending on experience and conditions.

19. Soak face down in still water baths under dim light, moving paper to clean water as needed. Wear gloves; immerse print with a glass rod. Image will develop by subtraction in between 10 minutes and 2 hours. At least 20 minutes is preferable. Develop by inspection.
20. Holding it vertically, let the print drip as dry as possible.
21. Place it on the baker's rack to dry overnight.

(These 12 printing steps (#10 - 21) must be carried out at least 4 times for 4-color separation negatives, and more often 8 times. Hence it is really accurate to count them as 96 steps, which makes 108 steps total.)

109. Let dry an extra 24 hours.
110. Soak 5 minutes.
111. Clear for 3-4 minutes, depending on conditions, face down in 5 or 6 liters 1.5 percent potassium metabisulphite solution. This solution can be used until it turns greenish (usually about 15 prints). At the end, turn the print over and leave it in the clearing bath for another 30 seconds
112. Wash 10 minutes face up in very gently running water. It is best to shut off the water before inserting or removing the print.
113. Dry overnight.

MOUNT IMAGE (about 12 days)
114. Cut archival card stock to 13 x 17".
115. Paint one side black.
116. Dry overnight.
117. Paint the reverse black or some other color.
118. Dry overnight.
119. Wrap edges with Thai paper.
120. Dry overnight.
121. Trim the finished gum print to borders.
122. Lay it face down on a clean card and apply PVA glue evenly. Wait a few seconds.
123. Turn the print over, position by eye, and lay it down on a piece of painted card.
124. Sandwiching it between sheets of clean wax paper, place it in a dry mount press for 15 minutes with the heat off.
125. Cut a sheet of Niedeggen paper to 11 x 14".

(Repeat steps 123-125 with the Niedeggen on the back of the card. So this takes us up through steps 127-29.)

130. Dry overnight.
131. With print vertical, spray with Golden MSA archival varnish.
132. Wait 15 min.
133. With print horizontal, spray a second coat.
134. Repeat steps 131-133, for four coats total.
135. Dry for at least 1 week. [I am now experimenting with shorter drying times.]
136. As varnish dries, it may lift corners of print from card. Where needed, glue these down and place in the press for 15 minutes.
137. Dry for at least three days.
138. Rub with Renaissance microcrystalline wax.
139. Dry overnight.
140. Sleeve.

Total time 28 days (at best).

3.2: Captions

All the images in this book were made between 2007 and 2012 inclusive.

Smiling, in black dress — Low resolution laptop photo (this kind of image is never more than 200 kilobytes, and usually much less).

The two Doloreses — From Oaxaca sketchbook. See the chapter "Mexican Watercolor Drawings."

Seated, in bra and panties — Selenium toned in camera 11 x 14" silver gelatin paper negative. Exposure was 16 seconds.

With hand against face — Laptop.

CONSTRUCTIONS
Cosmetic kit — From Oaxaca sketchbook. Most of these smaller drawings were scanned for me by Mr. Jason Helmar.

Denial, and Other Cosmetics
With flashing camera — Selenium toned 11 x 14" silver gelatin enlargement, made from 35 mm. negative.

With round mirror — Laptop.

Three "indigenous" drawings — From Oaxaca sketchbook.

Party girl, housewife, geologist — All laptop photos.

Holding 35 mm. camera — Japanese department store color print from 35 mm. color negative.

Dolores and her friends — First four images are laptop photos. The fifth is an American drugstore one-hour color print from a 35 mm. color negative.

Practicing and Recording
First three images (all color inset) — Laptop.

Formal portrait with weed in vase — Reversed scan of 8 x 10″ in camera silver gelatin negative.

Becoming Dolores
First ten images — Laptop.

In corset, holding whip — Reversed scan of 8 x 10″ in camera Ektachrome transparency, cross-processed as negative. One hot July night in around 1997 my friend William Linne found several boxes of expired sheet film in a trash can in Austin, Texas. "I love how lurid the colors are," he said, presenting me with my very own supply. "They're like candy." I used the stuff sparingly (mostly for night shots in the San Francisco streets), and stored it in the refrigerator. The Dolores Ektachromes were all shot in my studio in 2012, by which time the colors had mellowed again, the reds going plum, the blues getting purple. That was the end of the box, and Ektachrome a relic of the late Cretaceous Period. I was sorry.

In Between; Female Gazes; Male Gazes; Breasts
All laptop.

How You Are
First five portraits — Laptop.

Dolores as prostitute — Reversed scan of 8 x 10″ Ektachrome.

The "Calliope" passage
First portrait — Drugstore print from 35 mm. color negative.

Second and third portraits — Two increasingly "over the top" digital versions of the first, the color saturation and contrast being increased for a suitably grotesque effect.

The "black lipstick" passage
Both laptop.

The "birthing cave" sequence
All laptop, except for the last photo (fullpage night view from mouth of birthing cave), which is a selenium toned 11 x 14 silver gelatin enlargement from a 35 mm. black and white negative.

"Speak now, my heart"
All handpainted gum bichromate prints. The first four derive from 11 x 14″ negatives made for me by Chris Fraser from my laptop photos. Chris also made the fifth negative, which originated in a 35 mm. color negative.

PORTRAITS
Dress and door — From Oaxaca sketchbook.

Laptop Portraits

As stated.

Mexican Watercolor Drawings

Dolores in Oaxaca — Laptop.

Remaining two drawings — From Oaxaca sketchbook.

Oaxaca 2008

Ditto.

Xalapa, Veracruz, 2010

As stated. In spiral-bound sketchbook.

Veracruz, Veracruz, 2011

As stated. Loose sheets from watercolor blocks.

Woodblock Prints
Detail from "Happy Landings" — Scanned from the print.

Next five images — Laptop.

"Happy Landings" (two) — Scanned from prints.

Watercoloring a print — Laptop.

Remaining six images — Scanned from prints. The laser engraving was carried out by a husband and wife team in Long Beach, on a fine piece of cherry wood supplied by my friend Jake Dickinson.

Paper Negatives
All but the last two are selenium toned 8 x 10" or 11 x 14" silver gelatin in camera paper negatives, some hand colored afterward. I cannot tell a lie; the vulva belongs not to Dolores but to a certain pretty friend of mine (who also likes women, I am happy to report). Since Dolores likes to pretend, I figured I would just drop it into this sequence and hope for the best.

The final pair of paper negatives are gum prints. They were contact printed from inkjet-printed color *positives* (contracted for with Mr. Kent Lacin) from laptop camera files.

Silver Gelatin Positives
As noted in the text, the diptych was contact printed on 8 x 10" developing-out paper

under regular room light. The next three portraits are selenium toned 11 x 14" en-
largements from 35 mm. negatives. (I held back development on "Hoping to pass"
wishing to suppress some of Dolores's wrinkles. Perhaps this intention would have
been more artfully expressed in a gum print, but there you go.) "In Montana" is a
contrast-reversed scan from a 35 mm. negative — hence a positive in the meaning
of my section title. (Poor Dolores had just turned fifty-three not long before; gravity
continued its insidious work on her face.) To me the scan has more grain, clarity and
punch than my prints; I think I prefer the latter.

Color Film Positives

With the exception of "Katy's makeup," which employed drugstore film and process-
ing, and "Happy woman," which is a detail from a reverse-contrast scan of that good
old cross-processed Ektachrome (may it decompose gently), these are lab-grade
color machine prints from professional color negative film. I have digitally softened
and red-tinted "Black nightgown," in part out of pity for Dolores (whose portraits are
often cruel), and also out of curiosity, in case I ever felt like pushing those effects
further in a gum print.

Gum Bichromate Prints

Images 2-7, 9-12 and 15-17 are laptop photos. The rest are, indeed, gum prints,
which I have captioned more fully than usual, since this section discusses process in
some detail.

Or Whichever Other Innocuous State of Being - Laptop.

END MATTER

Dresses — From Oaxaca sketchbook.

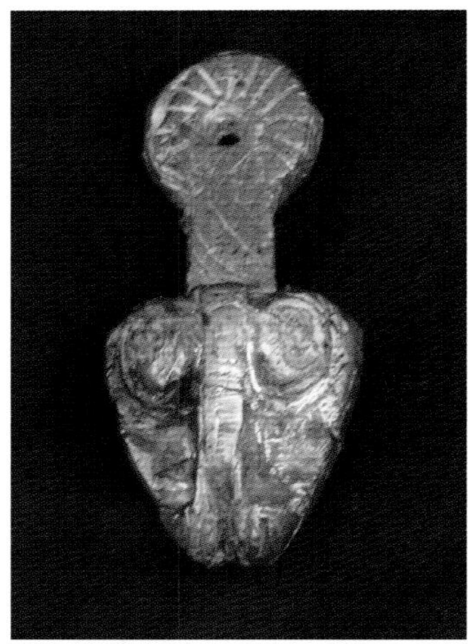

*Brass Venus figurine (lost
wax casting)*

3.3: Acknowledgements

As in my previous photo book *Imperial*, I express gratitude to all my photographic mentors and comrades: Jeff Cox, Chris Fraser, Kent Lacin (and of course his wife, Greta, who taught me the darkest secrets of German makeup), William Linne, Ken Miller, Jock Sturges, Mary Swisher, Tom Robinson, and Roger Vail. Mr. Jason Helmar, known to the trade as "We Control Our Future," scanned many images for me even as Dolores's slips and blouses hung drying on the backs of chairs around him.

The generosity of the American Academy of Arts and Letters and of Ohio State University made it possible for me to take the time to improve my gum printing. Geoffrey Smith and Lisa Iacabellis deserve my special thanks. My art and manuscript dealers, Priscilla Juvelis and George R. Minkoff, also bear considerable credit. Thank you all.

A portion of the opening essay and of the remarks on *How You Are* derive from a speech I gave in Norway at the Kapittel 11 Stavanger International Festival of Literature and Freedom of Speech. That year (2011) the subject was defiance. For this venue, which proved conducive to writing ghost stories, I am very grateful to Eirik Bø, Marit Egaas (and her husband Kurt Kristensen), Arild Rein and John Eirik Riley.

My agent, Susan Golomb, and her assistants Soumeya Bendimerad, Krista Ingebretson, Eliza Rothstein and Lauren Shekari are beautiful ladies who were kind to Dolores. Craig Cohen, Will Luckman, Robert Avellan and Nina Ventura deserve much appreciation for their hard work on the production and publication of this book. Thank you so much.

I would like to thank my long-suffering friends. As for James Hosking, Jeremy Lybarger, Joseph Mattson and Doug Rice, they went further than others, and should be called co-investigators and -instigators. The following people were charitable enough to serve as Dolores's makeup artists, suppliers and instructors: Mandy Aftel, Classy, Heidi, Lauren Hutton, Isabel, Katy, Takako Kawai, Paula Keyth, Lisa W. and Lisa X., both unsurnamed Melissas, a certain Dominique, Katie Peterson, Terrie Petree and Jean Stein. Ben Pax did not always like what he saw, but kept his mouth shut.

Dolores owes most of all to Teresa McFarland, makeup teacher, barhopper, paper sizer, big and little sister, transgender traveler, confidante, darkroom partner and muse. And I myself also thank her with all my heart.

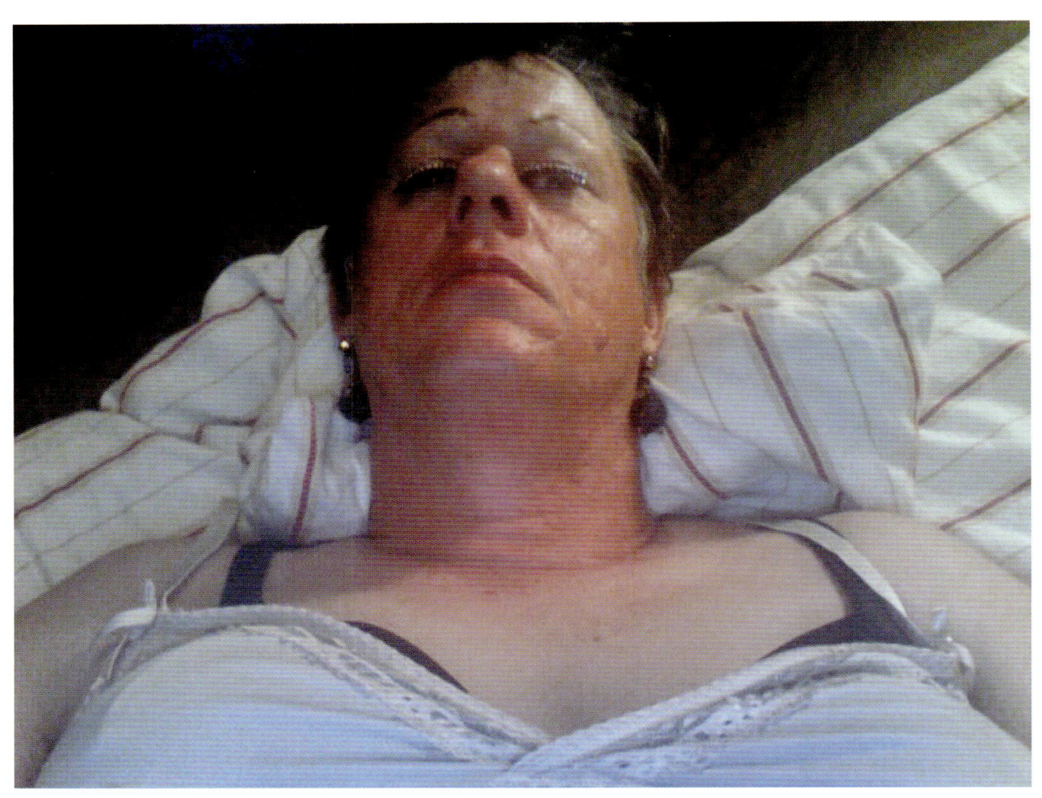

3.4: Or Whichever Other Innocuous State Of Being

And Dolores, her lips glossed coral pink, her dark eyebrows done into perfect arches of knowing surprise, her eyes kohled and mascaraed dramatically dark around and her flesh powdered perfectly white, set hopefully out. Perhaps she should have been apprehensive, for, if I may put the matter kindly, she stood a trifle tall for a woman . . . What do you suppose she wished for now? . . . Too many times now I have called her stupid. But the body is not wise, nor needs to be. To exist as touch of skin and sweetness of flesh, to long for the purity of sensation without knowledge, as if from the very mouth of Grinning Cave one were to see ecstasy in a single shooting star transecting our rock-framed world just before dawn, why can't this be womanhood, or whichever other innocuous state of being you care to name it? In brief, what has the vulva to do with conscious personality? And so who I am to denigrate Dolores simply because she cannot define herself? Whose dream on this earth is the brightest?

from *How You Are*

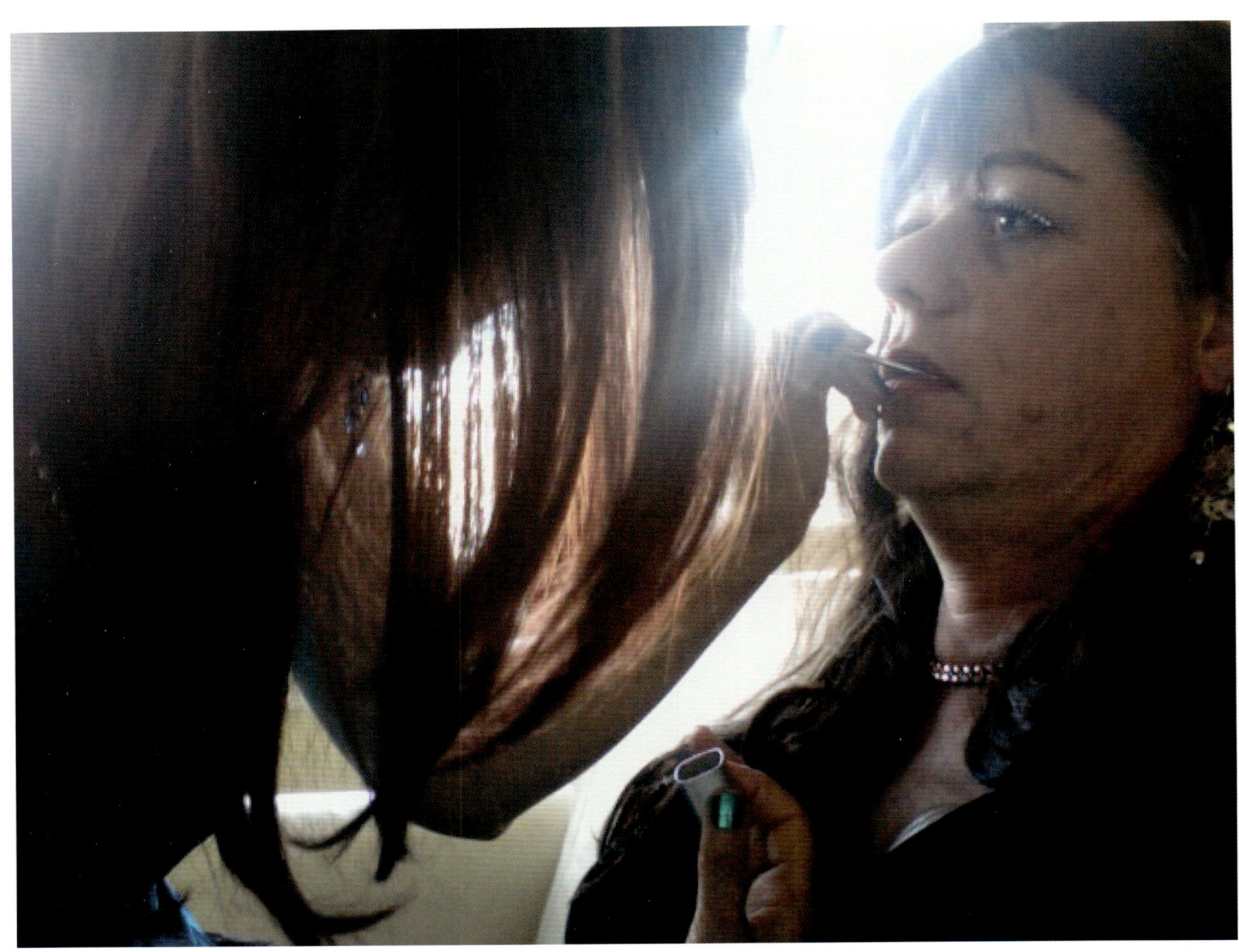

The Book of Dolores

© 2013 William T. Vollmann

All rights reserved. No part of this book may be reproduced in any manner in any media, or transmitted by any means whatsoever, electronic or mechanical (including photocopy, film or video recording, Internet posting, or any other information storage and retrieval system), without the prior written permission of the publisher.

The color photographs on pp. 22 and 150 were previously published in *Vice* magazine (vol. 12, no. 4) as an excertpt from William T. Vollmann's *Kissing the Mask* (Ecco, 2010) which included low-resolution black and white reproductions of the same.

Published in the United States by powerHouse Books,
a division of powerHouse Cultural Entertainment, Inc.
37 Main Street, Brooklyn, NY 11201-1021
telephone 212.604.9074, fax 212.366.5247
e-mail: info@powerHouseBooks.com
website: www.powerHouseBooks.com

First edition, 2013

Library of Congress Control Number: 2013942850

Hardcover ISBN 978-1-57687-657-2

Printing and binding by Midas Printing, Inc., China

Book design by Robert Avellan

10 9 8 7 6 5 4 3 2 1

Printed and bound in China